sleeper

out in the cold

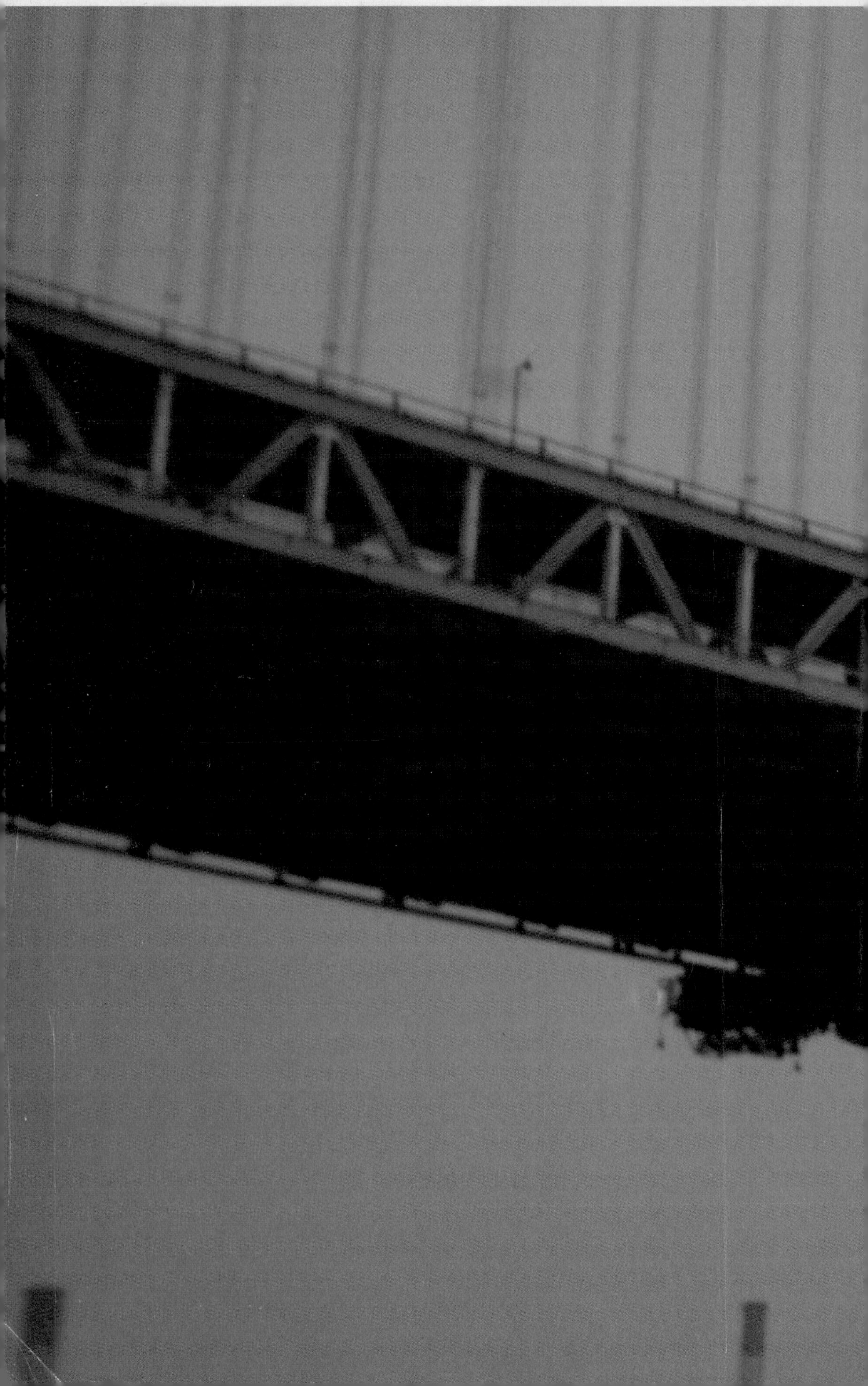

sleeper

out in the cold

Writer

ED BRUBAKER

Artist

SEAN PHILLIPS

Colors

Tony Aviña

with assistance from Randy Mayor issues #1-2

Letters

Bill Oakley issues #1-3,

Ken Lopez issues #4-6

SLEEPER created by Brubaker and Phillips

SLEEPER: OUT IN THE COLD, ISBN: 1-4012-0115-6 Published by WildStorm Productions. 888 Prospect St. #240, La Jolla, CA 92037. Cover and compilation copyright © 2003 WildStorm Productions, an imprint of DC Comics. All Rights Reserved. Originally published in single magazine form as Sleeper #1-6 copyright © 2003. WILDSTORM UNIVERSE, SLEEPER, all characters, the distinctive likenesses thereof and all related indicia are trademarks of DC Comics. The stories, characters, and incidents mentioned in this magazine are entirely fictional. Printed on recyclable paper. WildStorm does not read or accept unsolicited submissions of ideas, stories or artwork. Printed in Canada. Second Printing.

DC Comics, a Warner Bros. Entertainment Company.

Cover illustration & publication design by Sean Phillips

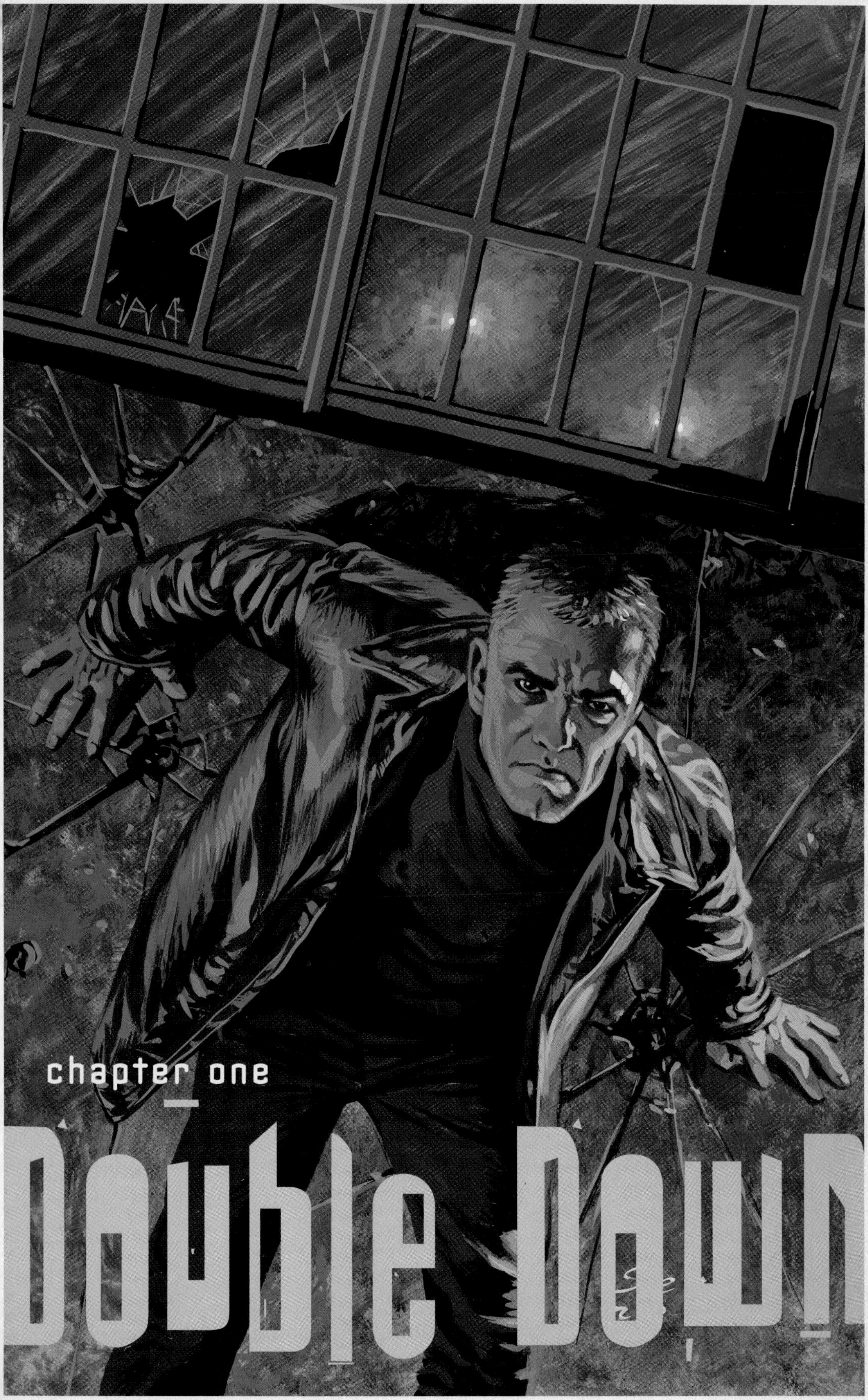
chapter one
Double Down

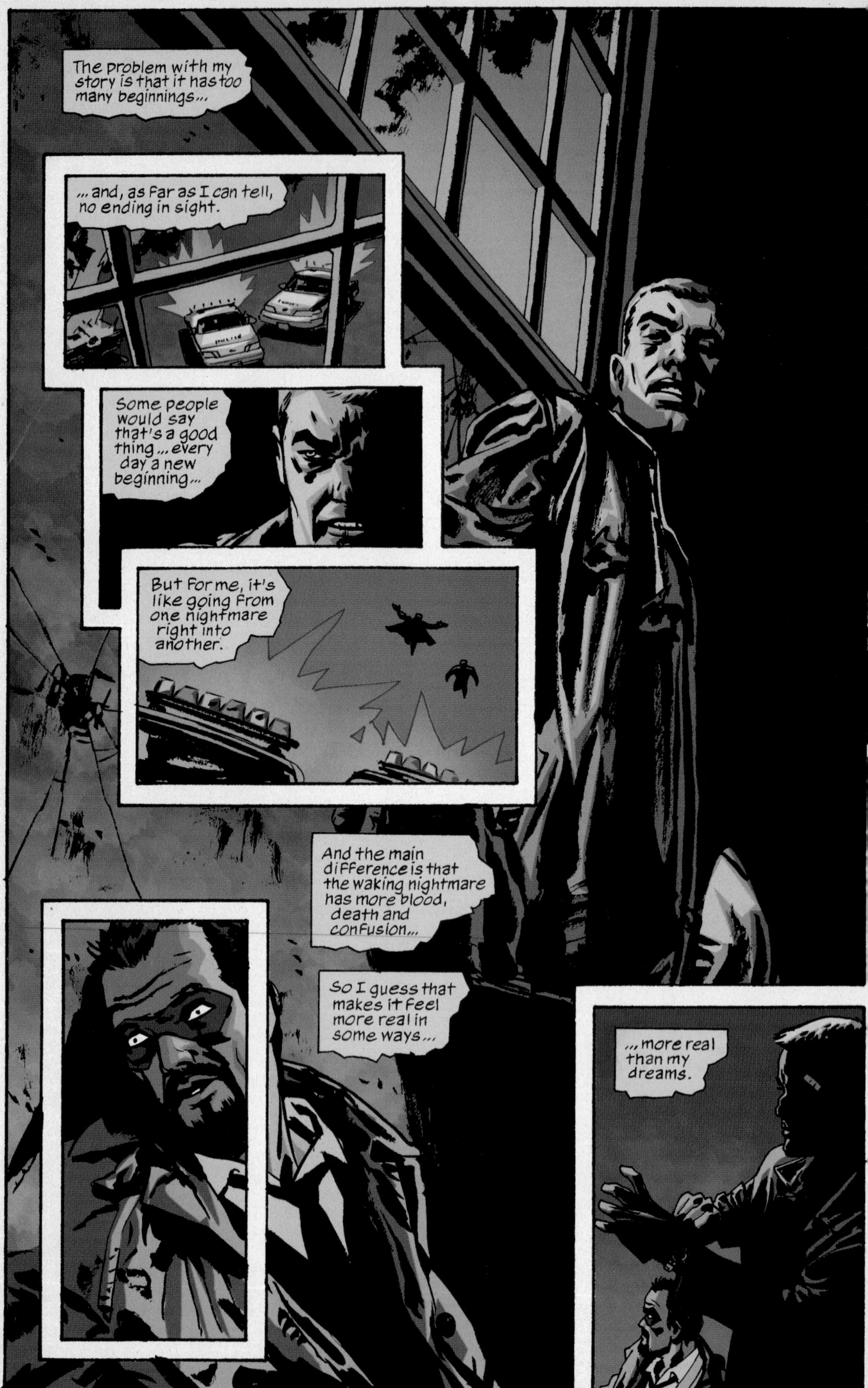
The problem with my story is that it has too many beginnings...
...and, as far as I can tell, no ending in sight.
Some people would say that's a good thing... every day a new beginning...
But for me, it's like going from one nightmare right into another.
And the main difference is that the waking nightmare has more blood, death and confusion...
So I guess that makes it feel more real in some ways...
...more real than my dreams.

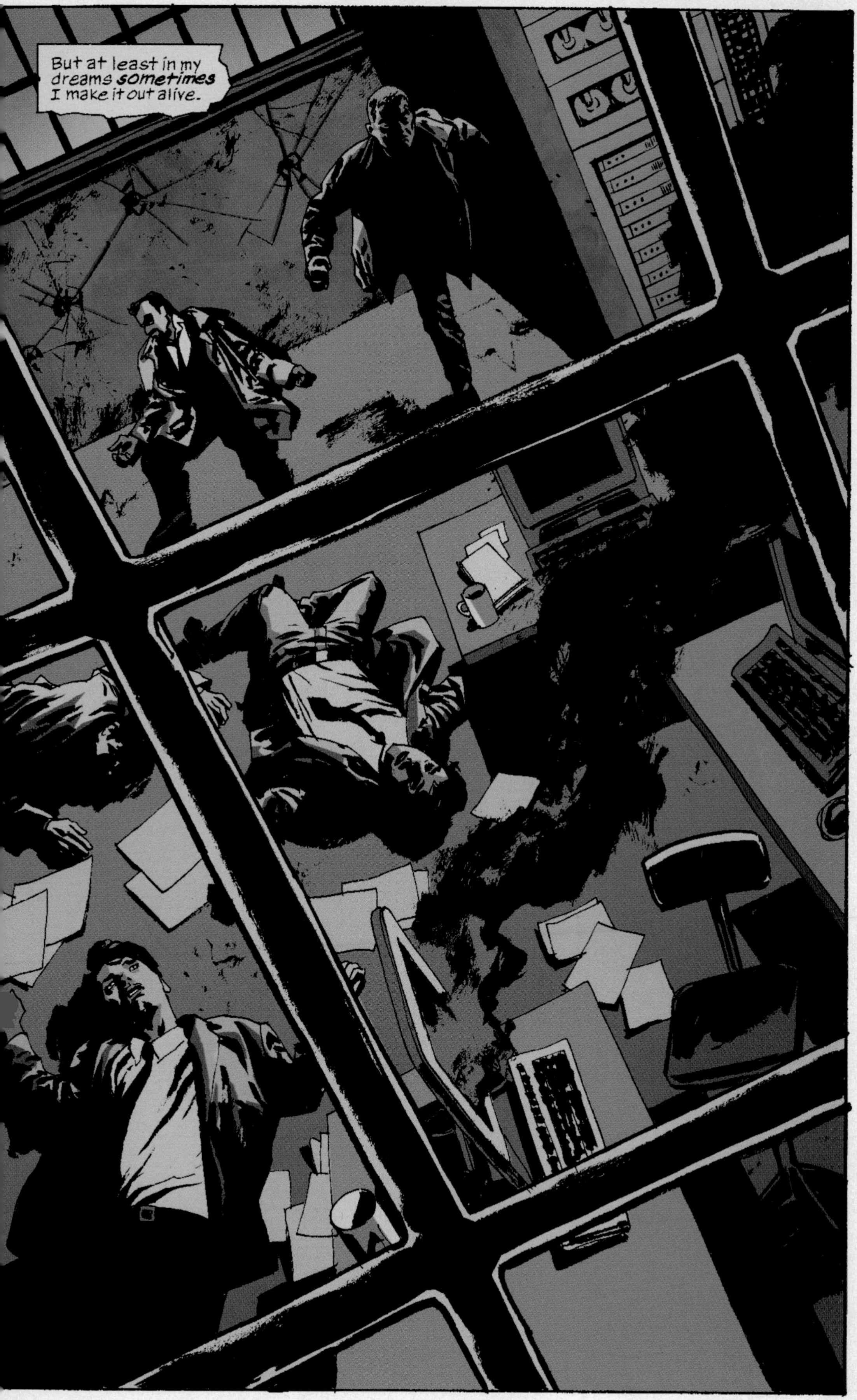
But at least in my dreams sometimes I make it out alive.

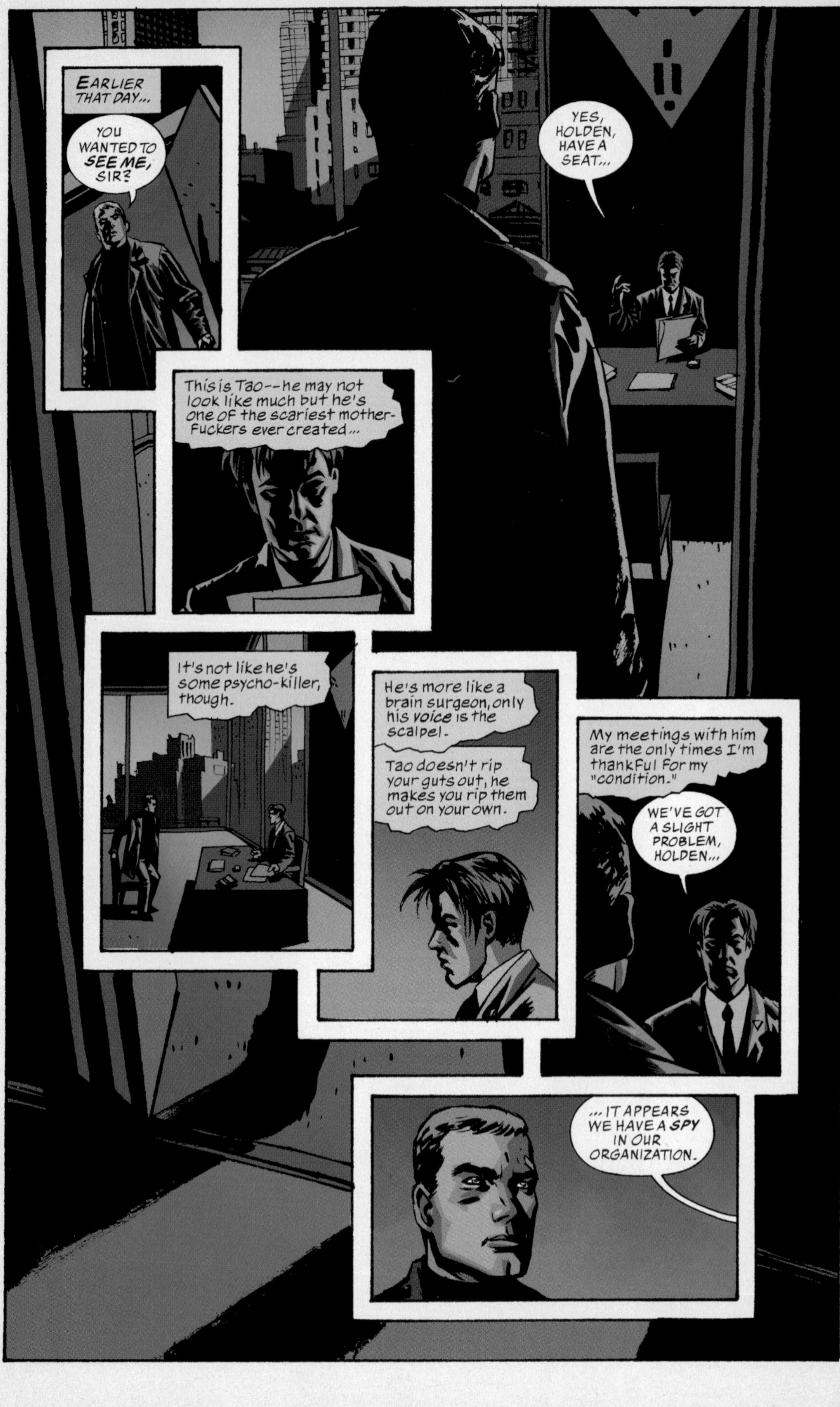
EARLIER THAT DAY...
YOU WANTED TO SEE ME, SIR?
YES, HOLDEN, HAVE A SEAT...
This is Tao--he may not look like much but he's one of the scariest mother-fuckers ever created...
It's not like he's some psycho-killer, though.
He's more like a brain surgeon, only his voice is the scalpel.
Tao doesn't rip your guts out, he makes you rip them out on your own.
My meetings with him are the only times I'm thankful for my "condition."
WE'VE GOT A SLIGHT PROBLEM, HOLDEN...
...IT APPEARS WE HAVE A SPY IN OUR ORGANIZATION.

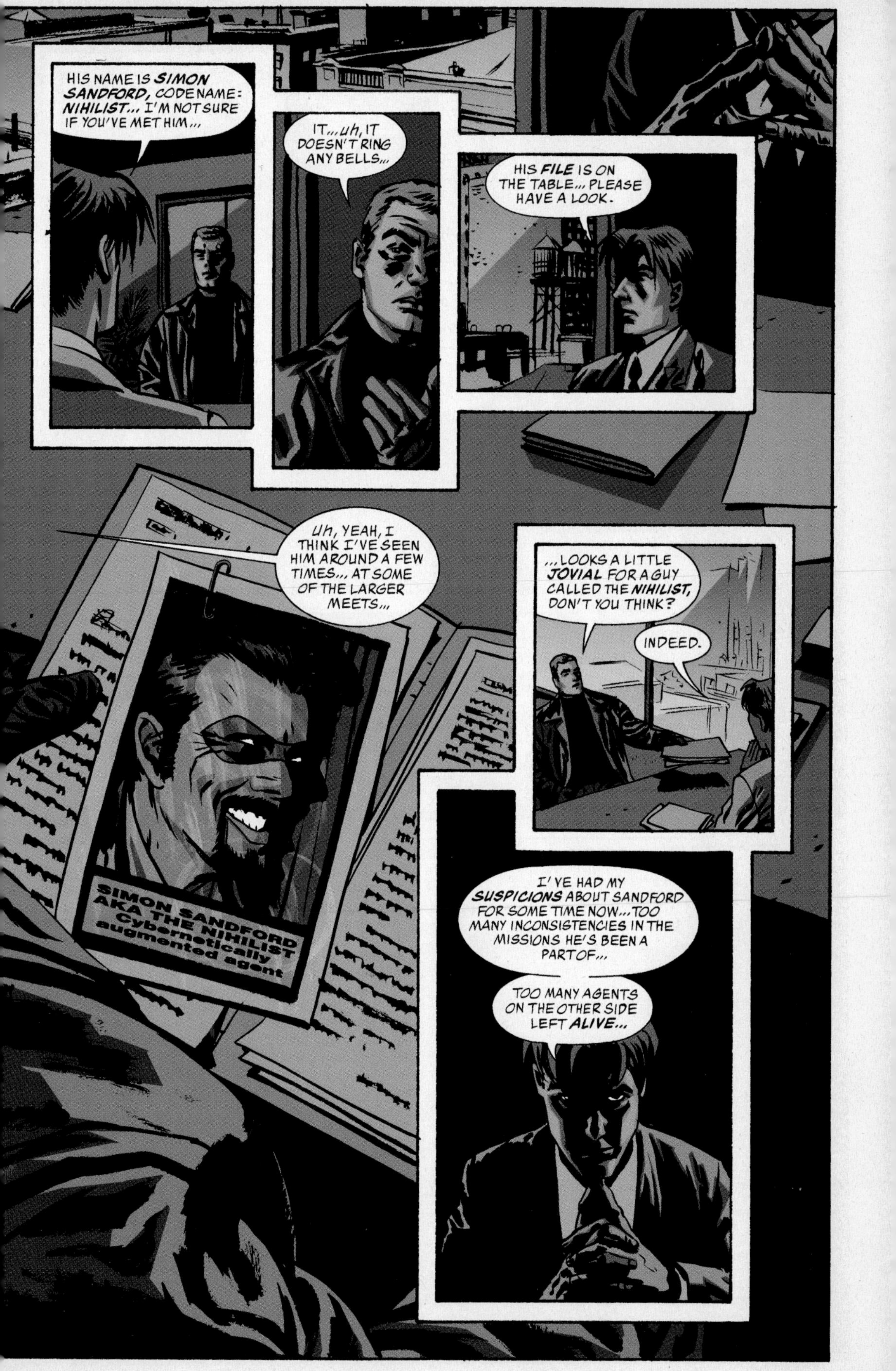
HIS NAME IS SIMON SANDFORD, CODENAME: NIHILIST... I'M NOT SURE IF YOU'VE MET HIM...
IT... uh, IT DOESN'T RING ANY BELLS...
HIS FILE IS ON THE TABLE... PLEASE HAVE A LOOK.
uh, YEAH, I THINK I'VE SEEN HIM AROUND A FEW TIMES... AT SOME OF THE LARGER MEETS...
SIMON SANDFORD AKA THE NIHILIST Cybernetically augmented agent
...LOOKS A LITTLE JOVIAL FOR A GUY CALLED THE NIHILIST, DON'T YOU THINK?
INDEED.
I'VE HAD MY SUSPICIONS ABOUT SANDFORD FOR SOME TIME NOW... TOO MANY INCONSISTENCIES IN THE MISSIONS HE'S BEEN A PART OF...
TOO MANY AGENTS ON THE OTHER SIDE LEFT ALIVE...

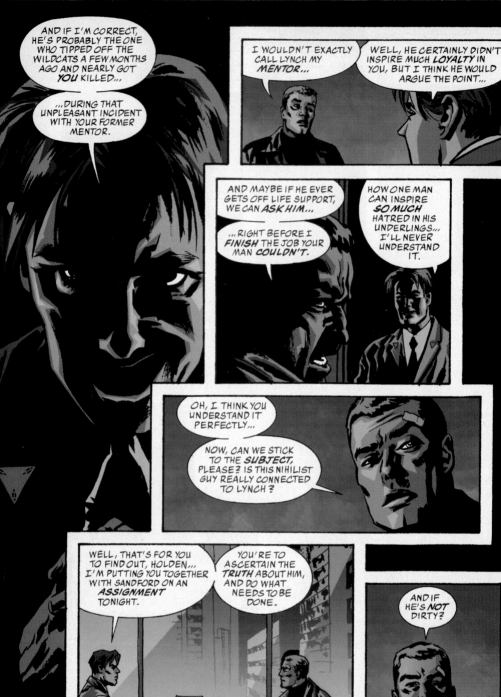

AND IF I'M CORRECT, HE'S PROBABLY THE ONE WHO TIPPED OFF THE WILDCATS A FEW MONTHS AGO AND NEARLY GOT *YOU* KILLED...

...DURING THAT UNPLEASANT INCIDENT WITH YOUR FORMER MENTOR.

I WOULDN'T EXACTLY CALL LYNCH MY *MENTOR*...

WELL, HE CERTAINLY DIDN'T INSPIRE MUCH *LOYALTY* IN YOU, BUT I THINK HE WOULD ARGUE THE POINT...

AND MAYBE IF HE EVER GETS OFF LIFE SUPPORT, WE CAN *ASK HIM*...

...RIGHT BEFORE I *FINISH* THE JOB YOUR MAN *COULDN'T*.

HOW ONE MAN CAN INSPIRE *SO MUCH* HATRED IN HIS UNDERLINGS... I'LL NEVER UNDERSTAND IT.

OH, I THINK YOU UNDERSTAND IT PERFECTLY...

NOW, CAN WE STICK TO THE *SUBJECT*, PLEASE? IS THIS NIHILIST GUY REALLY CONNECTED TO LYNCH?

WELL, THAT'S FOR YOU TO FIND OUT, HOLDEN... I'M PUTTING YOU TOGETHER WITH SANDFORD ON AN *ASSIGNMENT* TONIGHT.

YOU'RE TO ASCERTAIN THE *TRUTH* ABOUT HIM, AND DO WHAT NEEDS TO BE DONE.

AND IF HE'S *NOT* DIRTY?

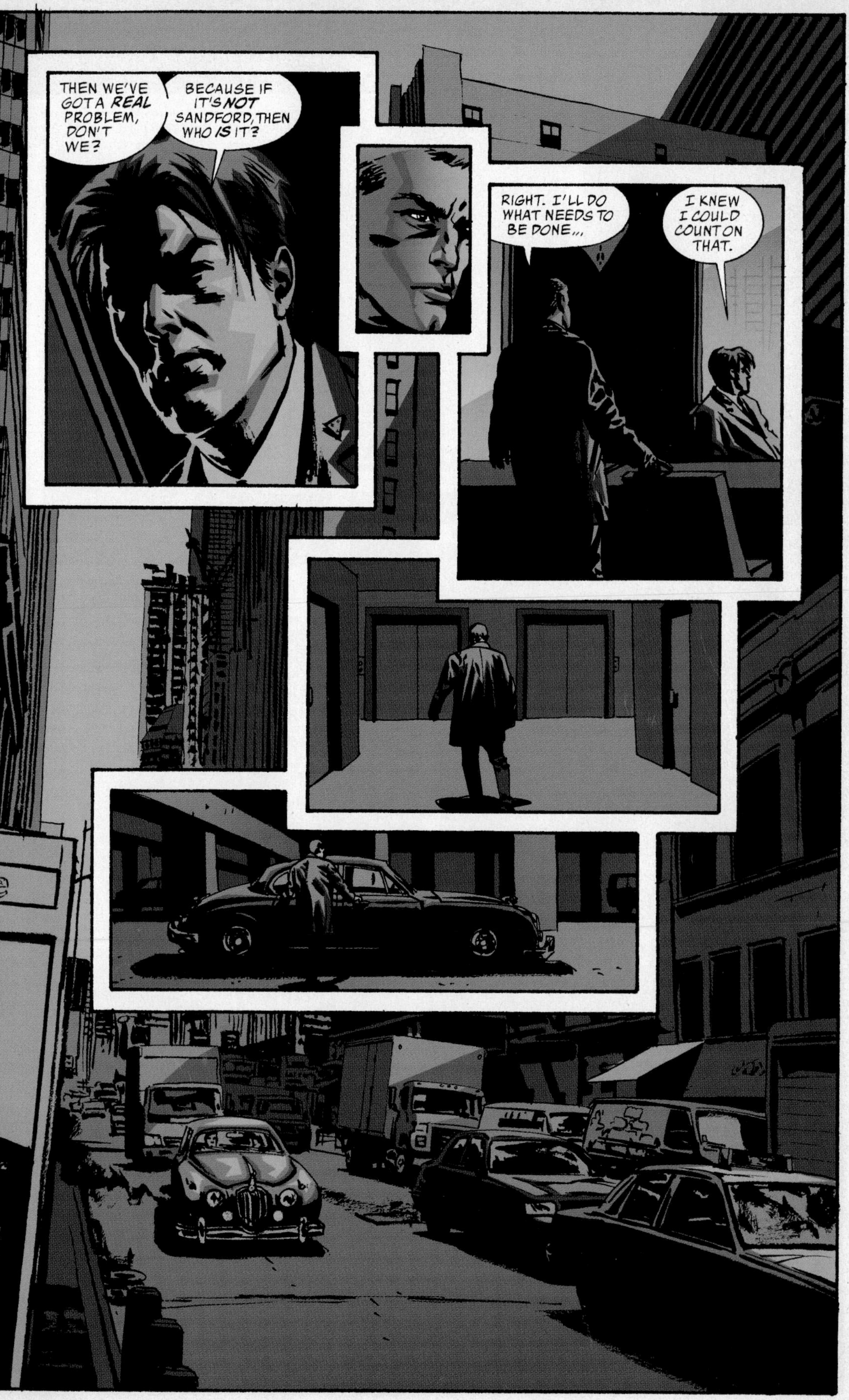
THEN WE'VE GOT A REAL PROBLEM, DON'T WE?
BECAUSE IF IT'S NOT SANDFORD, THEN WHO IS IT?
RIGHT. I'LL DO WHAT NEEDS TO BE DONE...
I KNEW I COULD COUNT ON THAT.

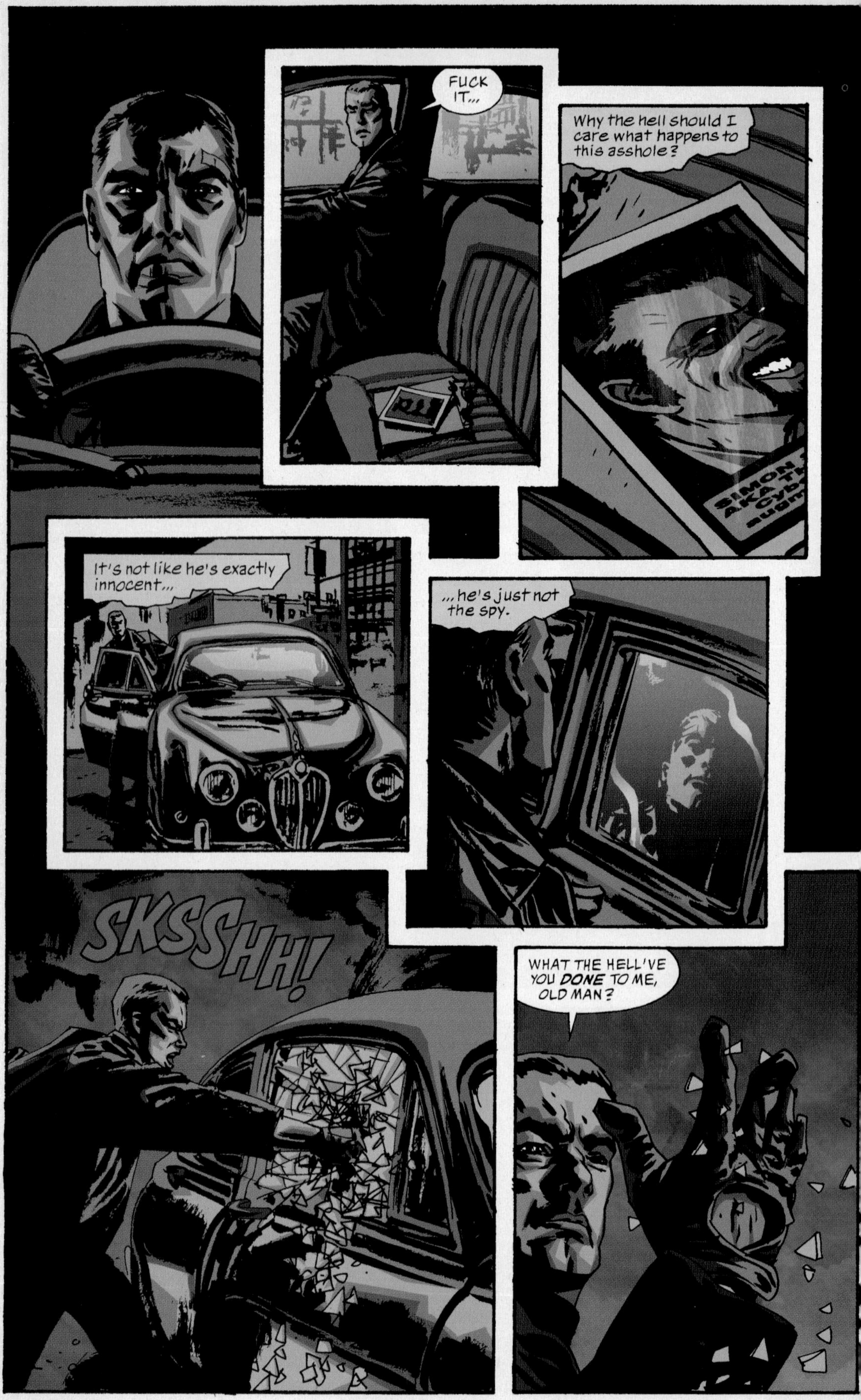
FUCK IT...
Why the hell should I care what happens to this asshole?
It's not like he's exactly innocent...
...he's just not the spy.
SKSSHH!
WHAT THE HELL'VE YOU DONE TO ME, OLD MAN?

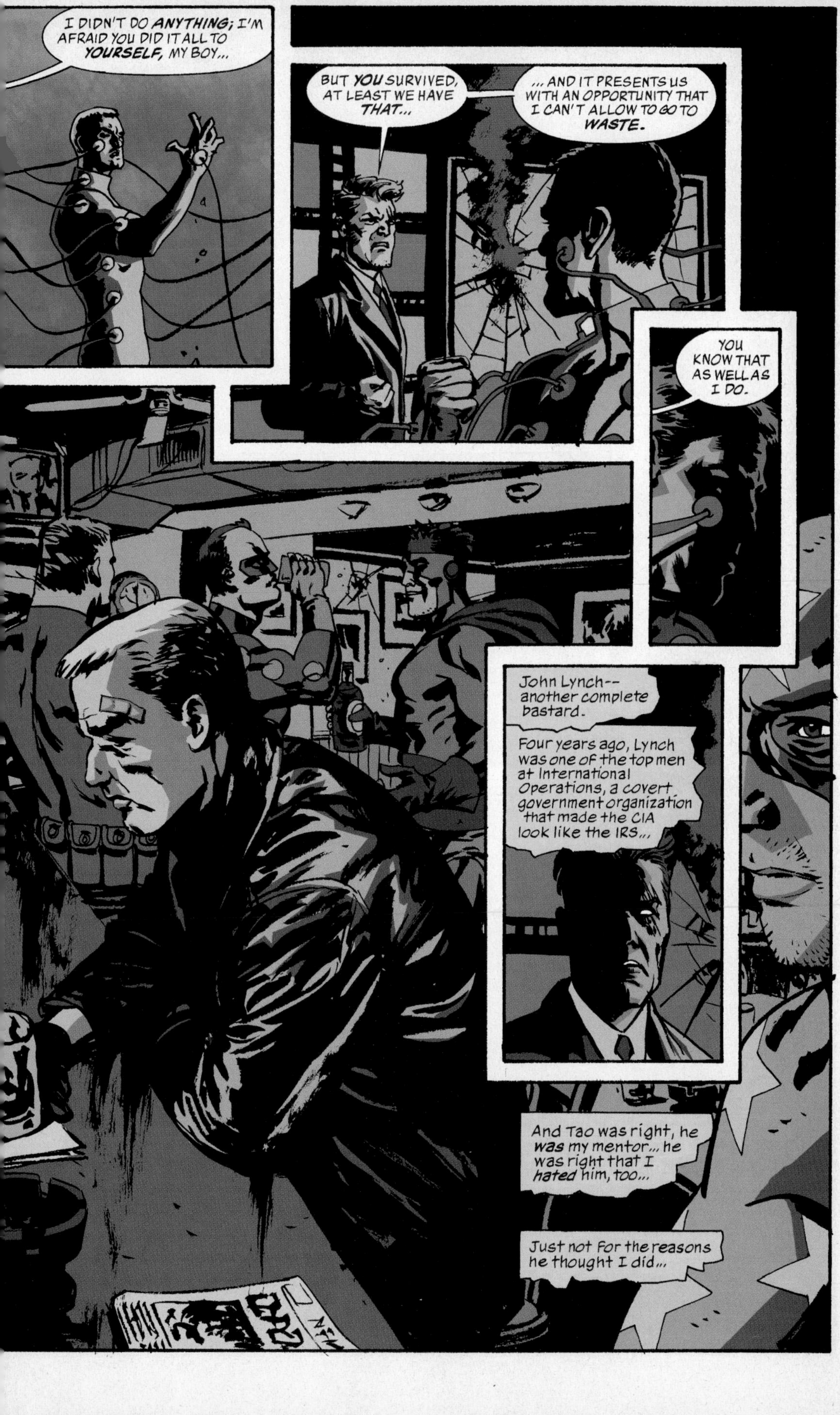

I DIDN'T DO ANYTHING; I'M AFRAID YOU DID IT ALL TO YOURSELF, MY BOY...
BUT YOU SURVIVED, AT LEAST WE HAVE THAT...
...AND IT PRESENTS US WITH AN OPPORTUNITY THAT I CAN'T ALLOW TO GO TO WASTE.
YOU KNOW THAT AS WELL AS I DO.
John Lynch-- another complete bastard.
Four years ago, Lynch was one of the top men at International Operations, a covert government organization that made the CIA look like the IRS...
And Tao was right, he was my mentor... he was right that I hated him, too...
Just not for the reasons he thought I did...

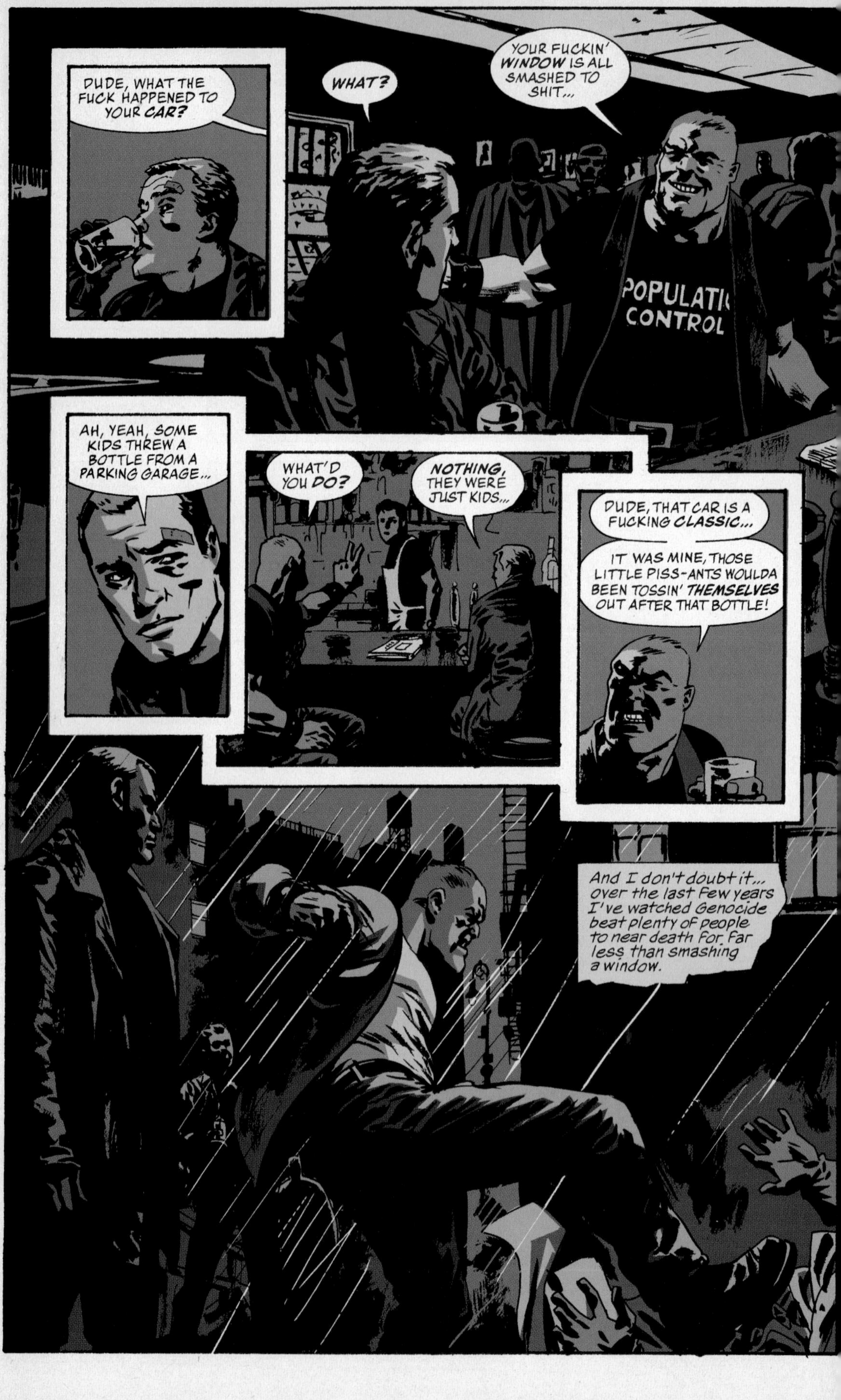

DUDE, WHAT THE FUCK HAPPENED TO YOUR CAR?
WHAT?
YOUR FUCKIN' WINDOW IS ALL SMASHED TO SHIT...
POPULATI CONTROL
AH, YEAH, SOME KIDS THREW A BOTTLE FROM A PARKING GARAGE...
WHAT'D YOU DO?
NOTHING, THEY WERE JUST KIDS...
DUDE, THAT CAR IS A FUCKING CLASSIC...
IT WAS MINE, THOSE LITTLE PISS-ANTS WOULDA BEEN TOSSIN' THEMSELVES OUT AFTER THAT BOTTLE!
And I don't doubt it... over the last few years I've watched Genocide beat plenty of people to near death for far less than smashing a window.

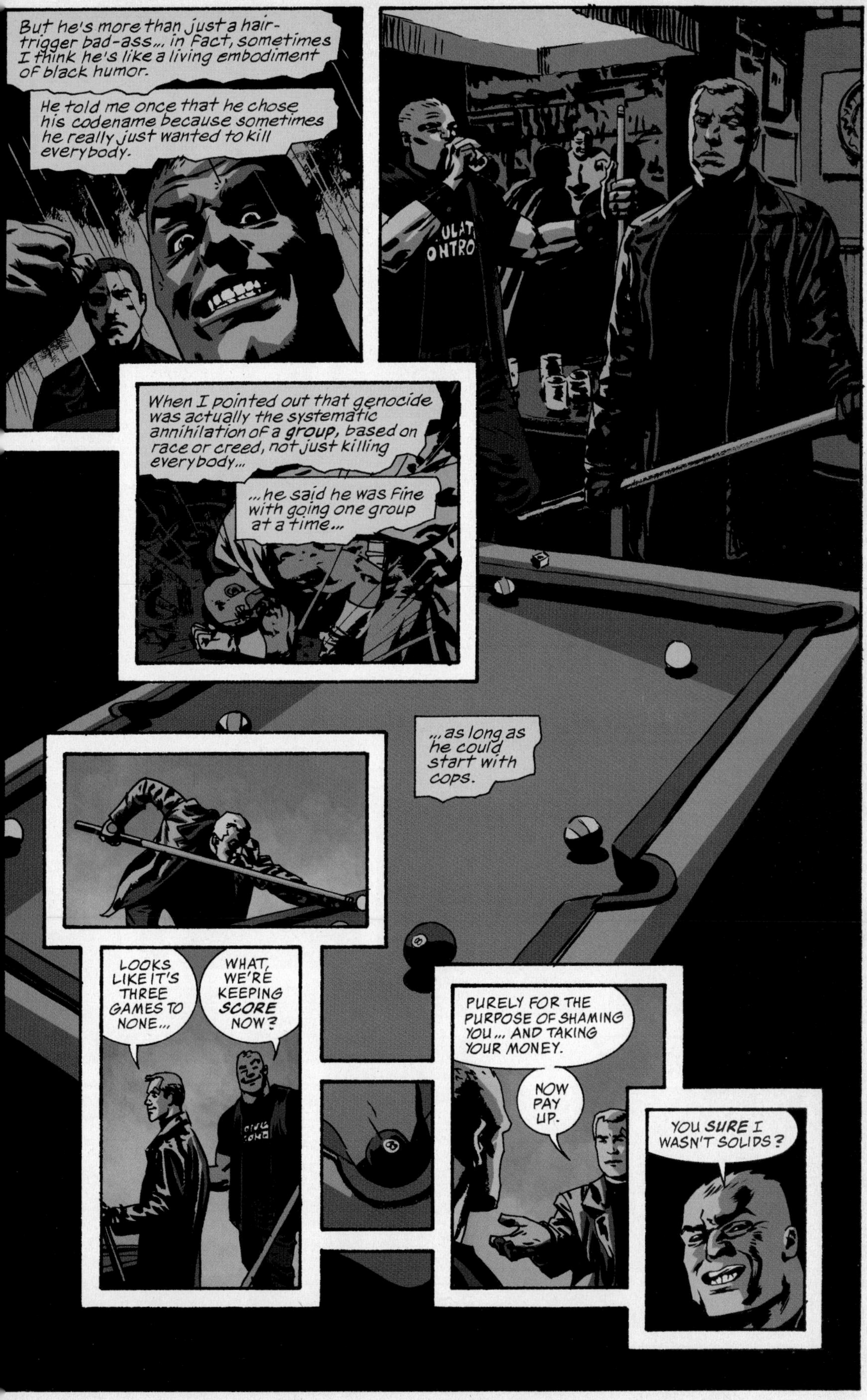
But he's more than just a hair-trigger bad-ass... in fact, sometimes I think he's like a living embodiment of black humor.
He told me once that he chose his codename because sometimes he really just wanted to kill everybody.
When I pointed out that genocide was actually the systematic annihilation of a group, based on race or creed, not just killing everybody...
...he said he was fine with going one group at a time...
...as long as he could start with cops.
LOOKS LIKE IT'S THREE GAMES TO NONE...
WHAT, WE'RE KEEPING SCORE NOW?
PURELY FOR THE PURPOSE OF SHAMING YOU... AND TAKING YOUR MONEY.
NOW PAY UP.
YOU SURE I WASN'T SOLIDS?

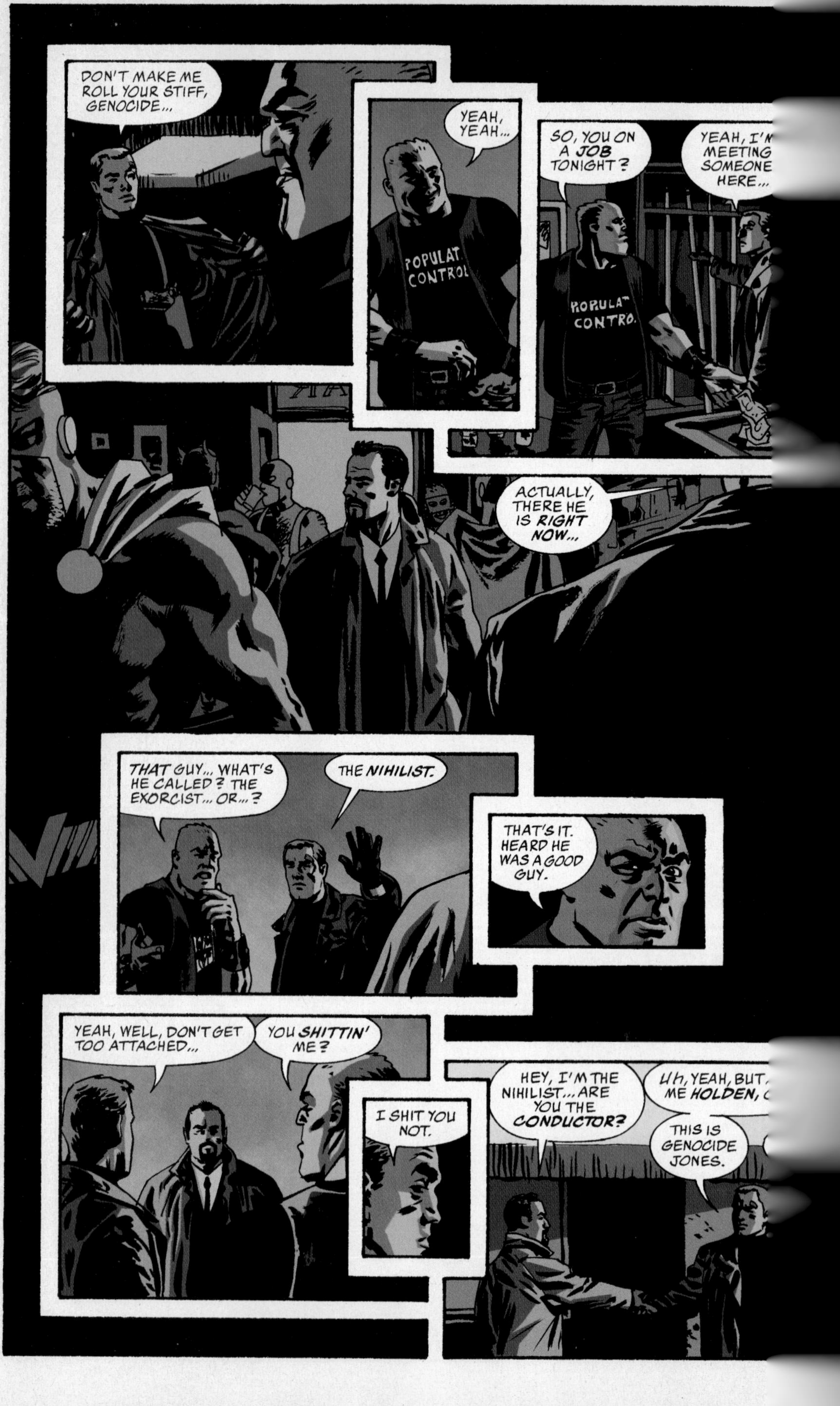
DON'T MAKE ME ROLL YOUR STIFF, GENOCIDE...
YEAH, YEAH...
POPULAT CONTROL
SO, YOU ON A JOB TONIGHT?
YEAH, I'M MEETING SOMEONE HERE...
ACTUALLY, THERE HE IS RIGHT NOW...
THAT GUY... WHAT'S HE CALLED? THE EXORCIST... OR...?
THE NIHILIST.
THAT'S IT. HEARD HE WAS A GOOD GUY.
YEAH, WELL, DON'T GET TOO ATTACHED...
YOU SHITTIN' ME?
I SHIT YOU NOT.
HEY, I'M THE NIHILIST... ARE YOU THE CONDUCTOR?
UH, YEAH, BUT... ME HOLDEN,
THIS IS GENOCIDE JONES.

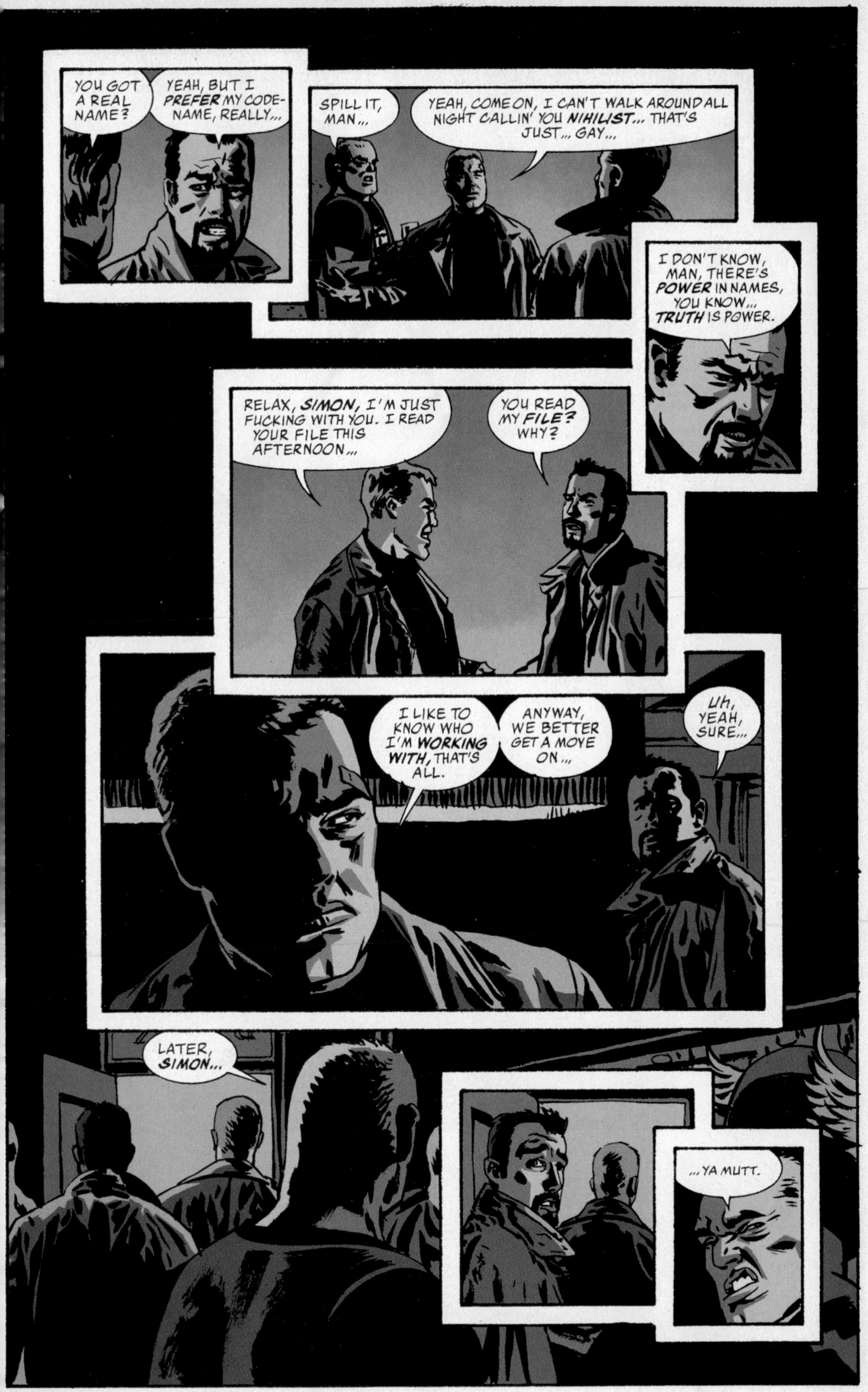
YOU GOT A REAL NAME?
YEAH, BUT I PREFER MY CODE-NAME, REALLY...
SPILL IT, MAN...
YEAH, COME ON, I CAN'T WALK AROUND ALL NIGHT CALLIN' YOU NIHILIST... THAT'S JUST... GAY...
I DON'T KNOW, MAN, THERE'S POWER IN NAMES, YOU KNOW... TRUTH IS POWER.
RELAX, SIMON, I'M JUST FUCKING WITH YOU. I READ YOUR FILE THIS AFTERNOON...
YOU READ MY FILE? WHY?
I LIKE TO KNOW WHO I'M WORKING WITH, THAT'S ALL.
ANYWAY, WE BETTER GET A MOVE ON...
UH, YEAH, SURE...
LATER, SIMON...
...YA MUTT.

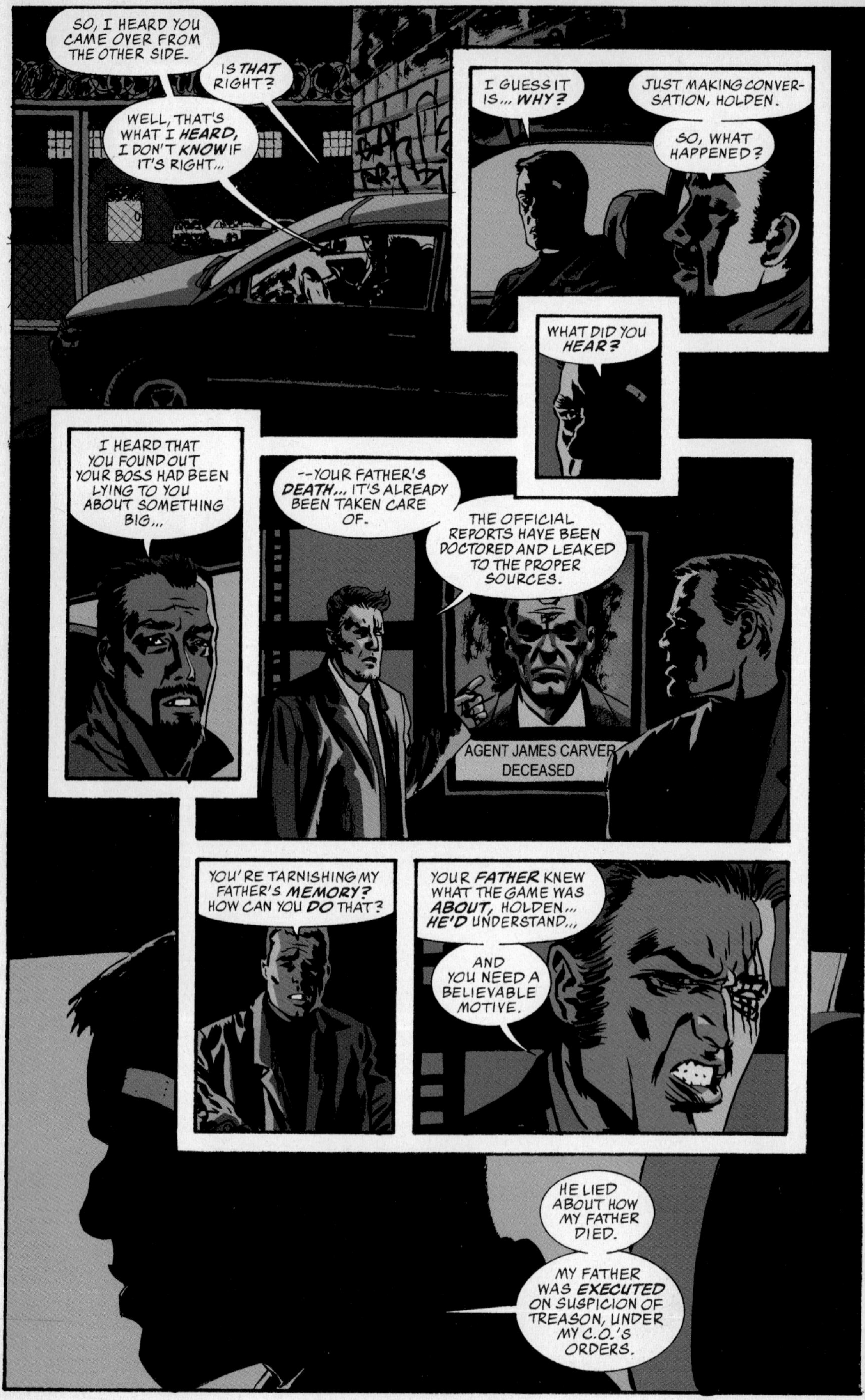
SO, I HEARD YOU CAME OVER FROM THE OTHER SIDE.
IS THAT RIGHT?
WELL, THAT'S WHAT I HEARD, I DON'T KNOW IF IT'S RIGHT...
I GUESS IT IS... WHY?
JUST MAKING CONVERSATION, HOLDEN.
SO, WHAT HAPPENED?
WHAT DID YOU HEAR?
I HEARD THAT YOU FOUND OUT YOUR BOSS HAD BEEN LYING TO YOU ABOUT SOMETHING BIG...
--YOUR FATHER'S DEATH... IT'S ALREADY BEEN TAKEN CARE OF.
THE OFFICIAL REPORTS HAVE BEEN DOCTORED AND LEAKED TO THE PROPER SOURCES.
AGENT JAMES CARVER DECEASED
YOU'RE TARNISHING MY FATHER'S MEMORY? HOW CAN YOU DO THAT?
YOUR FATHER KNEW WHAT THE GAME WAS ABOUT, HOLDEN... HE'D UNDERSTAND...
AND YOU NEED A BELIEVABLE MOTIVE.
HE LIED ABOUT HOW MY FATHER DIED.
MY FATHER WAS EXECUTED ON SUSPICION OF TREASON, UNDER MY C.O.'S ORDERS.

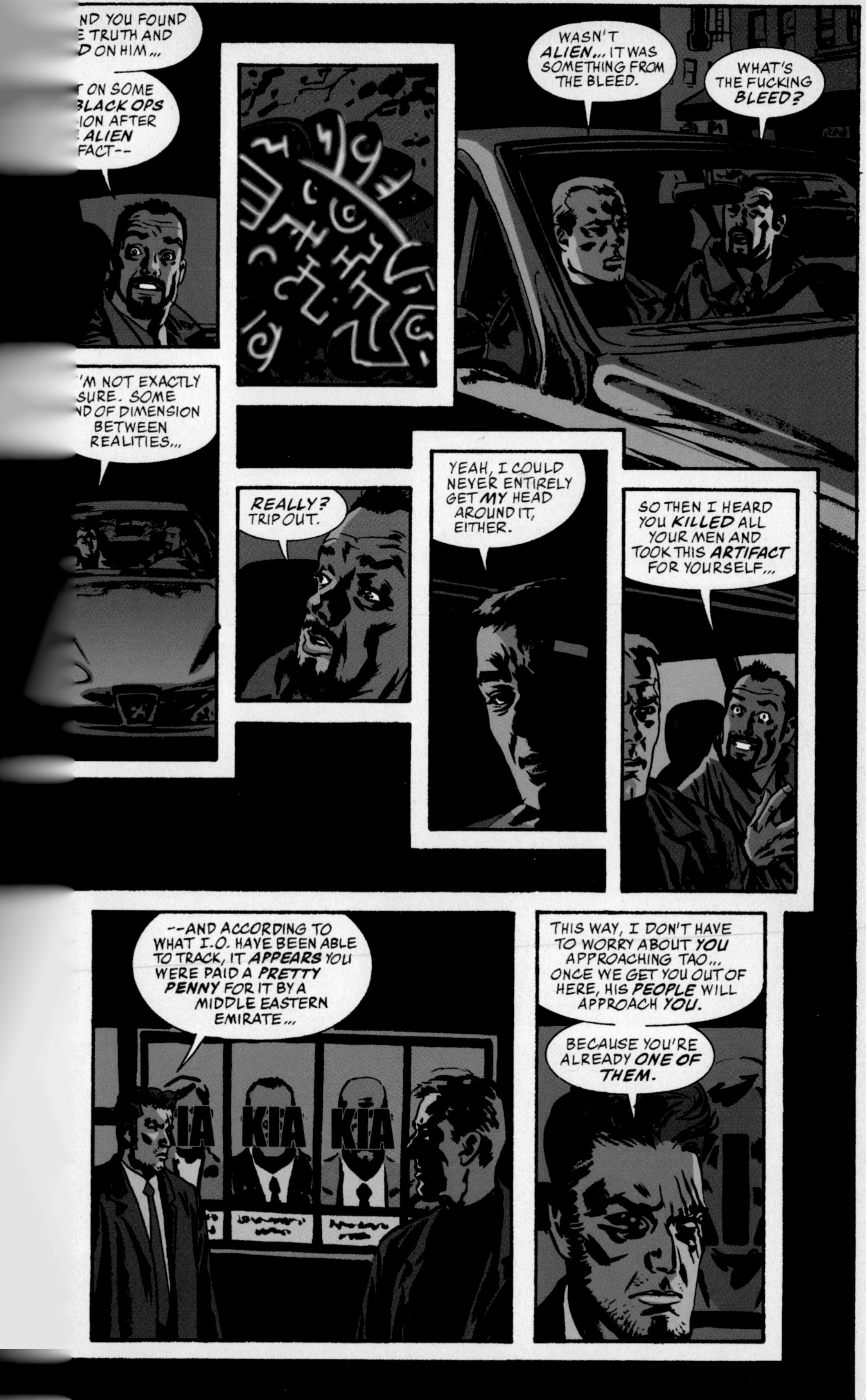
ND YOU FOUND
E TRUTH AND
D ON HIM...
T ON SOME
BLACK OPS
ION AFTER
ALIEN
FACT--
WASN'T ALIEN... IT WAS SOMETHING FROM THE BLEED.
WHAT'S THE FUCKING BLEED?
'M NOT EXACTLY
SURE. SOME
ND OF DIMENSION
BETWEEN
REALITIES...
REALLY? TRIP OUT.
YEAH, I COULD NEVER ENTIRELY GET MY HEAD AROUND IT, EITHER.
SO THEN I HEARD YOU KILLED ALL YOUR MEN AND TOOK THIS ARTIFACT FOR YOURSELF...
--AND ACCORDING TO WHAT I.O. HAVE BEEN ABLE TO TRACK, IT APPEARS YOU WERE PAID A PRETTY PENNY FOR IT BY A MIDDLE EASTERN EMIRATE...
KIA
KIA
KIA
THIS WAY, I DON'T HAVE TO WORRY ABOUT YOU APPROACHING TAO... ONCE WE GET YOU OUT OF HERE, HIS PEOPLE WILL APPROACH YOU.
BECAUSE YOU'RE ALREADY ONE OF THEM.

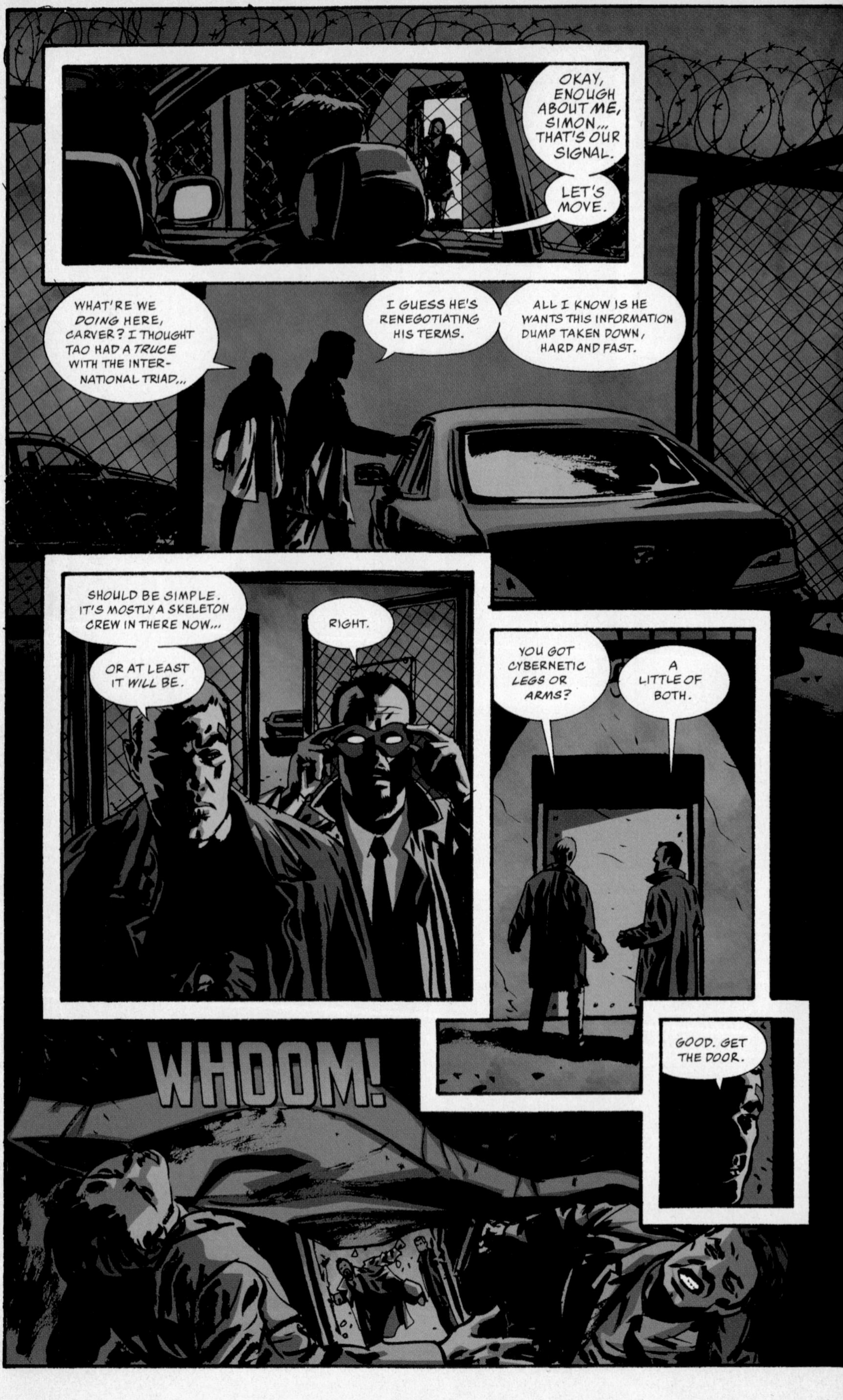
OKAY, ENOUGH ABOUT ME, SIMON... THAT'S OUR SIGNAL.
LET'S MOVE.
WHAT'RE WE DOING HERE, CARVER? I THOUGHT TAO HAD A TRUCE WITH THE INTERNATIONAL TRIAD...
I GUESS HE'S RENEGOTIATING HIS TERMS.
ALL I KNOW IS HE WANTS THIS INFORMATION DUMP TAKEN DOWN, HARD AND FAST.
SHOULD BE SIMPLE. IT'S MOSTLY A SKELETON CREW IN THERE NOW...
OR AT LEAST IT WILL BE.
RIGHT.
YOU GOT CYBERNETIC LEGS OR ARMS?
A LITTLE OF BOTH.
GOOD. GET THE DOOR.
WHOOM!

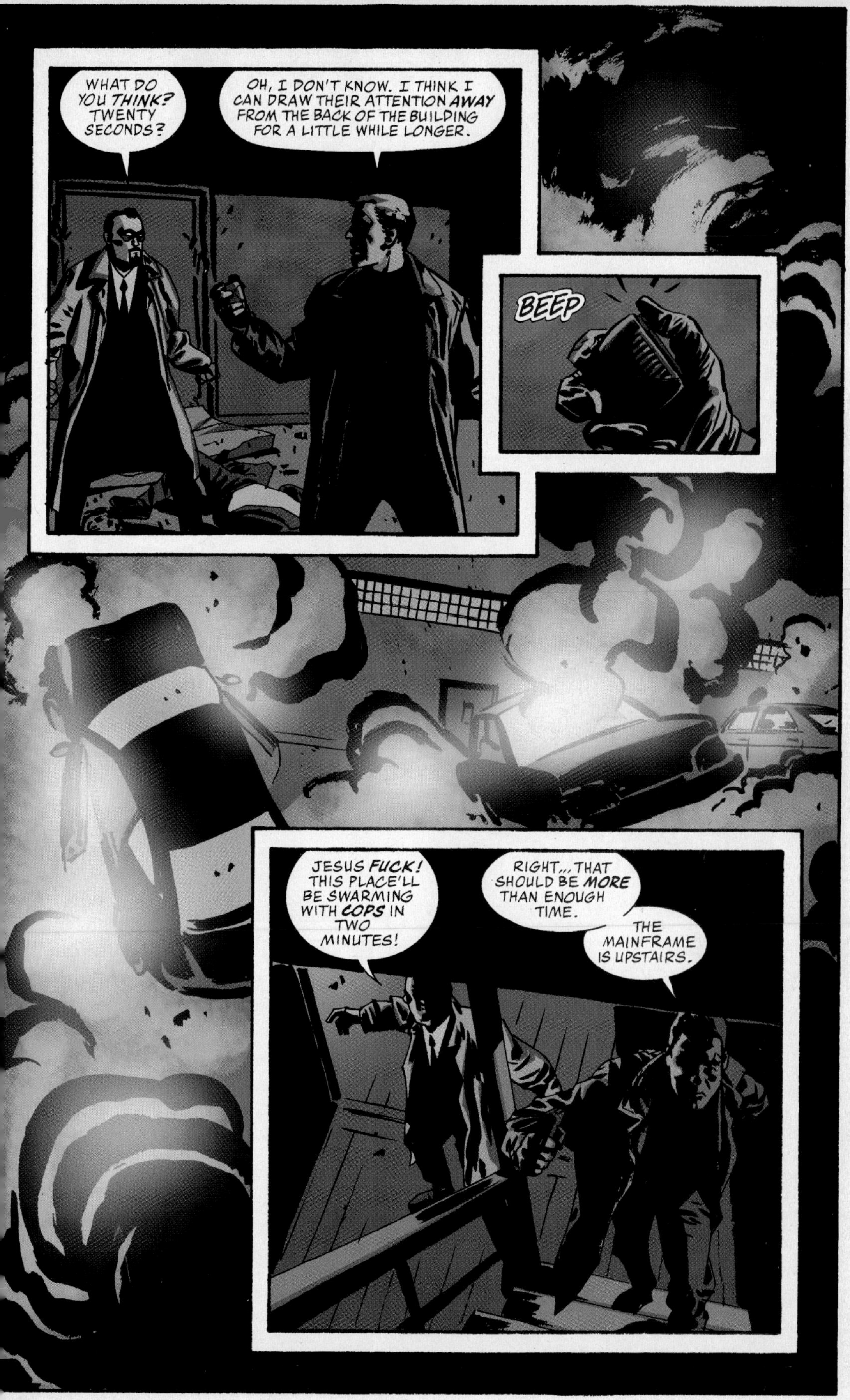
WHAT DO YOU THINK? TWENTY SECONDS?
OH, I DON'T KNOW. I THINK I CAN DRAW THEIR ATTENTION AWAY FROM THE BACK OF THE BUILDING FOR A LITTLE WHILE LONGER.
BEEP
JESUS FUCK! THIS PLACE'LL BE SWARMING WITH COPS IN TWO MINUTES!
RIGHT... THAT SHOULD BE MORE THAN ENOUGH TIME.
THE MAINFRAME IS UPSTAIRS.

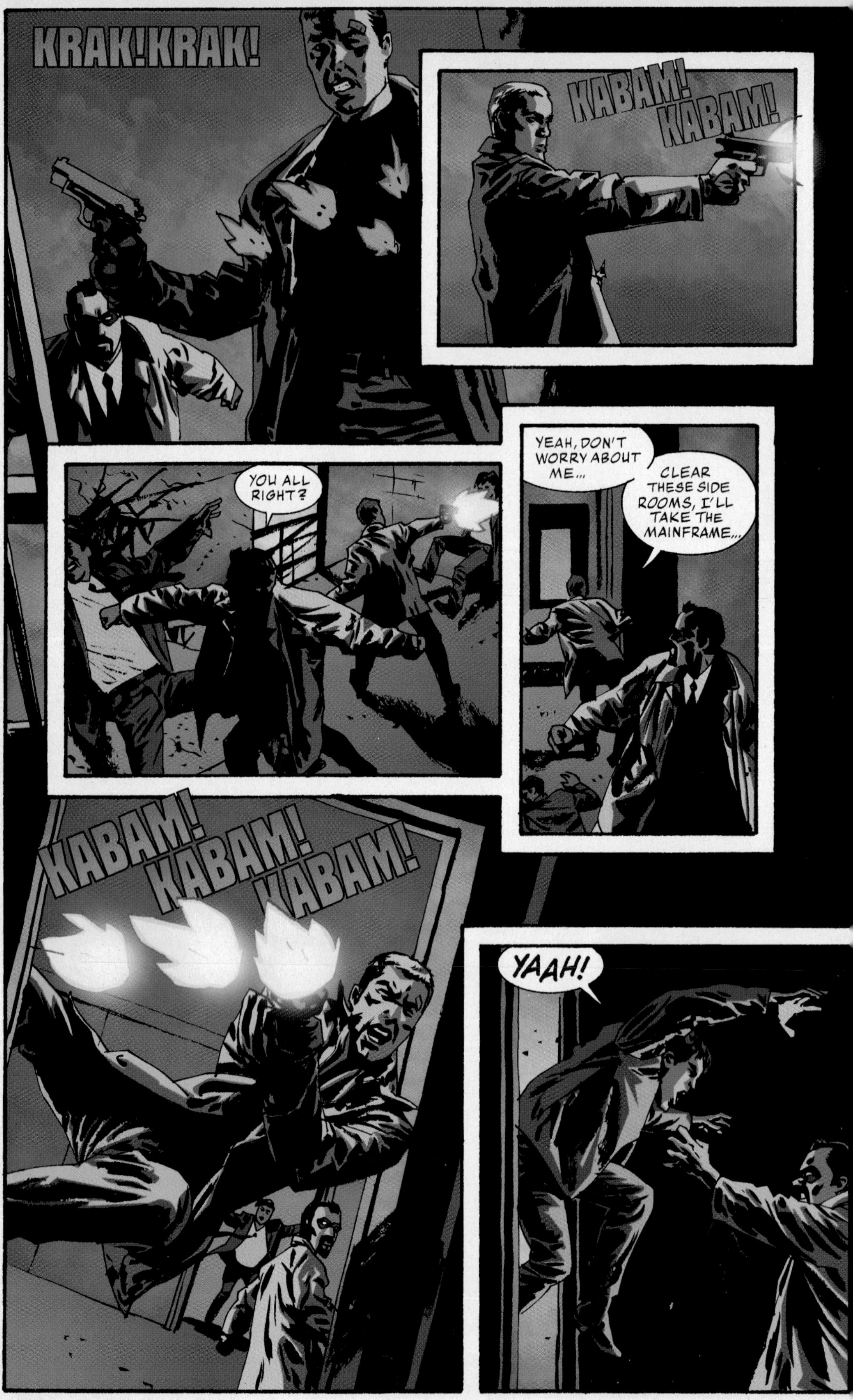
KRAK! KRAK!
KABAM! KABAM!
YOU ALL RIGHT?
YEAH, DON'T WORRY ABOUT ME...
CLEAR THESE SIDE ROOMS, I'LL TAKE THE MAINFRAME...
KABAM! KABAM! KABAM!
YAAH!

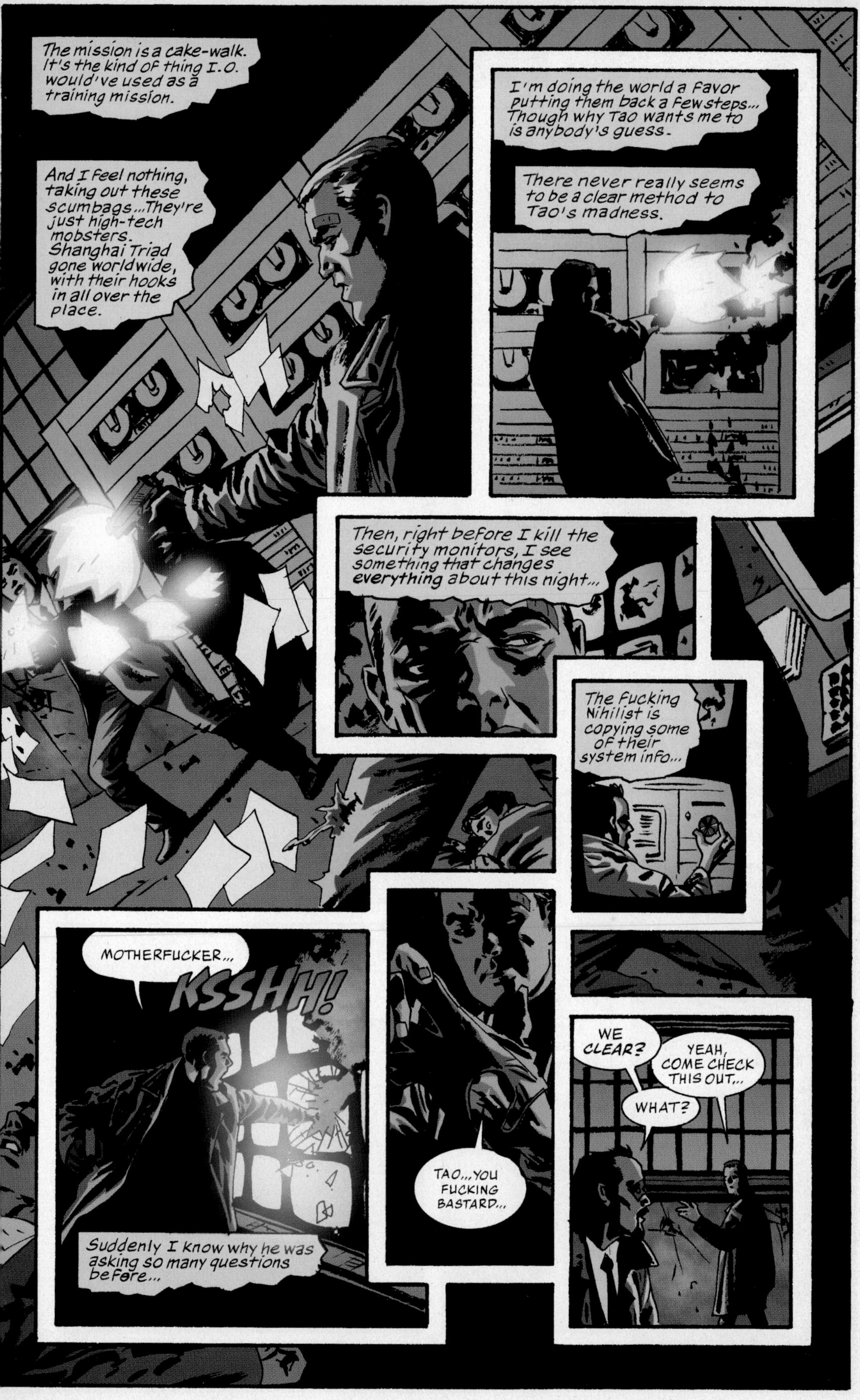

The mission is a cake-walk. It's the kind of thing I.O. would've used as a training mission.
And I feel nothing, taking out these scumbags...They're just high-tech mobsters. Shanghai Triad gone worldwide, with their hooks in all over the place.
I'm doing the world a favor putting them back a few steps... Though why Tao wants me to is anybody's guess.
There never really seems to be a clear method to Tao's madness.
Then, right before I kill the security monitors, I see something that changes everything about this night...
The fucking Nihilist is copying some of their system info...
MOTHERFUCKER...
KSSHH!
Suddenly I know why he was asking so many questions before...
TAO...YOU FUCKING BASTARD...
WE CLEAR?
YEAH, COME CHECK THIS OUT...
WHAT?

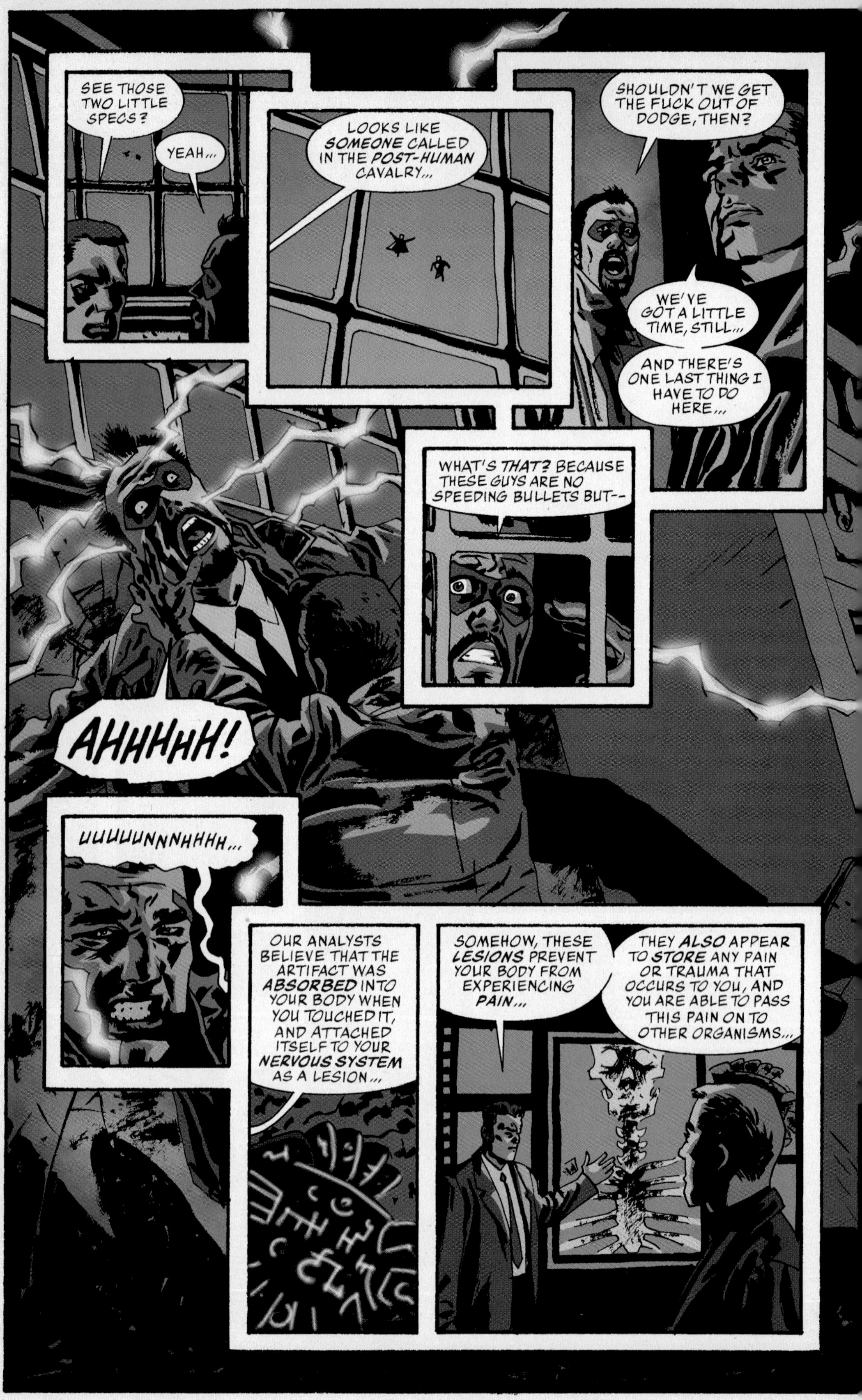
SEE THOSE TWO LITTLE SPECS?
YEAH...
LOOKS LIKE SOMEONE CALLED IN THE POST-HUMAN CAVALRY...
SHOULDN'T WE GET THE FUCK OUT OF DODGE, THEN?
WE'VE GOT A LITTLE TIME, STILL...
AND THERE'S ONE LAST THING I HAVE TO DO HERE...
WHAT'S THAT? BECAUSE THESE GUYS ARE NO SPEEDING BULLETS BUT--
AHHHHH!
UUUUUNNHHHH...
OUR ANALYSTS BELIEVE THAT THE ARTIFACT WAS ABSORBED INTO YOUR BODY WHEN YOU TOUCHED IT, AND ATTACHED ITSELF TO YOUR NERVOUS SYSTEM AS A LESION...
SOMEHOW, THESE LESIONS PREVENT YOUR BODY FROM EXPERIENCING PAIN...
THEY ALSO APPEAR TO STORE ANY PAIN OR TRAUMA THAT OCCURS TO YOU, AND YOU ARE ABLE TO PASS THIS PAIN ON TO OTHER ORGANISMS...

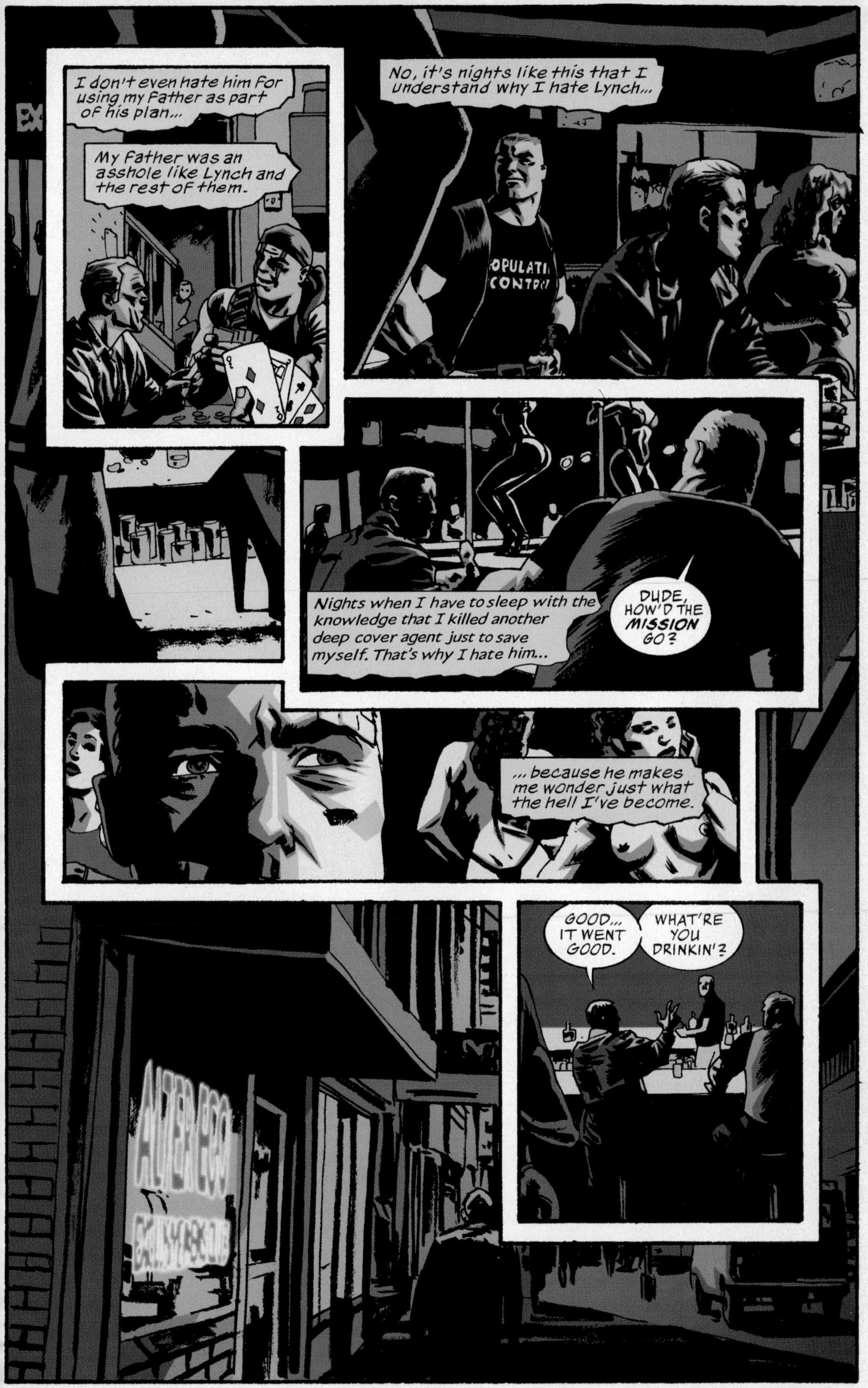
I don't even hate him for using my father as part of his plan...
My father was an asshole like Lynch and the rest of them.
No, it's nights like this that I understand why I hate Lynch...
POPULATI CONTR
Nights when I have to sleep with the knowledge that I killed another deep cover agent just to save myself. That's why I hate him...
DUDE, HOW'D THE MISSION GO?
...because he makes me wonder just what the hell I've become.
GOOD... IT WENT GOOD.
WHAT'RE YOU DRINKIN'?
ALTER EGO

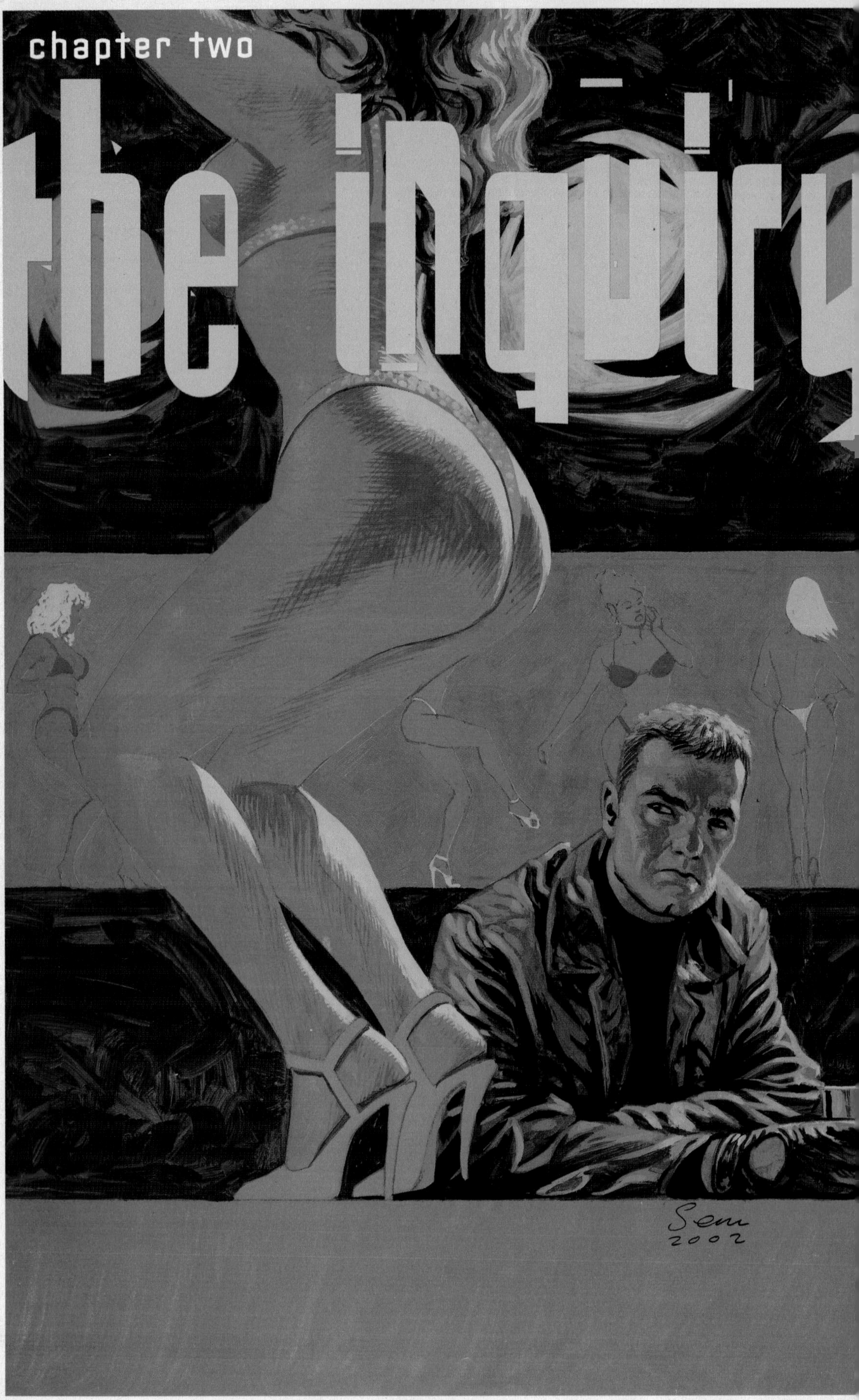
chapter two
the inquiry
Sean
2002

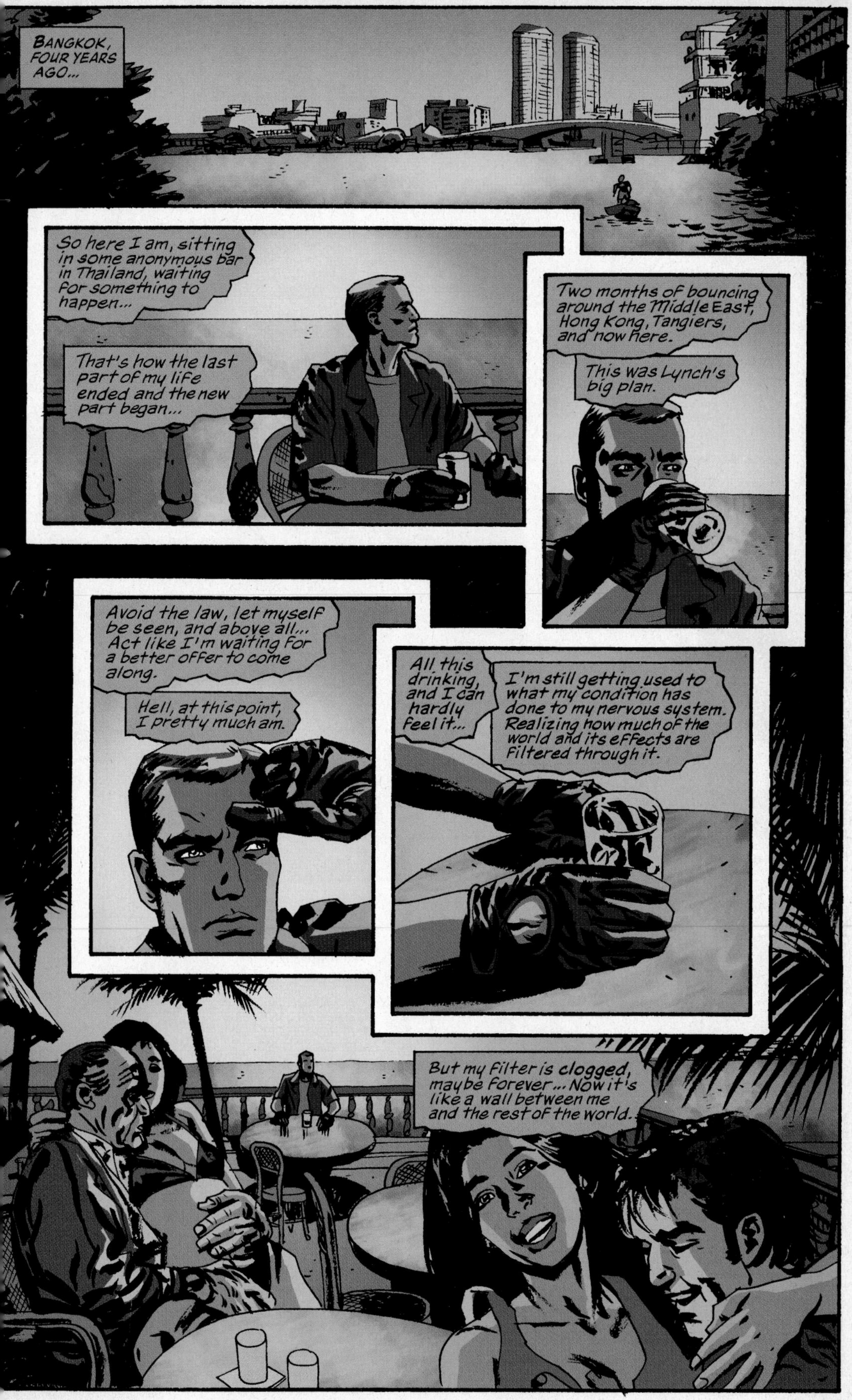
BANGKOK, FOUR YEARS AGO...
So here I am, sitting in some anonymous bar in Thailand, waiting for something to happen...
That's how the last part of my life ended and the new part began...
Two months of bouncing around the Middle East, Hong Kong, Tangiers, and now here.
This was Lynch's big plan.
Avoid the law, let myself be seen, and above all... Act like I'm waiting for a better offer to come along.
Hell, at this point, I pretty much am.
All this drinking, and I can hardly feel it...
I'm still getting used to what my condition has done to my nervous system. Realizing how much of the world and its effects are filtered through it.
But my filter is clogged, maybe forever... Now it's like a wall between me and the rest of the world.

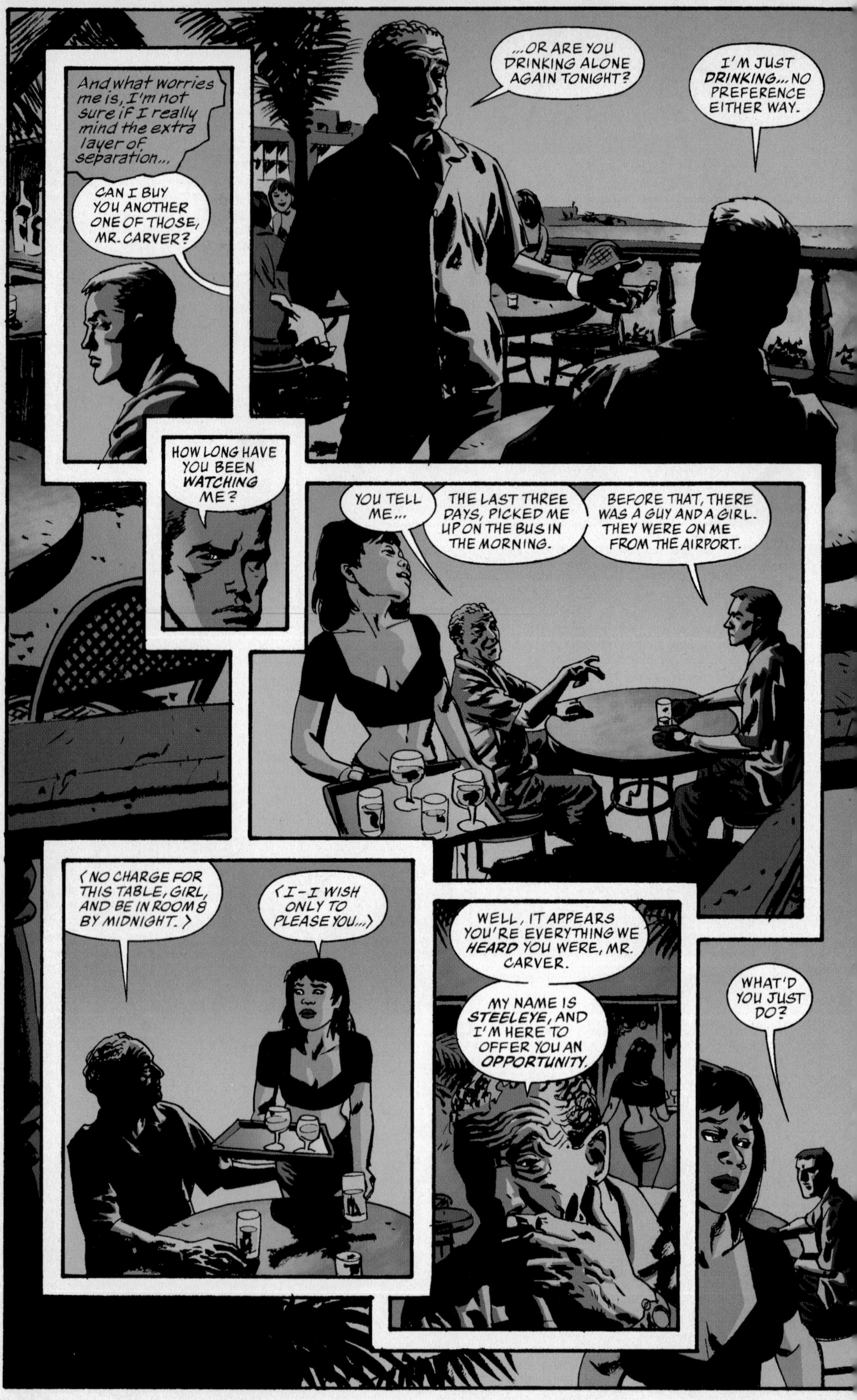
And what worries me is, I'm not sure if I really mind the extra layer of separation...
CAN I BUY YOU ANOTHER ONE OF THOSE, MR. CARVER?
...OR ARE YOU DRINKING ALONE AGAIN TONIGHT?
I'M JUST DRINKING... NO PREFERENCE EITHER WAY.
HOW LONG HAVE YOU BEEN WATCHING ME?
YOU TELL ME...
THE LAST THREE DAYS, PICKED ME UP ON THE BUS IN THE MORNING.
BEFORE THAT, THERE WAS A GUY AND A GIRL. THEY WERE ON ME FROM THE AIRPORT.
<NO CHARGE FOR THIS TABLE, GIRL, AND BE IN ROOM 8 BY MIDNIGHT.>
<I-I WISH ONLY TO PLEASE YOU...>
WELL, IT APPEARS YOU'RE EVERYTHING WE HEARD YOU WERE, MR. CARVER.
MY NAME IS STEELEYE, AND I'M HERE TO OFFER YOU AN OPPORTUNITY.
WHAT'D YOU JUST DO?

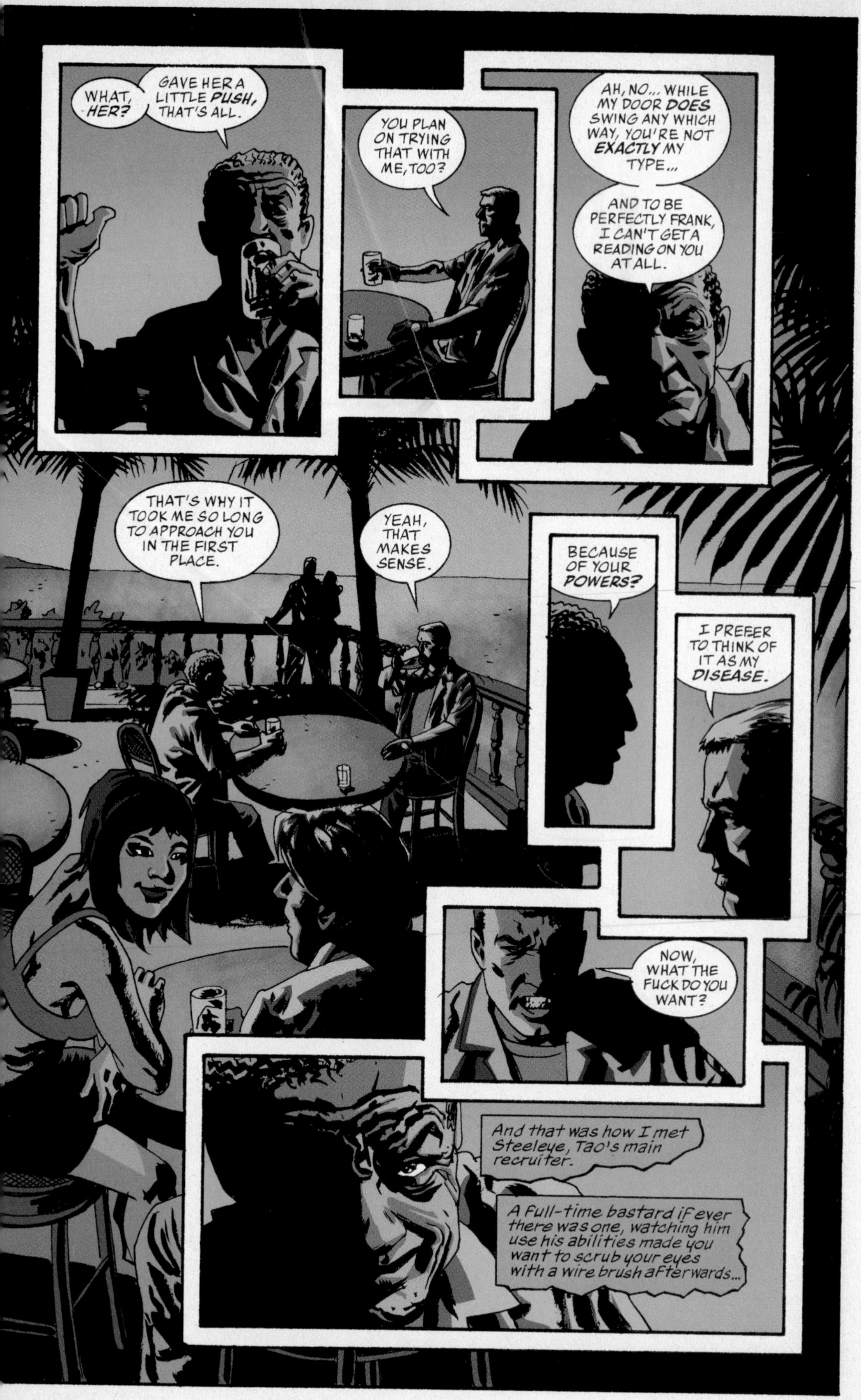
WHAT, HER?
GAVE HER A LITTLE PUSH, THAT'S ALL.
YOU PLAN ON TRYING THAT WITH ME, TOO?
AH, NO... WHILE MY DOOR DOES SWING ANY WHICH WAY, YOU'RE NOT EXACTLY MY TYPE...
AND TO BE PERFECTLY FRANK, I CAN'T GET A READING ON YOU AT ALL.
THAT'S WHY IT TOOK ME SO LONG TO APPROACH YOU IN THE FIRST PLACE.
YEAH, THAT MAKES SENSE.
BECAUSE OF YOUR POWERS?
I PREFER TO THINK OF IT AS MY DISEASE.
NOW, WHAT THE FUCK DO YOU WANT?
And that was how I met Steeleye, Tao's main recruiter.
A full-time bastard if ever there was one, watching him use his abilities made you want to scrub your eyes with a wire brush afterwards...

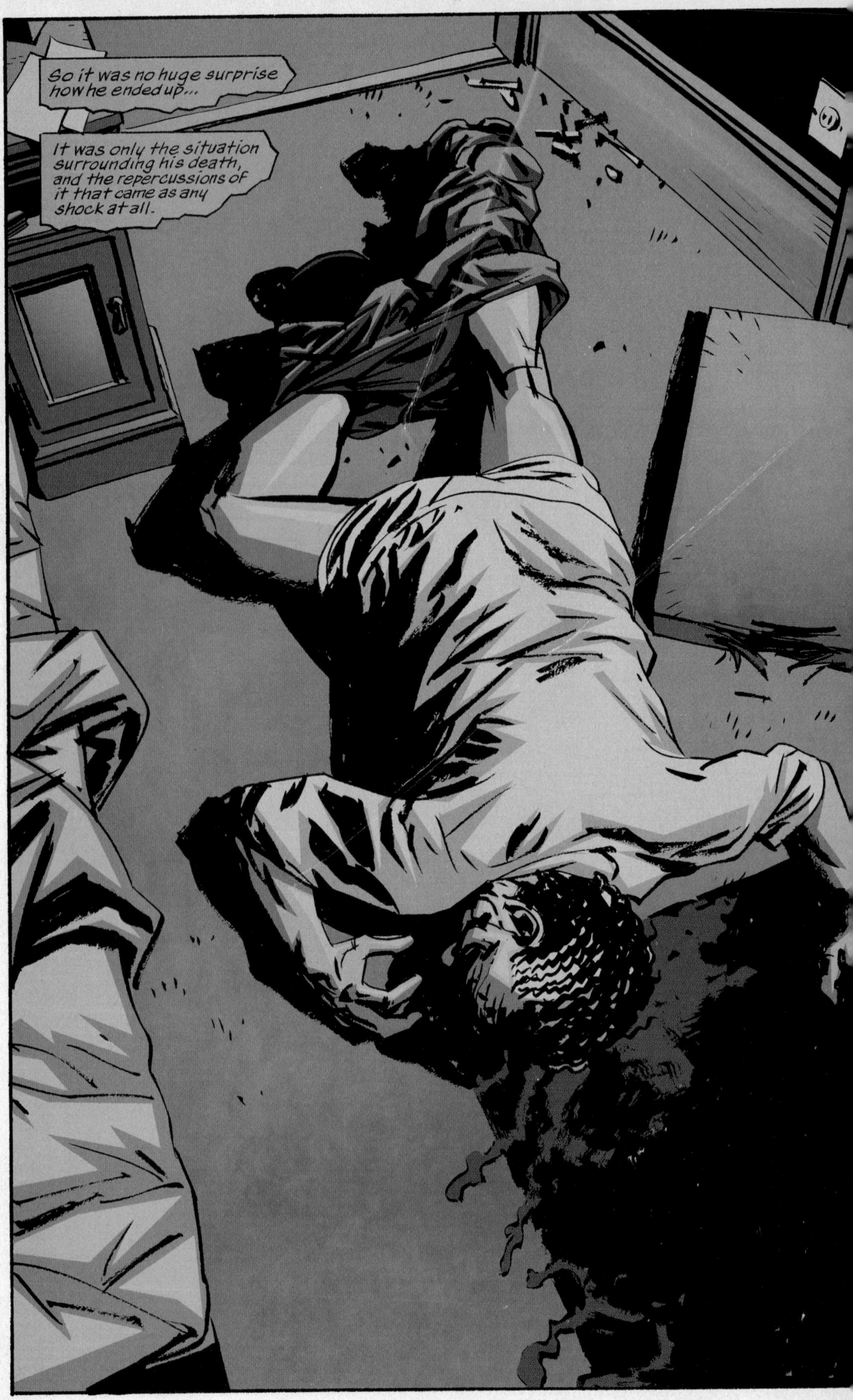
So it was no huge surprise how he ended up...
It was only the situation surrounding his death, and the repercussions of it that came as any shock at all.

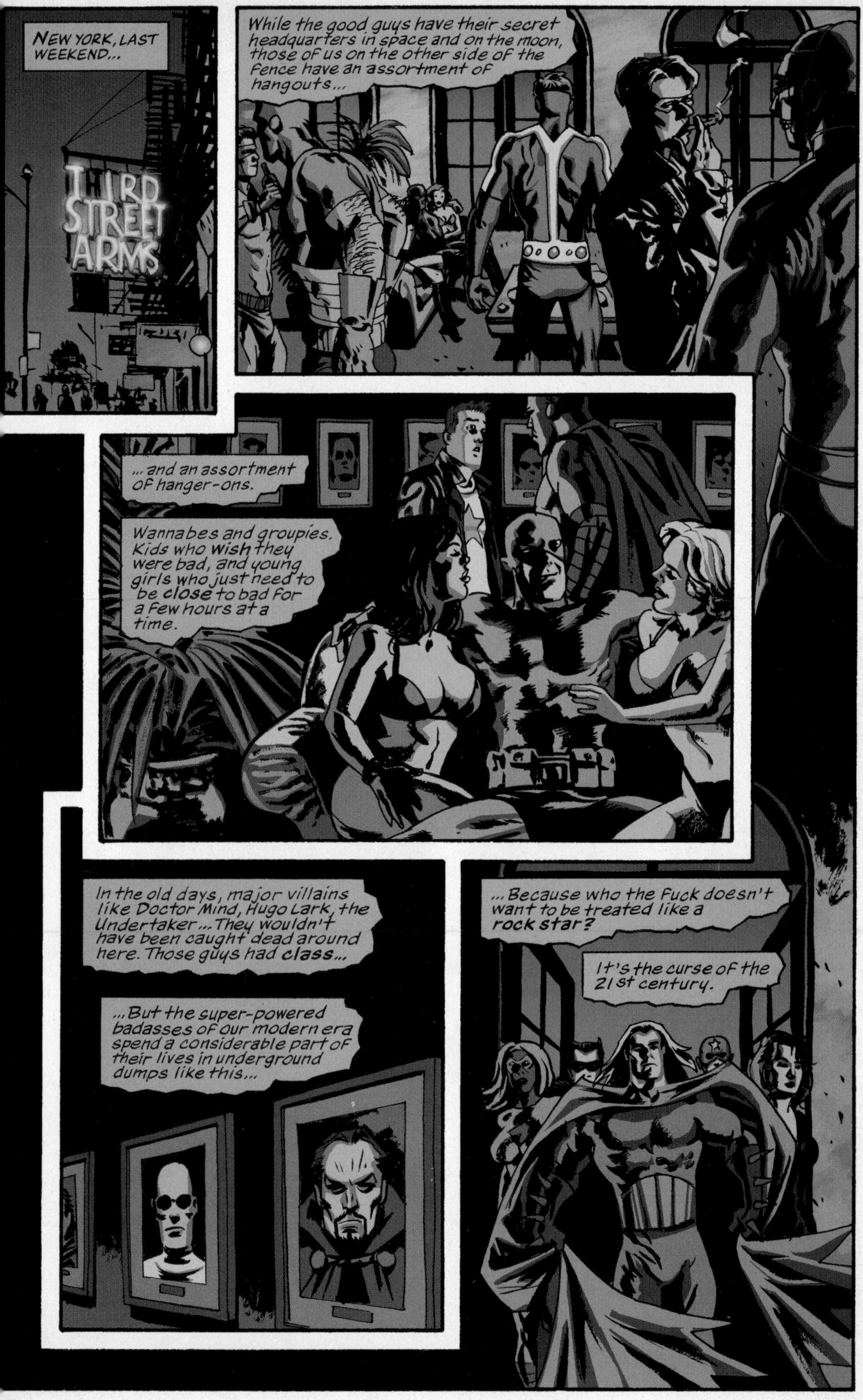
NEW YORK, LAST WEEKEND...
THIRD STREET ARMS
While the good guys have their secret headquarters in space and on the moon, those of us on the other side of the fence have an assortment of hangouts...
...and an assortment of hanger-ons.
Wannabes and groupies. Kids who wish they were bad, and young girls who just need to be close to bad for a few hours at a time.
In the old days, major villains like Doctor Mind, Hugo Lark, the Undertaker... They wouldn't have been caught dead around here. Those guys had class...
...But the super-powered badasses of our modern era spend a considerable part of their lives in underground dumps like this...
...Because who the fuck doesn't want to be treated like a rock star?
It's the curse of the 21st century.

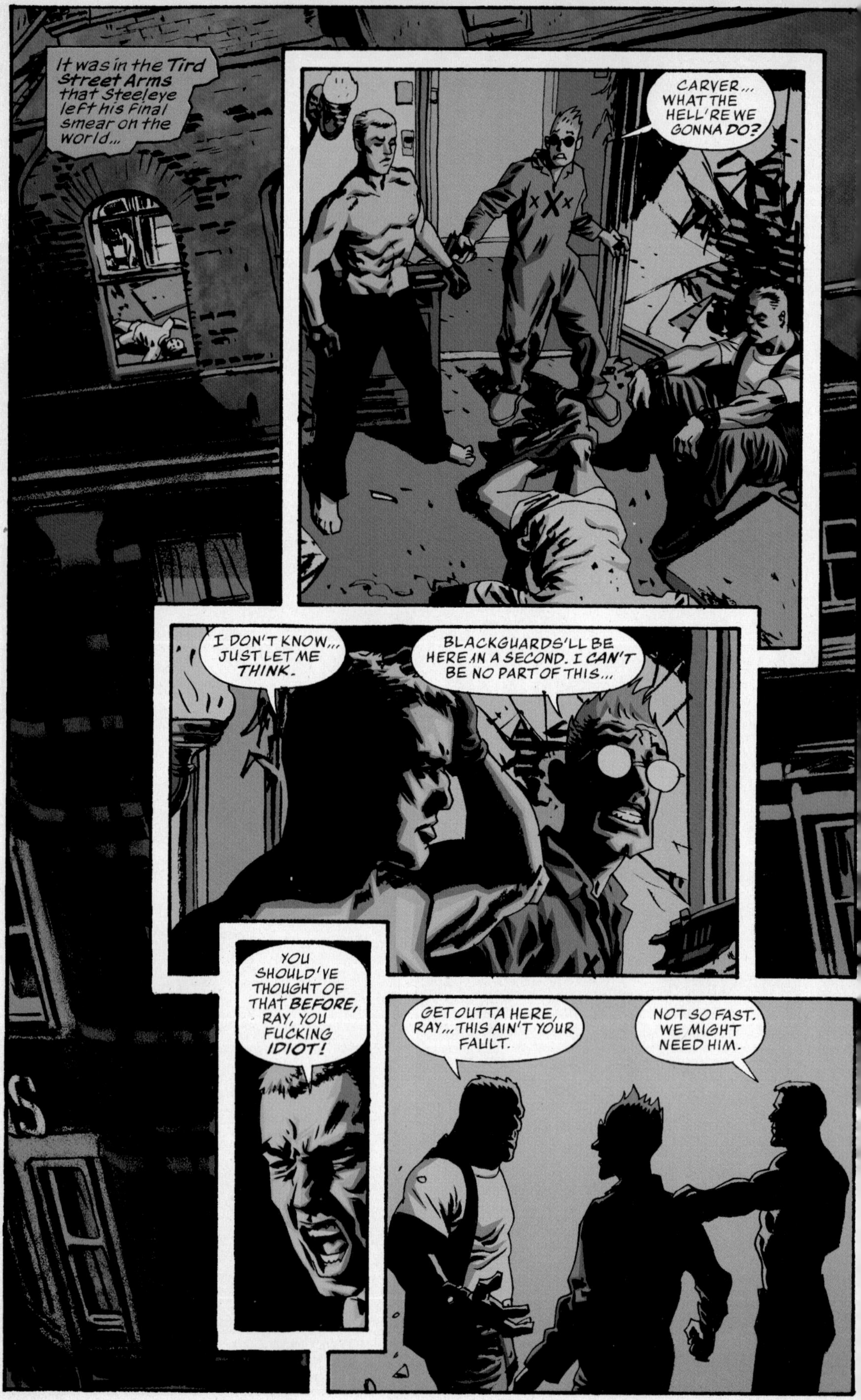
It was in the Tird Street Arms that Steeleye left his final smear on the world...
CARVER... WHAT THE HELL'RE WE GONNA DO?
I DON'T KNOW... JUST LET ME THINK.
BLACKGUARDS'LL BE HERE AN A SECOND. I CAN'T BE NO PART OF THIS...
YOU SHOULD'VE THOUGHT OF THAT BEFORE, RAY, YOU FUCKING IDIOT!
GET OUTTA HERE, RAY... THIS AIN'T YOUR FAULT.
NOT SO FAST. WE MIGHT NEED HIM.

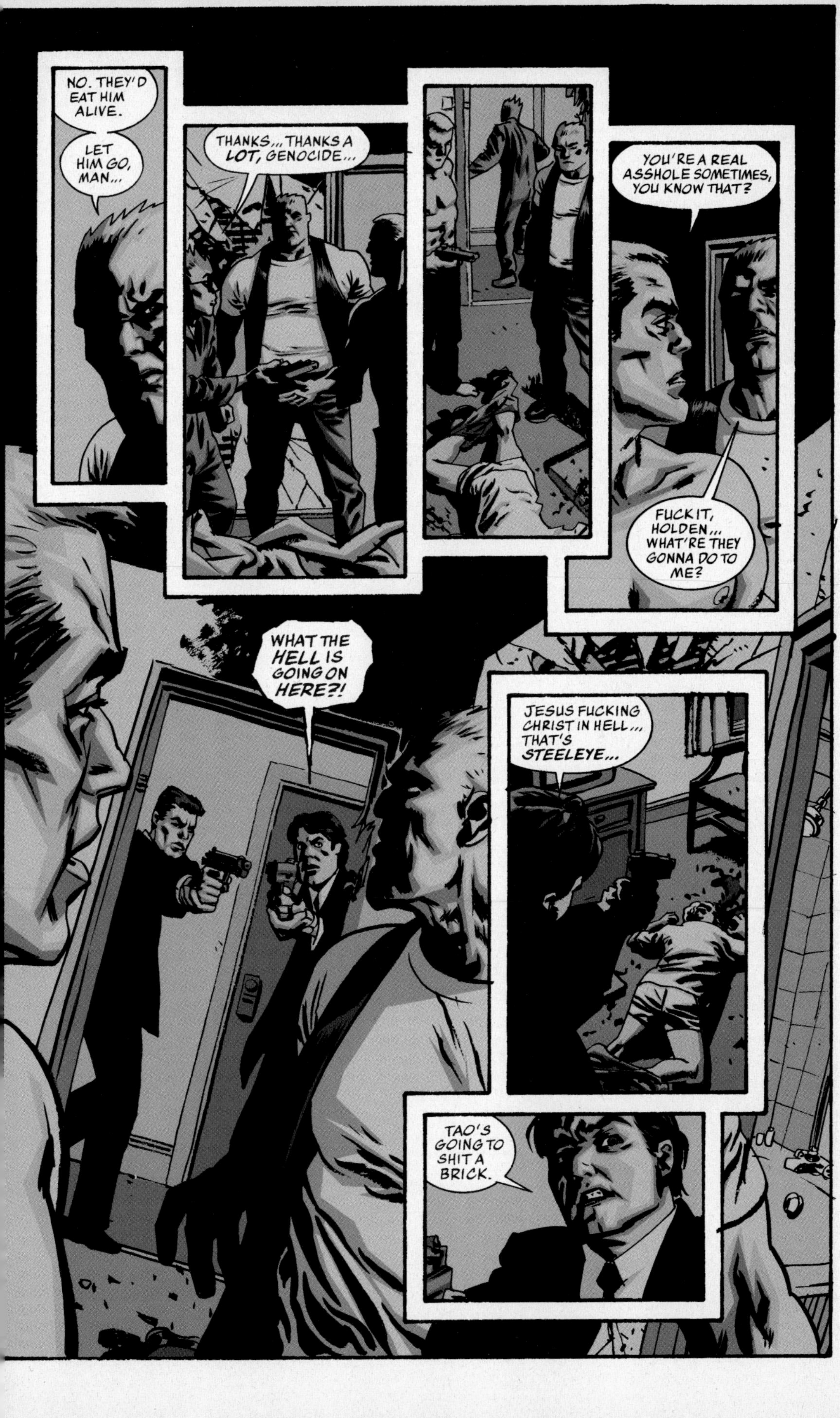
NO. THEY'D EAT HIM ALIVE.
LET HIM GO, MAN...
THANKS... THANKS A LOT, GENOCIDE...
YOU'RE A REAL ASSHOLE SOMETIMES, YOU KNOW THAT?
FUCK IT, HOLDEN... WHAT'RE THEY GONNA DO TO ME?
WHAT THE HELL IS GOING ON HERE?!
JESUS FUCKING CHRIST IN HELL... THAT'S STEELEYE...
TAO'S GOING TO SHIT A BRICK.

Of course, that's not a very accurate description. Tao doesn't shit bricks. He doesn't even get mad.

He just deals with problems in a meticulous and methodical way.

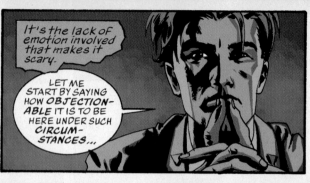

It's the lack of emotion involved that makes it scary.

LET ME START BY SAYING HOW OBJECTIONABLE IT IS TO BE HERE UNDER SUCH CIRCUMSTANCES...

...STEELEYE WAS A VALUED MEMBER OF OUR ORGANIZATION. MORE THAN THAT, HE WAS A PRODIGAL.

SO, I WANT TO KNOW EXACTLY WHAT HAPPENED.

AND THEN WE'LL SORT OUT WHAT TO DO WITH THE BOTH OF YOU.

Under normal circumstances, if either Genocide or I had killed another operative, it wouldn't be such a big deal.

Nobody would be thrilled, necessarily, but there wouldn't be an inquiry. Hell, half the time someone ended up dead, you could almost assume Tao wanted it that way.

But Steeleye's death was different because we had broken chain of command.

And understanding what that means goes back to my original mission...

WE KNOW THAT A *POST-HUMAN ORGANIZATION* EXISTS, AND THAT TAO IS RUNNING IT...

...WHAT WE *DON'T KNOW* IS WHAT ITS *PURPOSE* IS, AND HOW IT *OPERATES.*

KIDNAPPING AND MURDER ROME 3/22/98

FIREBOMBING RENO 7/11/97

TO ALL EYES, HIS ACTIVITIES *APPEAR* RANDOM. TOO RANDOM TO REALLY BE SO...

BUT *YOU* ARE GOING TO *CHANGE* ALL THAT.

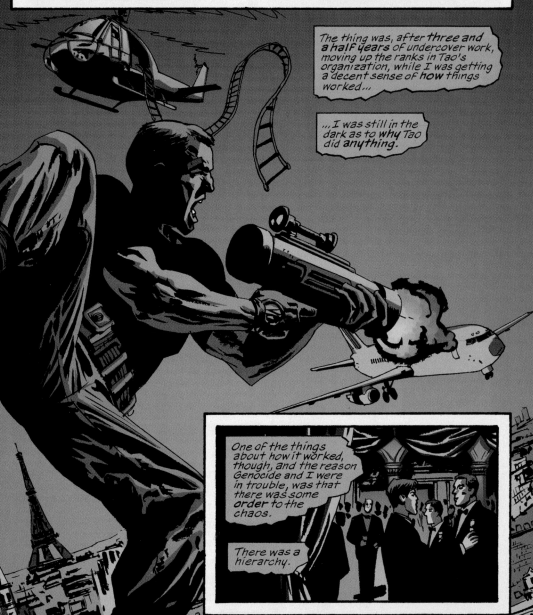

The thing was, after *three and a half years* of undercover work, moving up the ranks in Tao's organization, while I was getting a decent sense of *how* things worked...

...I was still in the dark as to *why* Tao did *anything.*

One of the things about how it worked, though, and the reason Genocide and I were in trouble, was that there was some *order* to the chaos.

There was a hierarchy.

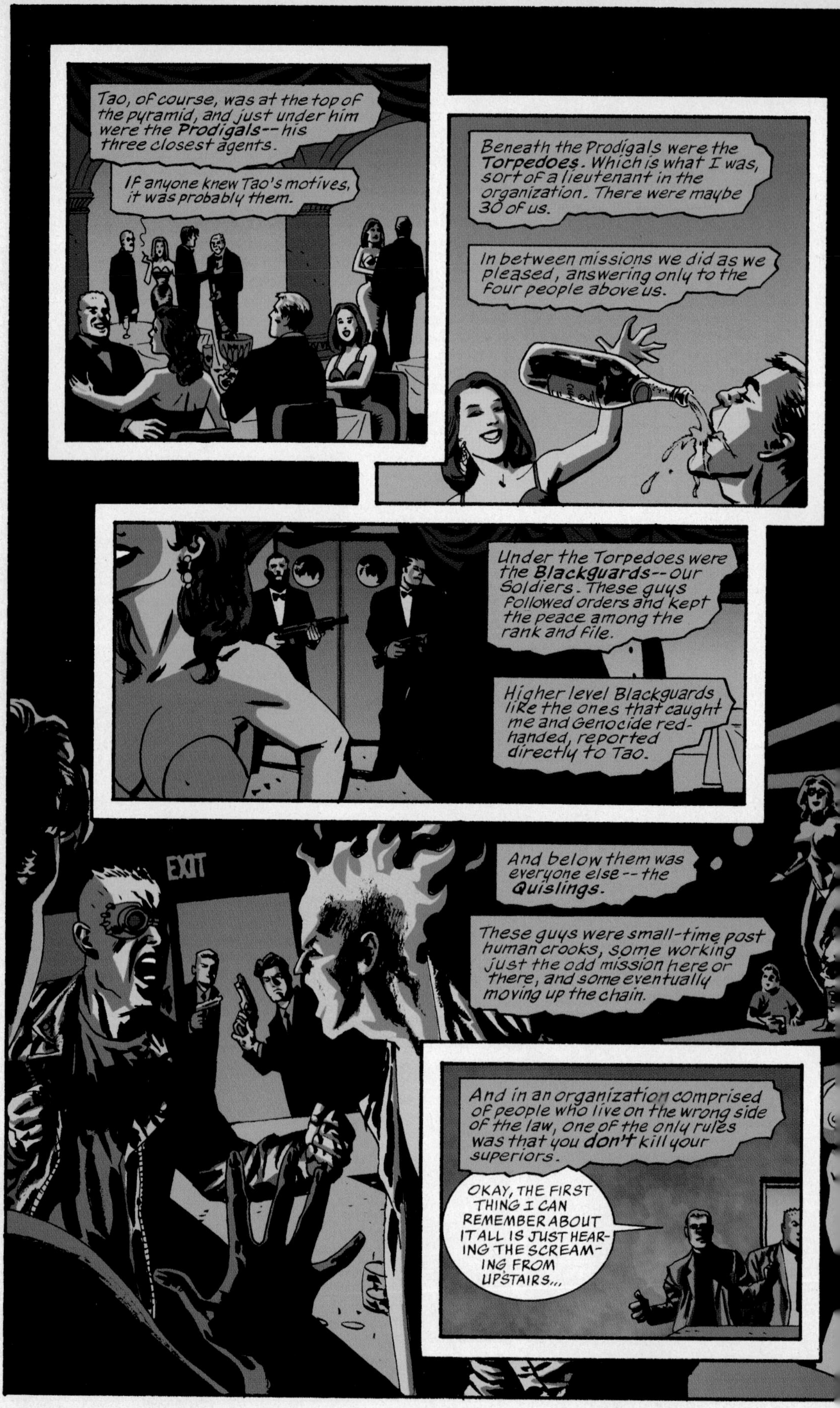
Tao, of course, was at the top of the pyramid, and just under him were the Prodigals-- his three closest agents.
If anyone knew Tao's motives, it was probably them.
Beneath the Prodigals were the Torpedoes. Which is what I was, sort of a lieutenant in the organization. There were maybe 30 of us.
In between missions we did as we pleased, answering only to the four people above us.
Under the Torpedoes were the Blackguards-- our Soldiers. These guys followed orders and kept the peace among the rank and file.
Higher level Blackguards like the ones that caught me and Genocide red-handed, reported directly to Tao.
EXIT
And below them was everyone else-- the Quislings.
These guys were small-time post human crooks, some working just the odd mission here or there, and some eventually moving up the chain.
And in an organization comprised of people who live on the wrong side of the law, one of the only rules was that you don't kill your superiors.
OKAY, THE FIRST THING I CAN REMEMBER ABOUT IT ALL IS JUST HEARING THE SCREAMING FROM UPSTAIRS...

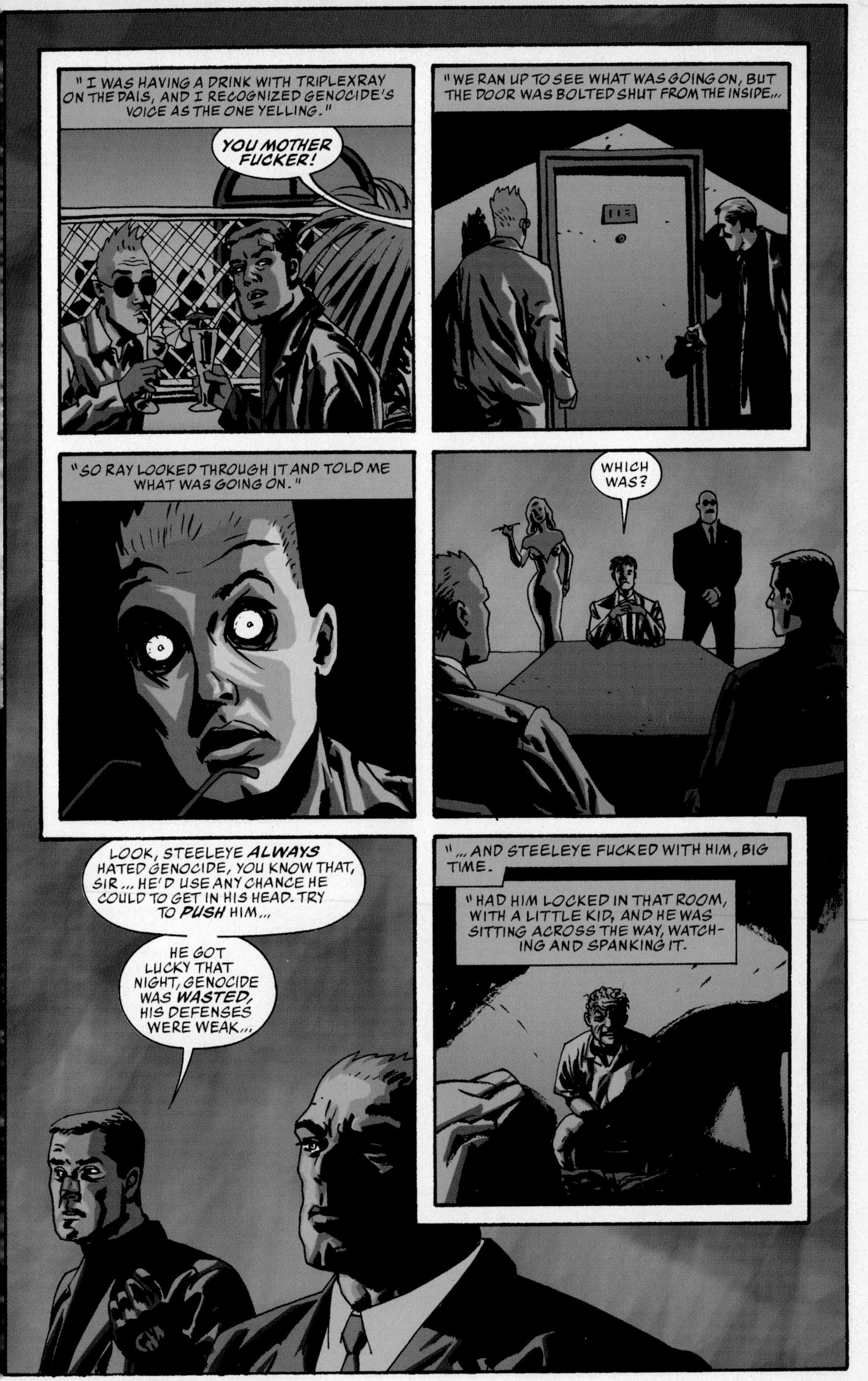

"I WAS HAVING A DRINK WITH TRIPLEXRAY ON THE DAIS, AND I RECOGNIZED GENOCIDE'S VOICE AS THE ONE YELLING."
YOU MOTHER FUCKER!
"WE RAN UP TO SEE WHAT WAS GOING ON, BUT THE DOOR WAS BOLTED SHUT FROM THE INSIDE...
"SO RAY LOOKED THROUGH IT AND TOLD ME WHAT WAS GOING ON."
WHICH WAS?
LOOK, STEELEYE ALWAYS HATED GENOCIDE, YOU KNOW THAT, SIR... HE'D USE ANY CHANCE HE COULD TO GET IN HIS HEAD. TRY TO PUSH HIM...
HE GOT LUCKY THAT NIGHT, GENOCIDE WAS WASTED, HIS DEFENSES WERE WEAK...
"...AND STEELEYE FUCKED WITH HIM, BIG TIME.
"HAD HIM LOCKED IN THAT ROOM, WITH A LITTLE KID, AND HE WAS SITTING ACROSS THE WAY, WATCHING AND SPANKING IT.

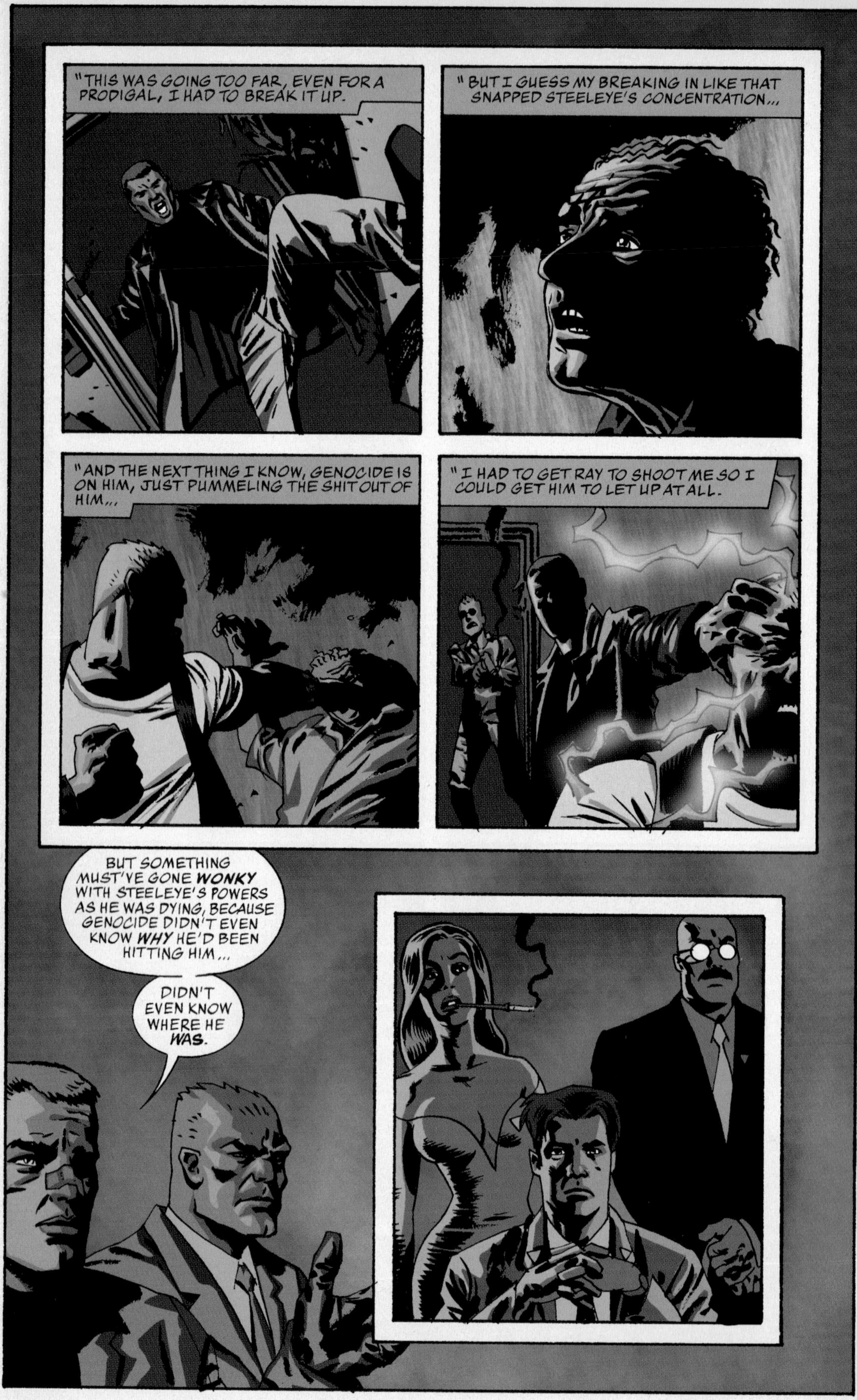
"THIS WAS GOING TOO FAR, EVEN FOR A PRODIGAL, I HAD TO BREAK IT UP.
"BUT I GUESS MY BREAKING IN LIKE THAT SNAPPED STEELEYE'S CONCENTRATION...
"AND THE NEXT THING I KNOW, GENOCIDE IS ON HIM, JUST PUMMELING THE SHIT OUT OF HIM...
"I HAD TO GET RAY TO SHOOT ME SO I COULD GET HIM TO LET UP AT ALL.
BUT SOMETHING MUST'VE GONE WONKY WITH STEELEYE'S POWERS AS HE WAS DYING, BECAUSE GENOCIDE DIDN'T EVEN KNOW WHY HE'D BEEN HITTING HIM...
DIDN'T EVEN KNOW WHERE HE WAS.

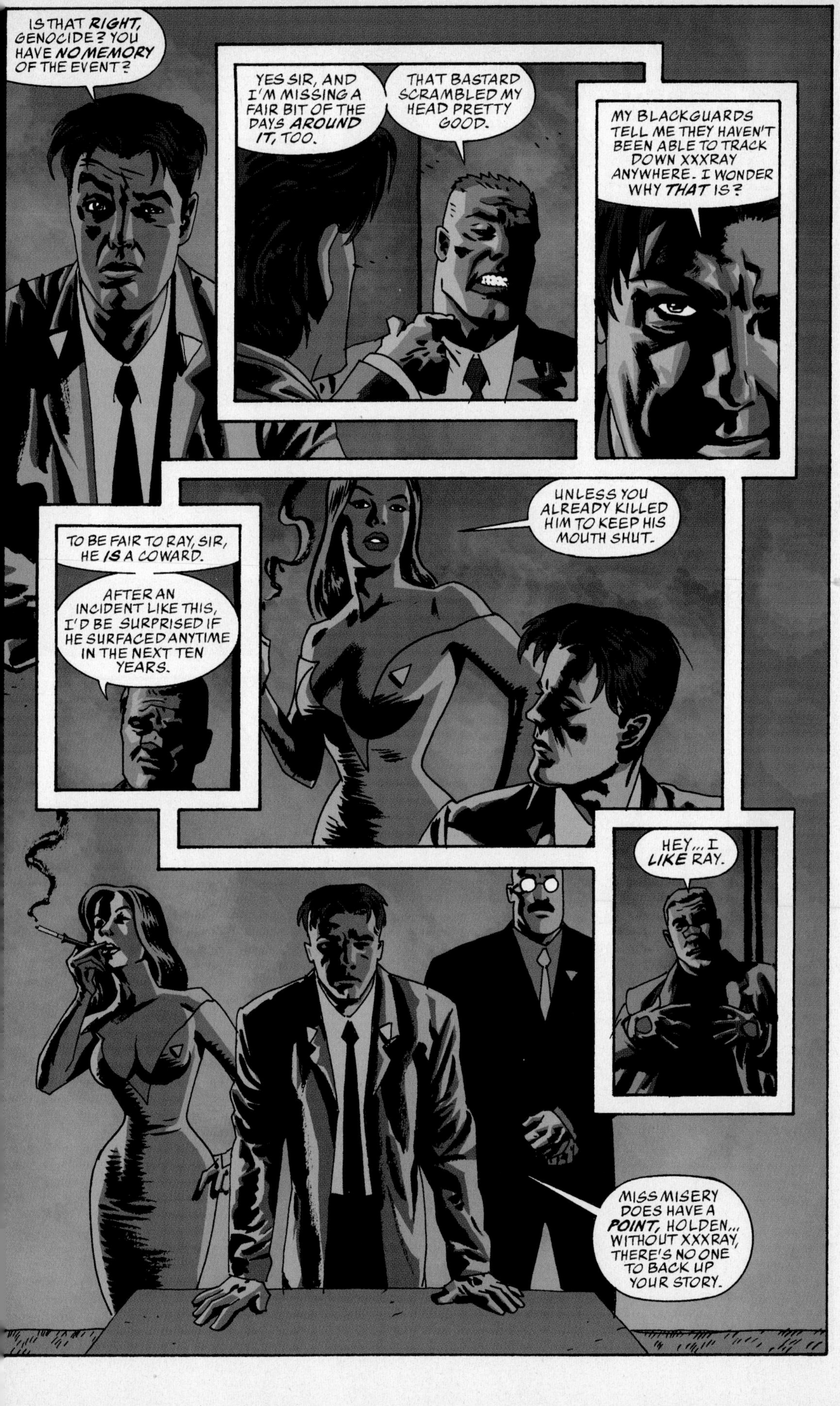
IS THAT RIGHT, GENOCIDE? YOU HAVE NO MEMORY OF THE EVENT?
YES SIR, AND I'M MISSING A FAIR BIT OF THE DAYS AROUND IT, TOO.
THAT BASTARD SCRAMBLED MY HEAD PRETTY GOOD.
MY BLACKGUARDS TELL ME THEY HAVEN'T BEEN ABLE TO TRACK DOWN XXXRAY ANYWHERE. I WONDER WHY THAT IS?
UNLESS YOU ALREADY KILLED HIM TO KEEP HIS MOUTH SHUT.
TO BE FAIR TO RAY, SIR, HE IS A COWARD.
AFTER AN INCIDENT LIKE THIS, I'D BE SURPRISED IF HE SURFACED ANYTIME IN THE NEXT TEN YEARS.
HEY... I LIKE RAY.
MISS MISERY DOES HAVE A POINT, HOLDEN... WITHOUT XXXRAY, THERE'S NO ONE TO BACK UP YOUR STORY.

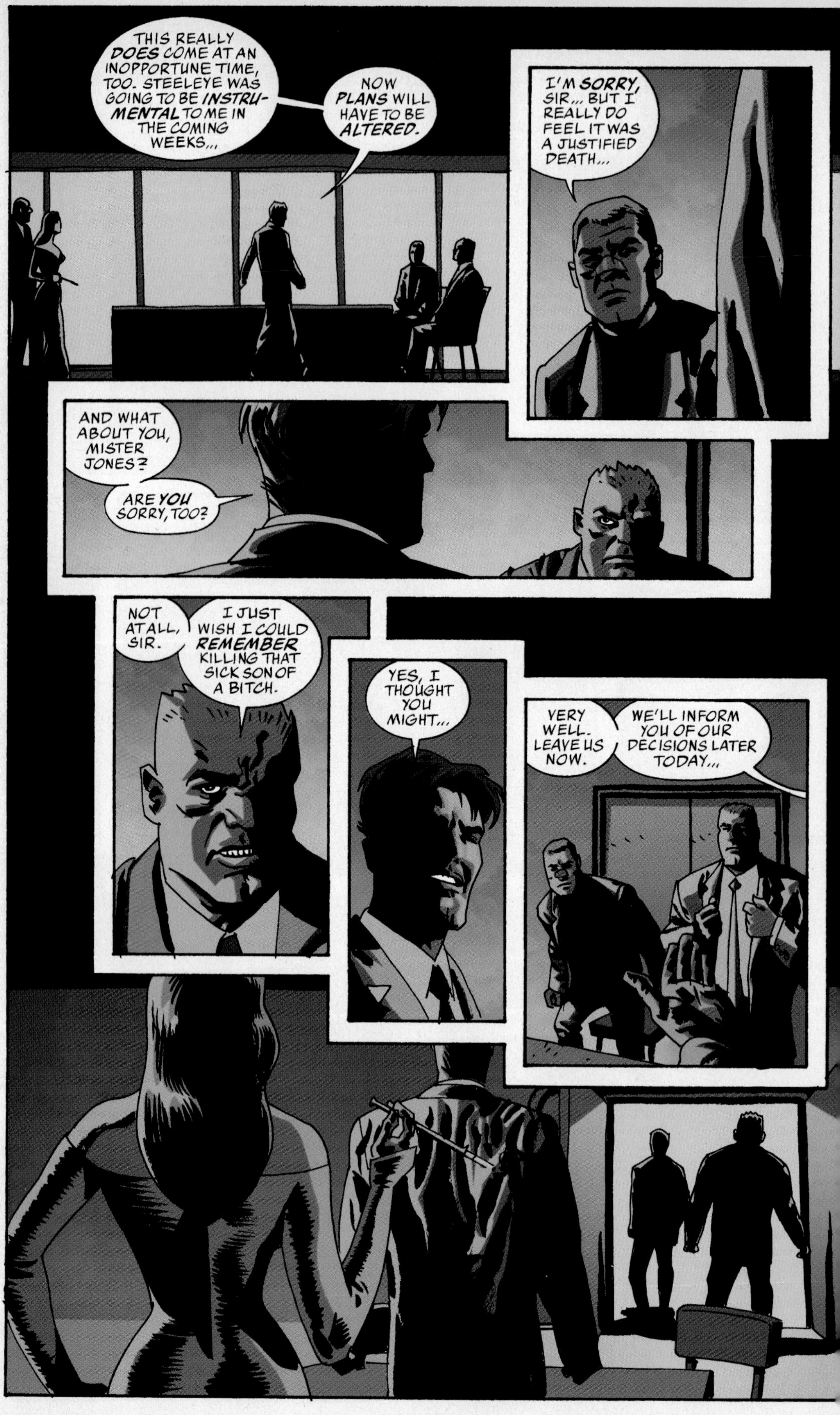
THIS REALLY DOES COME AT AN INOPPORTUNE TIME, TOO. STEELEYE WAS GOING TO BE INSTRUMENTAL TO ME IN THE COMING WEEKS...
NOW PLANS WILL HAVE TO BE ALTERED.
I'M SORRY, SIR... BUT I REALLY DO FEEL IT WAS A JUSTIFIED DEATH...
AND WHAT ABOUT YOU, MISTER JONES?
ARE YOU SORRY, TOO?
NOT AT ALL, SIR.
I JUST WISH I COULD REMEMBER KILLING THAT SICK SON OF A BITCH.
YES, I THOUGHT YOU MIGHT...
VERY WELL. LEAVE US NOW.
WE'LL INFORM YOU OF OUR DECISIONS LATER TODAY...

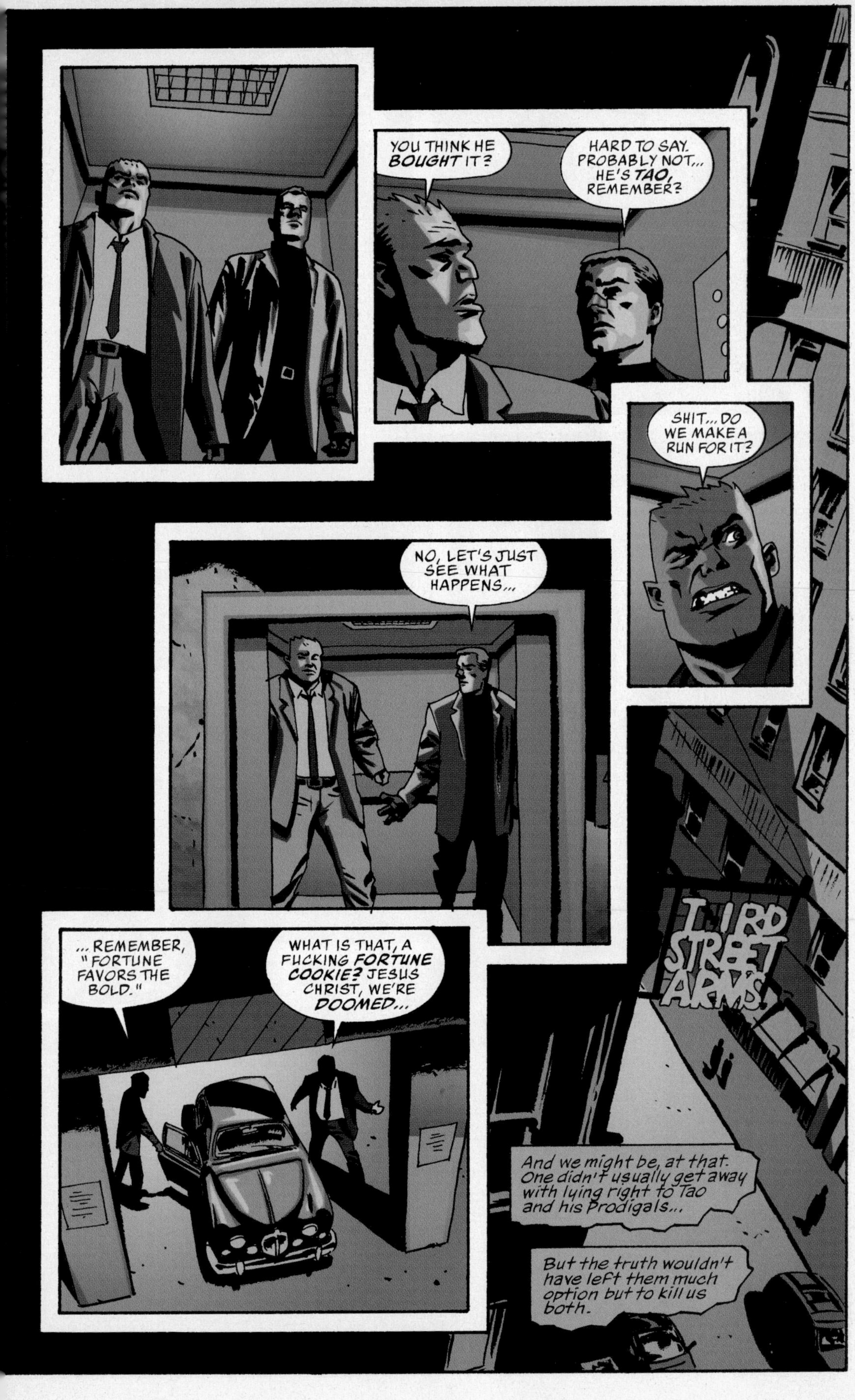
YOU THINK HE BOUGHT IT?
HARD TO SAY. PROBABLY NOT... HE'S TAO, REMEMBER?
SHIT... DO WE MAKE A RUN FOR IT?
NO, LET'S JUST SEE WHAT HAPPENS...
... REMEMBER, "FORTUNE FAVORS THE BOLD."
WHAT IS THAT, A FUCKING FORTUNE COOKIE? JESUS CHRIST, WE'RE DOOMED...
THIRD STREET ARMS
And we might be, at that. One didn't usually get away with lying right to Tao and his Prodigals...
But the truth wouldn't have left them much option but to kill us both.

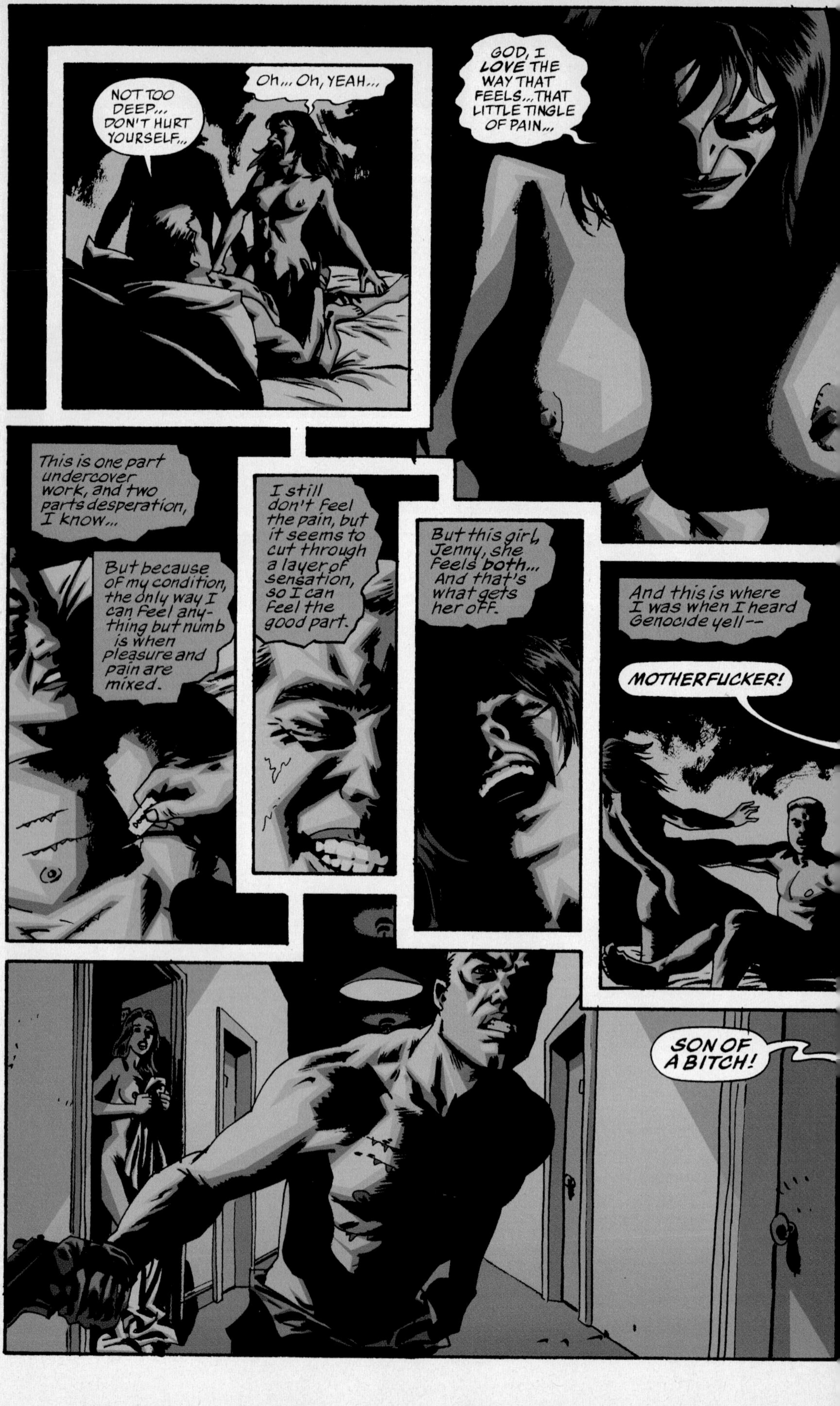
Oh... Oh, YEAH...
NOT TOO DEEP... DON'T HURT YOURSELF...
GOD, I LOVE THE WAY THAT FEELS... THAT LITTLE TINGLE OF PAIN...
This is one part undercover work, and two parts desperation, I know...
But because of my condition, the only way I can feel anything but numb is when pleasure and pain are mixed.
I still don't feel the pain, but it seems to cut through a layer of sensation, so I can feel the good part.
But this girl, Jenny, she feels both... And that's what gets her off.
And this is where I was when I heard Genocide yell--
MOTHERFUCKER!
SON OF A BITCH!

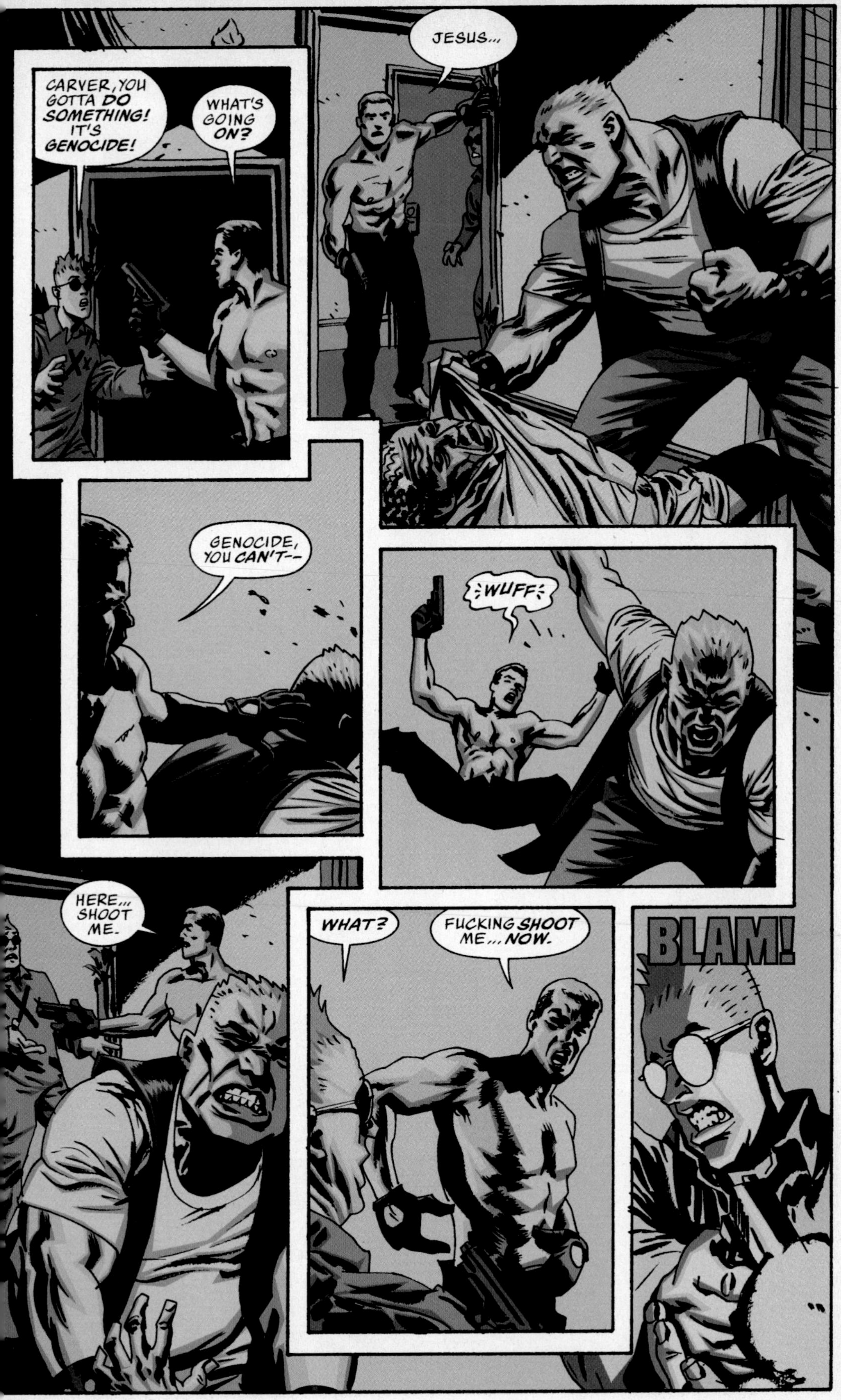
CARVER, YOU GOTTA DO SOMETHING! IT'S GENOCIDE!
WHAT'S GOING ON?
JESUS...
GENOCIDE, YOU CAN'T--
WUFF
HERE... SHOOT ME.
WHAT?
FUCKING SHOOT ME... NOW.
BLAM!

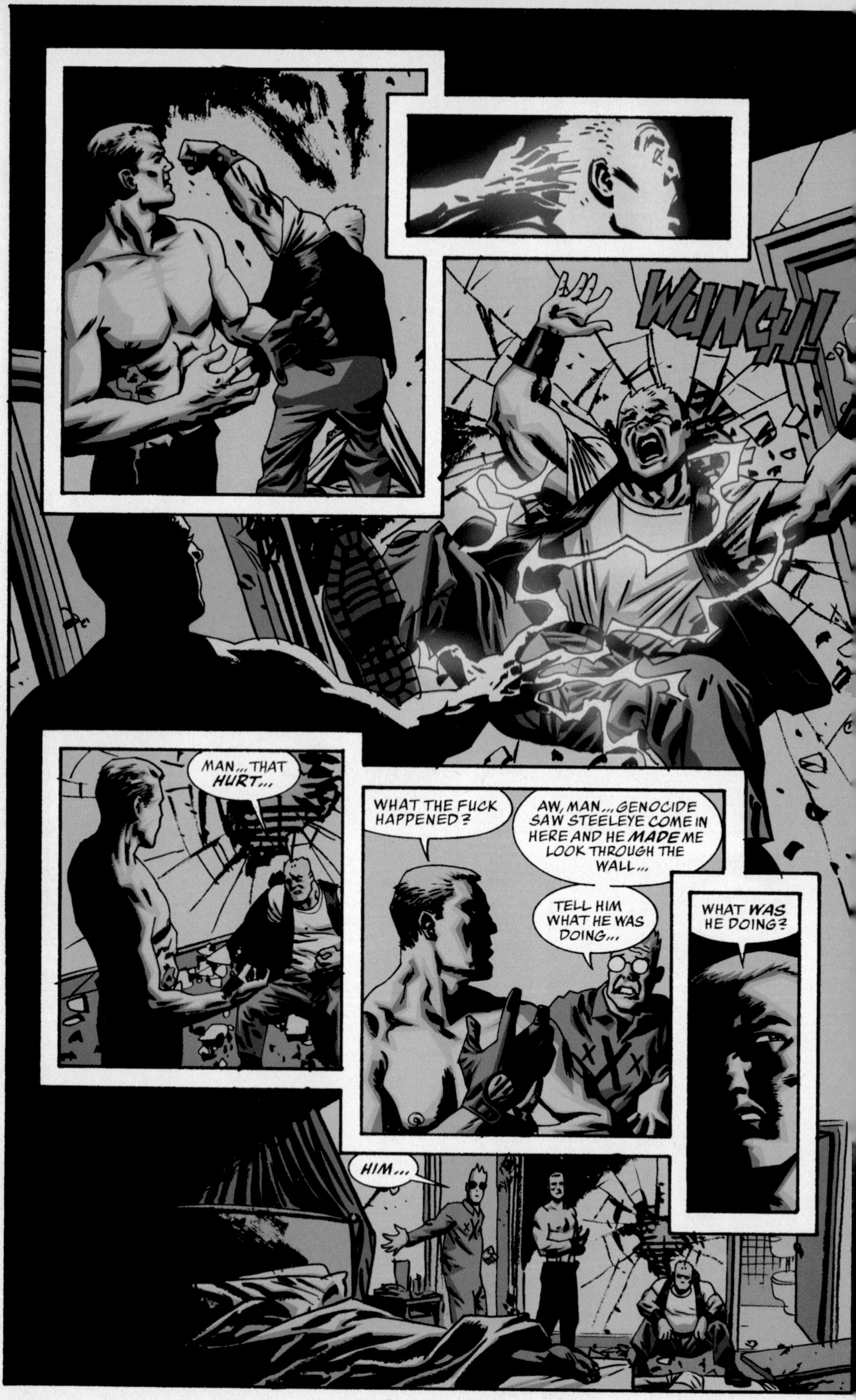
WUNCH!
MAN... THAT HURT...
WHAT THE FUCK HAPPENED?
AW, MAN... GENOCIDE SAW STEELEYE COME IN HERE AND HE MADE ME LOOK THROUGH THE WALL...
TELL HIM WHAT HE WAS DOING...
WHAT WAS HE DOING?
HIM...

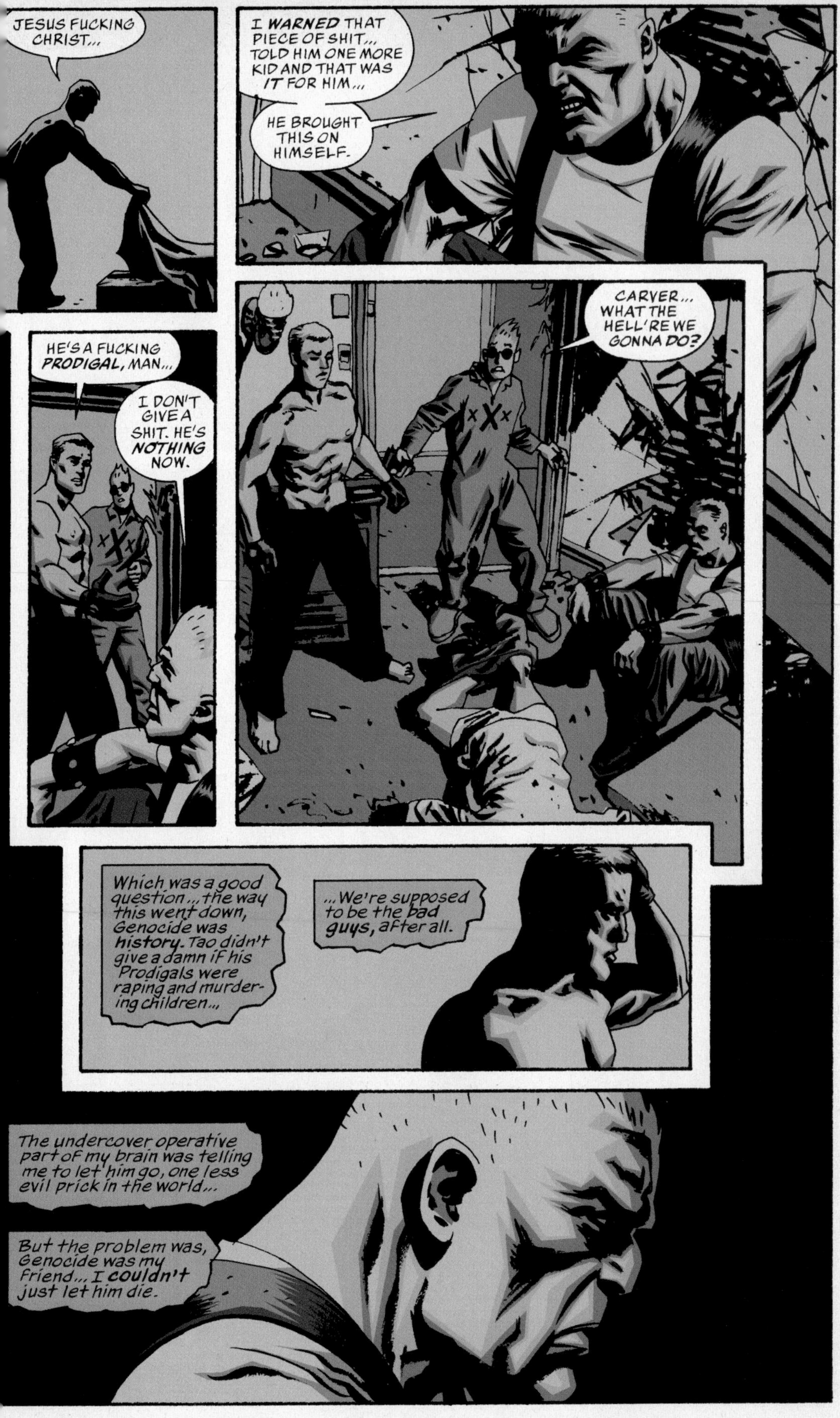
JESUS FUCKING CHRIST...
I WARNED THAT PIECE OF SHIT... TOLD HIM ONE MORE KID AND THAT WAS IT FOR HIM...
HE BROUGHT THIS ON HIMSELF.
HE'S A FUCKING PRODIGAL, MAN...
I DON'T GIVE A SHIT. HE'S NOTHING NOW.
CARVER... WHAT THE HELL'RE WE GONNA DO?
Which was a good question... the way this went down, Genocide was history. Tao didn't give a damn if his Prodigals were raping and murdering children...
...We're supposed to be the bad guys, after all.
The undercover operative part of my brain was telling me to let him go, one less evil prick in the world...
But the problem was, Genocide was my friend... I couldn't just let him die.

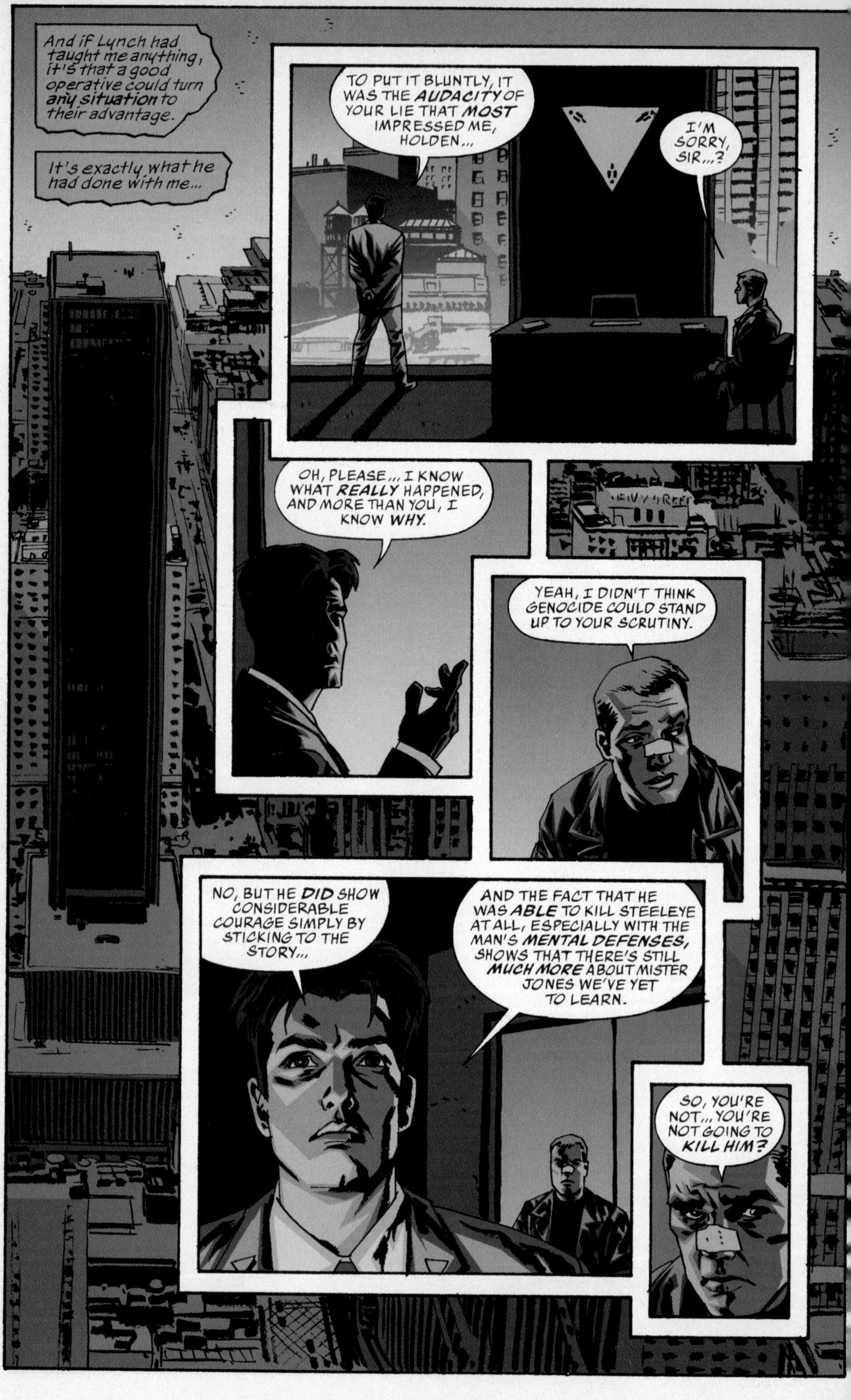
And if Lynch had taught me anything, it's that a good operative could turn any situation to their advantage.
It's exactly what he had done with me...
TO PUT IT BLUNTLY, IT WAS THE AUDACITY OF YOUR LIE THAT MOST IMPRESSED ME, HOLDEN...
I'M SORRY, SIR...?
OH, PLEASE... I KNOW WHAT REALLY HAPPENED, AND MORE THAN YOU, I KNOW WHY.
YEAH, I DIDN'T THINK GENOCIDE COULD STAND UP TO YOUR SCRUTINY.
NO, BUT HE DID SHOW CONSIDERABLE COURAGE SIMPLY BY STICKING TO THE STORY...
AND THE FACT THAT HE WAS ABLE TO KILL STEELEYE AT ALL, ESPECIALLY WITH THE MAN'S MENTAL DEFENSES, SHOWS THAT THERE'S STILL MUCH MORE ABOUT MISTER JONES WE'VE YET TO LEARN.
SO, YOU'RE NOT... YOU'RE NOT GOING TO KILL HIM?

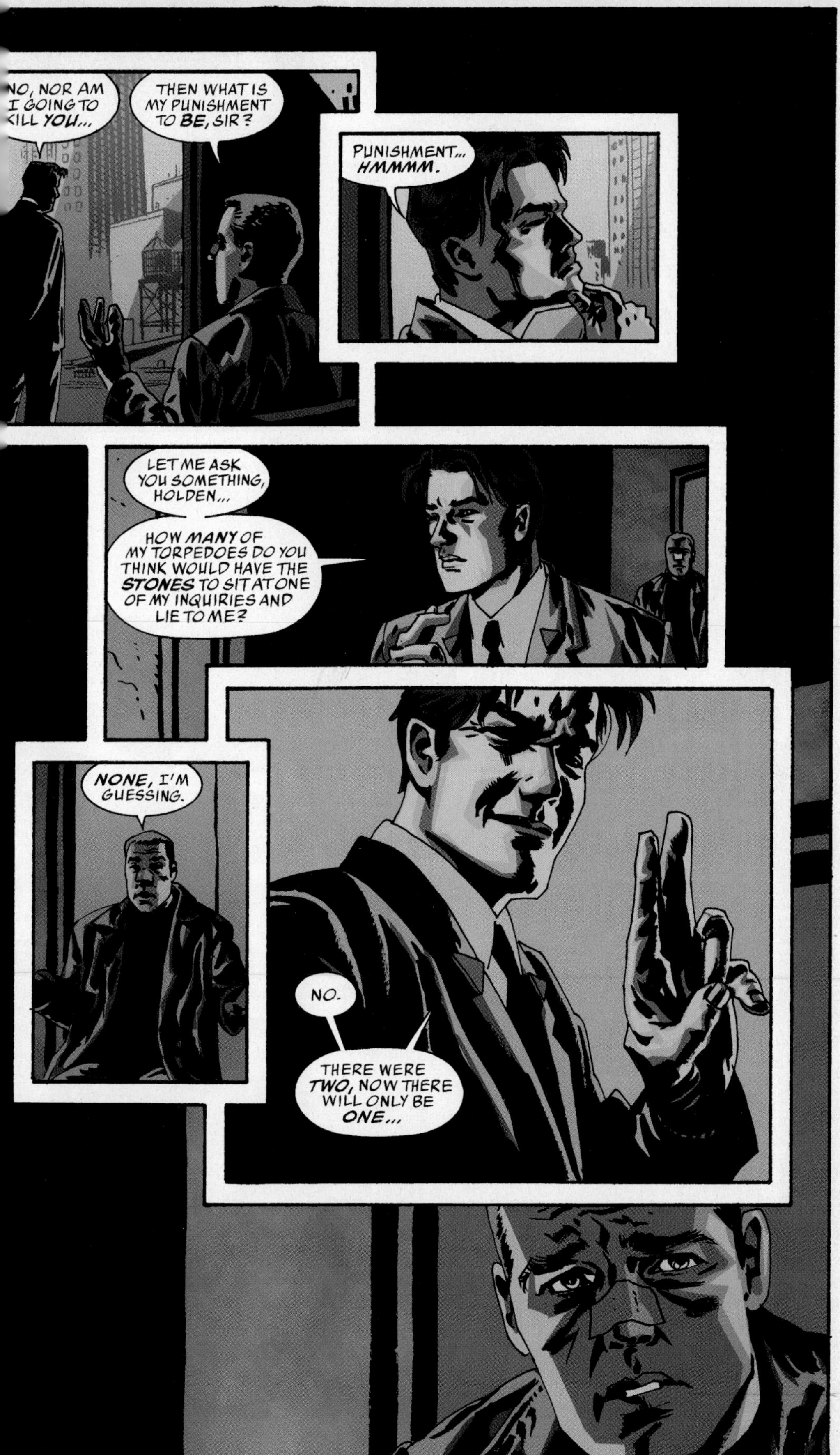
NO, NOR AM I GOING TO KILL YOU...
THEN WHAT IS MY PUNISHMENT TO BE, SIR?
PUNISHMENT... HMMMM.
LET ME ASK YOU SOMETHING, HOLDEN...
HOW MANY OF MY TORPEDOES DO YOU THINK WOULD HAVE THE STONES TO SIT AT ONE OF MY INQUIRIES AND LIE TO ME?
NONE, I'M GUESSING.
NO.
THERE WERE TWO, NOW THERE WILL ONLY BE ONE...

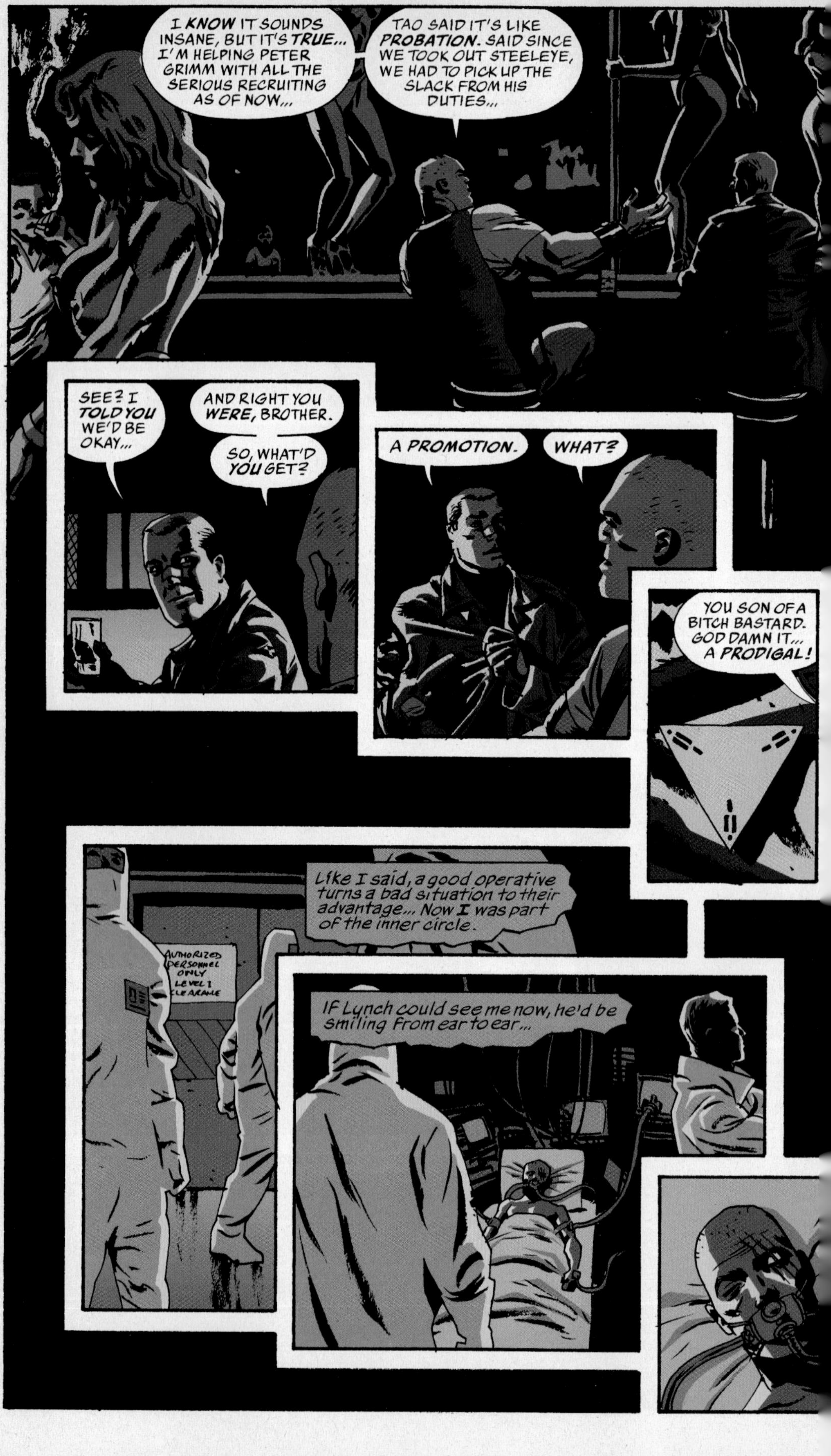
I KNOW IT SOUNDS INSANE, BUT IT'S TRUE... I'M HELPING PETER GRIMM WITH ALL THE SERIOUS RECRUITING AS OF NOW...
TAO SAID IT'S LIKE PROBATION. SAID SINCE WE TOOK OUT STEELEYE, WE HAD TO PICK UP THE SLACK FROM HIS DUTIES...
SEE? I TOLD YOU WE'D BE OKAY...
AND RIGHT YOU WERE, BROTHER.
SO, WHAT'D YOU GET?
A PROMOTION.
WHAT?
YOU SON OF A BITCH BASTARD. GOD DAMN IT... A PRODIGAL!
Like I said, a good operative turns a bad situation to their advantage... Now I was part of the inner circle.
AUTHORIZED PERSONNEL ONLY LEVEL 1 CLEARANCE
If Lynch could see me now, he'd be smiling from ear to ear...

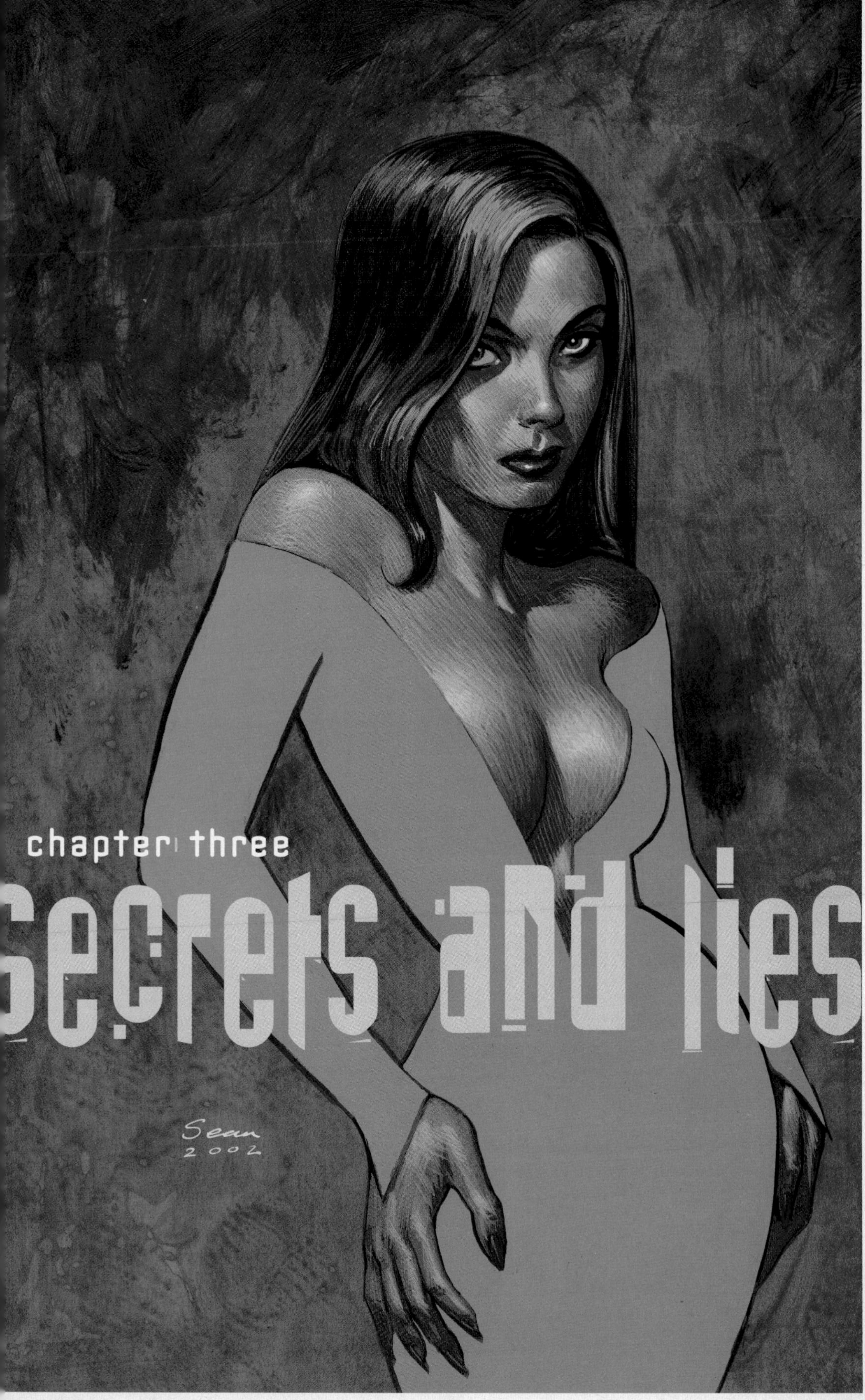
chapter three
secrets and lies
Sean
2002

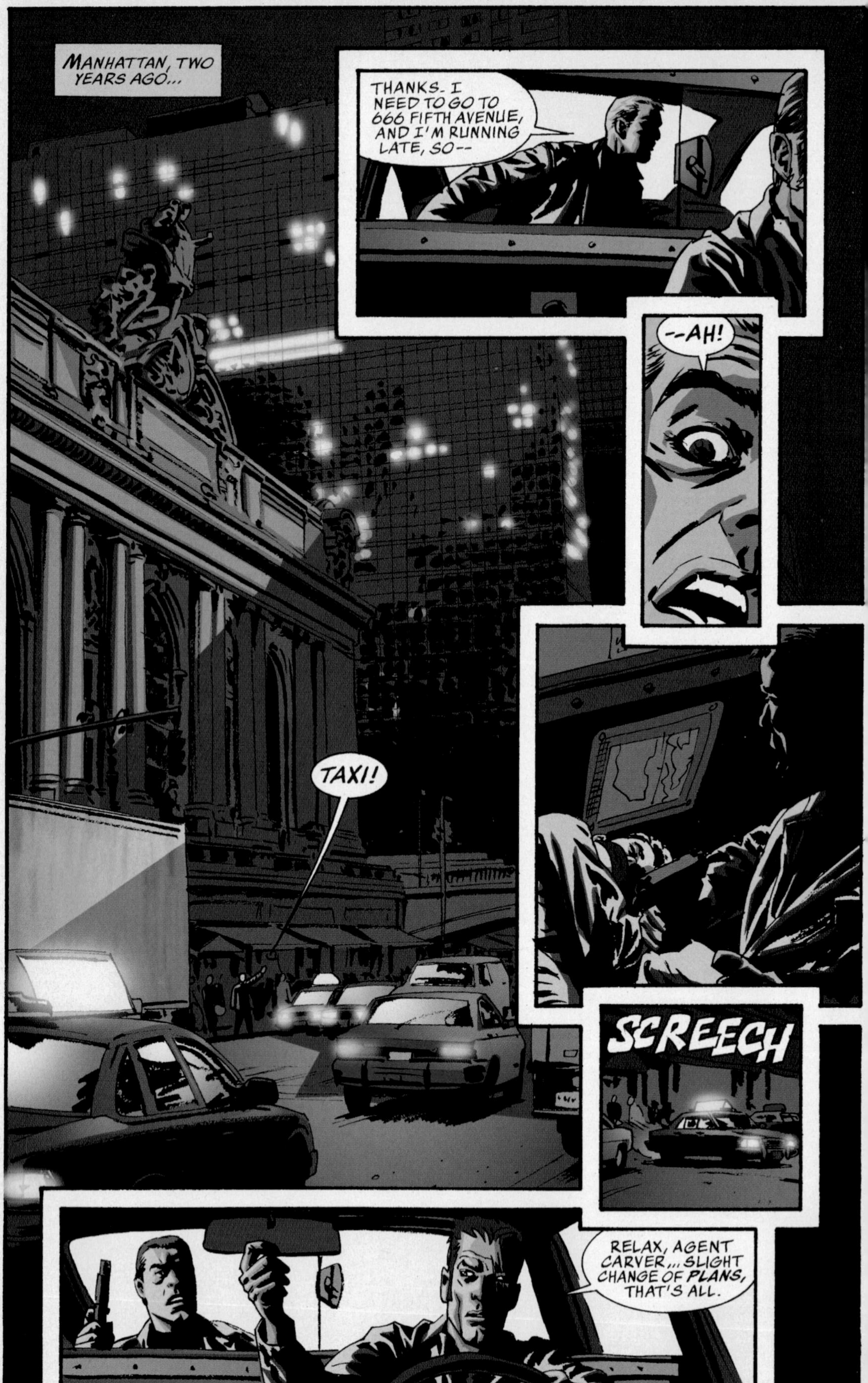
MANHATTAN, TWO YEARS AGO...
TAXI!
THANKS. I NEED TO GO TO 666 FIFTH AVENUE, AND I'M RUNNING LATE, SO--
--AH!
SCREECH
RELAX, AGENT CARVER... SLIGHT CHANGE OF PLANS, THAT'S ALL.

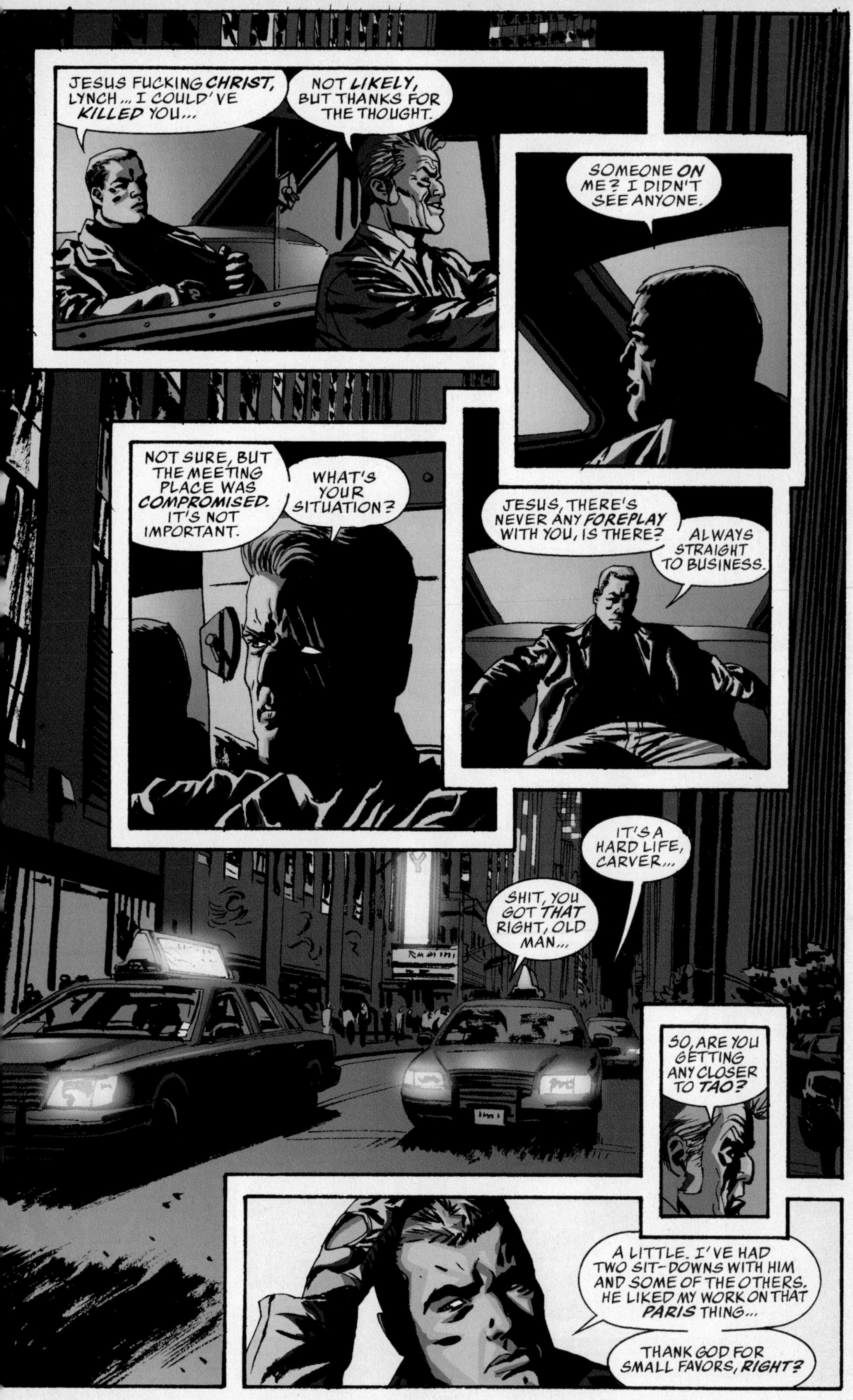
JESUS FUCKING CHRIST, LYNCH... I COULD'VE KILLED YOU...
NOT LIKELY, BUT THANKS FOR THE THOUGHT.
SOMEONE ON ME? I DIDN'T SEE ANYONE.
NOT SURE, BUT THE MEETING PLACE WAS COMPROMISED. IT'S NOT IMPORTANT.
WHAT'S YOUR SITUATION?
JESUS, THERE'S NEVER ANY FOREPLAY WITH YOU, IS THERE?
ALWAYS STRAIGHT TO BUSINESS.
IT'S A HARD LIFE, CARVER...
SHIT, YOU GOT THAT RIGHT, OLD MAN...
SO, ARE YOU GETTING ANY CLOSER TO TAO?
A LITTLE. I'VE HAD TWO SIT-DOWNS WITH HIM AND SOME OF THE OTHERS. HE LIKED MY WORK ON THAT PARIS THING...
THANK GOD FOR SMALL FAVORS, RIGHT?

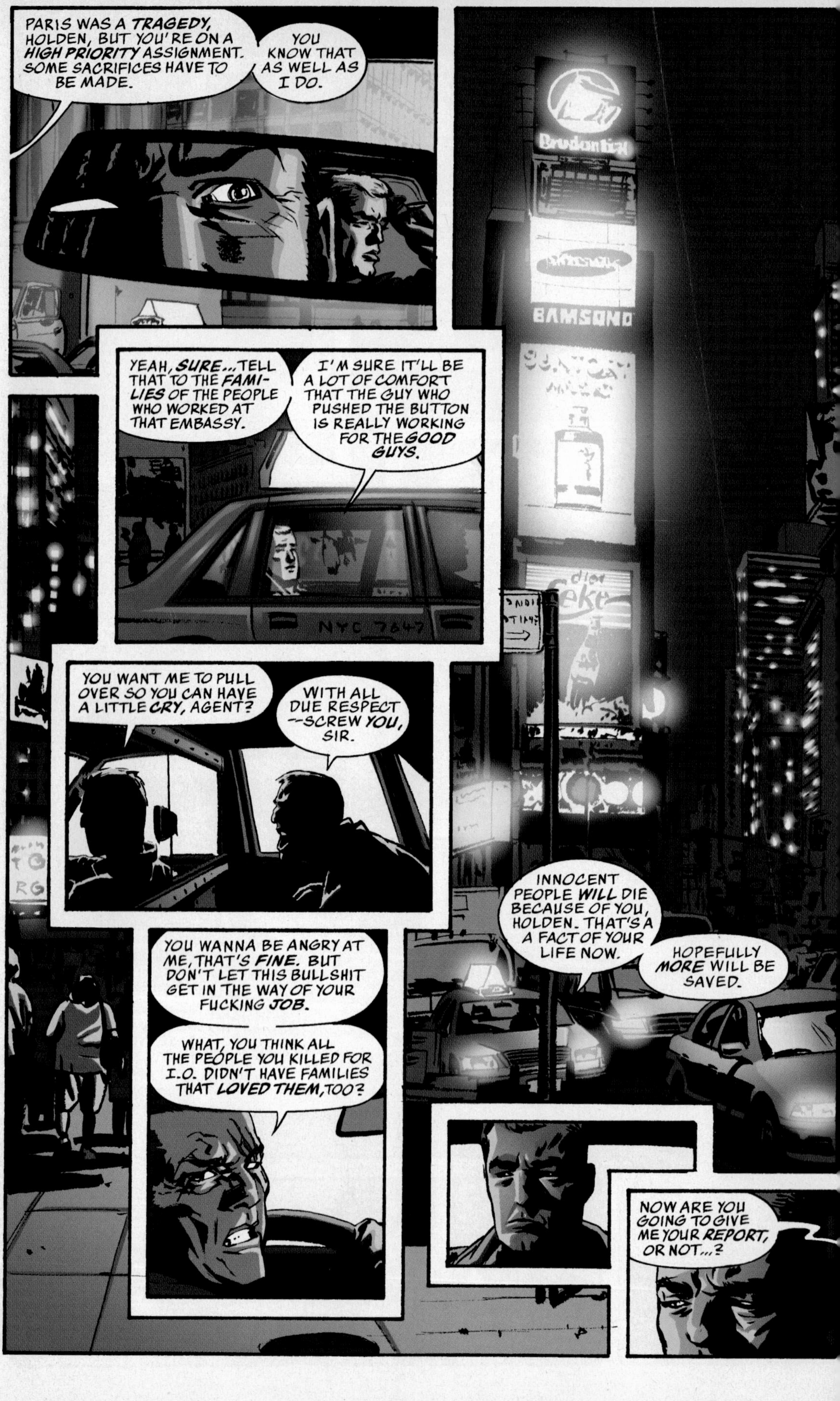

PARIS WAS A TRAGEDY, HOLDEN, BUT YOU'RE ON A HIGH PRIORITY ASSIGNMENT. SOME SACRIFICES HAVE TO BE MADE.
YOU KNOW THAT AS WELL AS I DO.
YEAH, SURE... TELL THAT TO THE FAMILIES OF THE PEOPLE WHO WORKED AT THAT EMBASSY.
I'M SURE IT'LL BE A LOT OF COMFORT THAT THE GUY WHO PUSHED THE BUTTON IS REALLY WORKING FOR THE GOOD GUYS.
NYC 7647
YOU WANT ME TO PULL OVER SO YOU CAN HAVE A LITTLE CRY, AGENT?
WITH ALL DUE RESPECT --SCREW YOU, SIR.
YOU WANNA BE ANGRY AT ME, THAT'S FINE. BUT DON'T LET THIS BULLSHIT GET IN THE WAY OF YOUR FUCKING JOB.
WHAT, YOU THINK ALL THE PEOPLE YOU KILLED FOR I.O. DIDN'T HAVE FAMILIES THAT LOVED THEM, TOO?
INNOCENT PEOPLE WILL DIE BECAUSE OF YOU, HOLDEN. THAT'S A FACT OF YOUR LIFE NOW.
HOPEFULLY MORE WILL BE SAVED.
NOW ARE YOU GOING TO GIVE ME YOUR REPORT, OR NOT...?

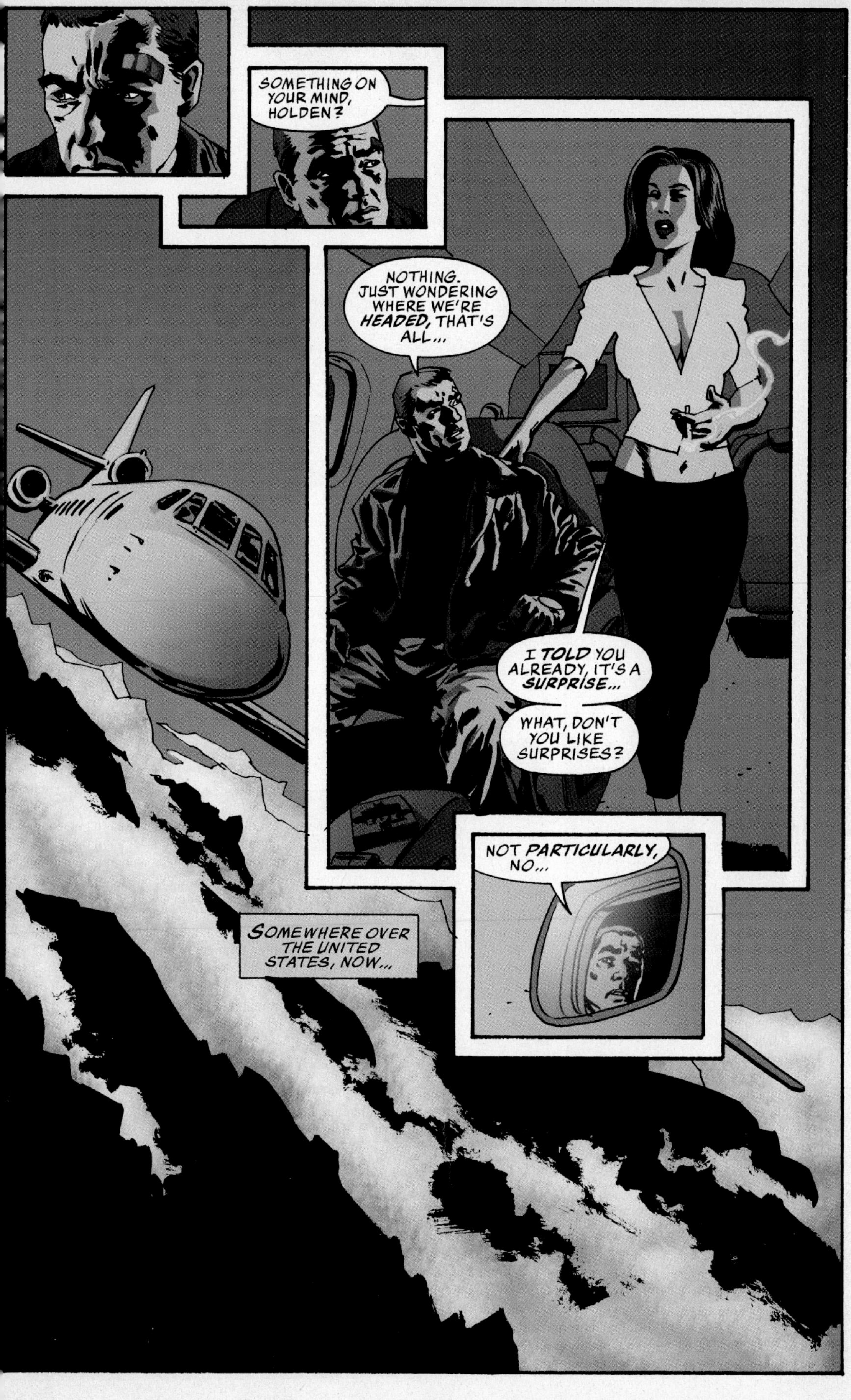
SOMETHING ON YOUR MIND, HOLDEN?
NOTHING. JUST WONDERING WHERE WE'RE HEADED, THAT'S ALL...
I TOLD YOU ALREADY, IT'S A SURPRISE...
WHAT, DON'T YOU LIKE SURPRISES?
SOMEWHERE OVER THE UNITED STATES, NOW...
NOT PARTICULARLY, NO...

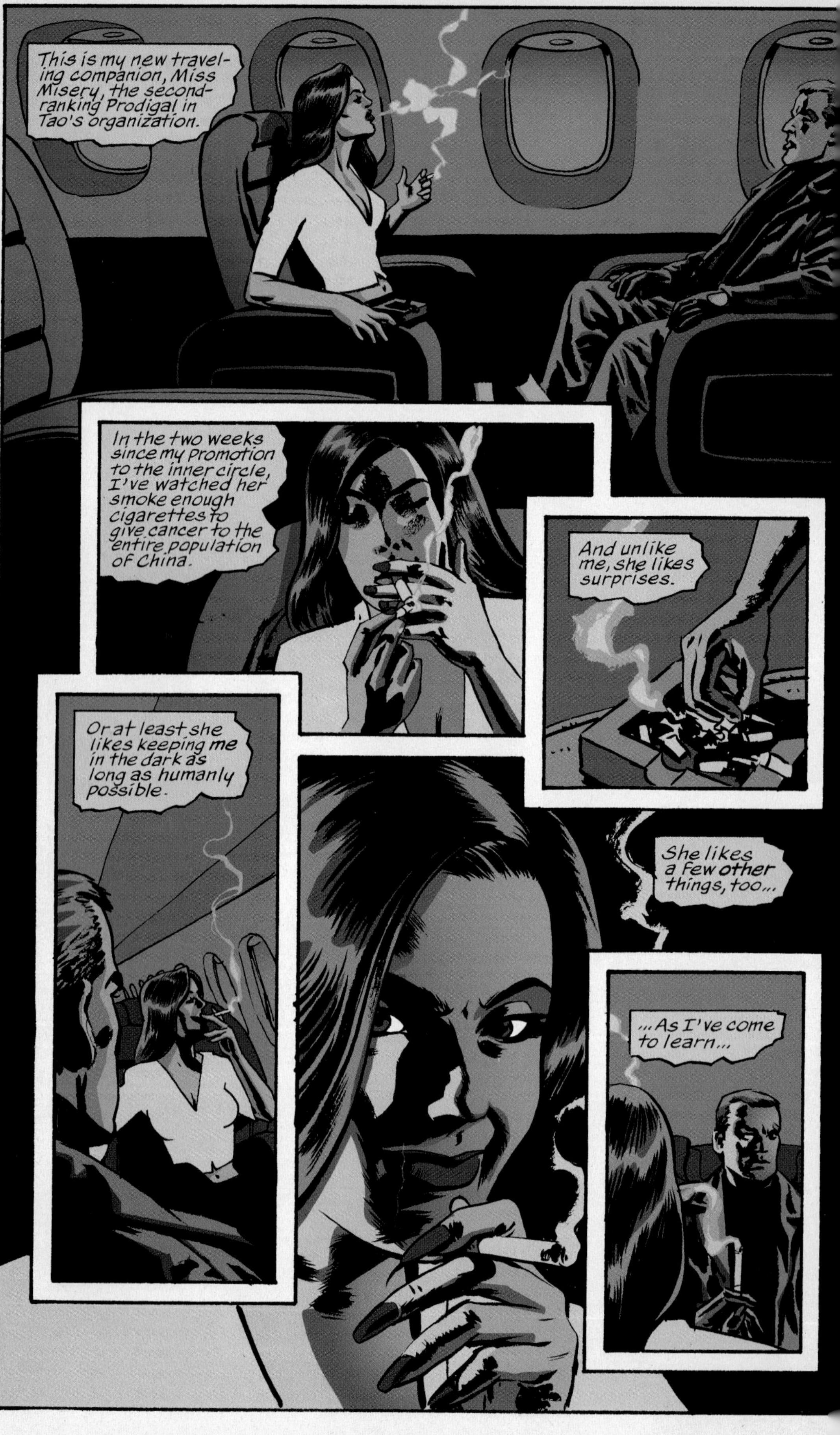
This is my new traveling companion, Miss Misery, the second-ranking Prodigal in Tao's organization.
In the two weeks since my promotion to the inner circle, I've watched her smoke enough cigarettes to give cancer to the entire population of China.
And unlike me, she likes surprises.
Or at least she likes keeping me in the dark as long as humanly possible.
She likes a few other things, too...
...As I've come to learn...

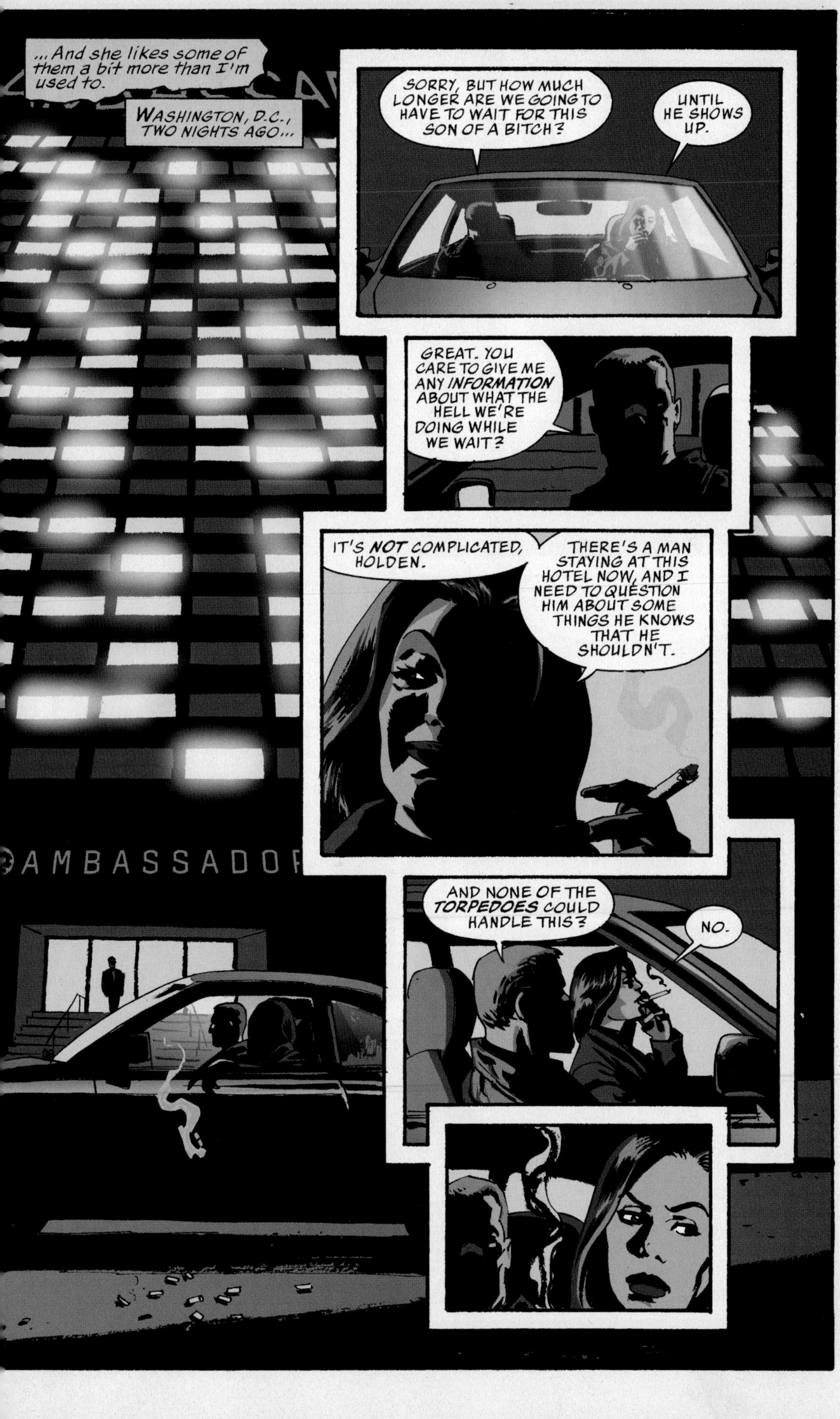
...And she likes some of them a bit more than I'm used to.
WASHINGTON, D.C., TWO NIGHTS AGO...
AMBASSADOR
SORRY, BUT HOW MUCH LONGER ARE WE GOING TO HAVE TO WAIT FOR THIS SON OF A BITCH?
UNTIL HE SHOWS UP.
GREAT. YOU CARE TO GIVE ME ANY INFORMATION ABOUT WHAT THE HELL WE'RE DOING WHILE WE WAIT?
IT'S NOT COMPLICATED, HOLDEN.
THERE'S A MAN STAYING AT THIS HOTEL NOW, AND I NEED TO QUESTION HIM ABOUT SOME THINGS HE KNOWS THAT HE SHOULDN'T.
AND NONE OF THE TORPEDOES COULD HANDLE THIS?
NO.

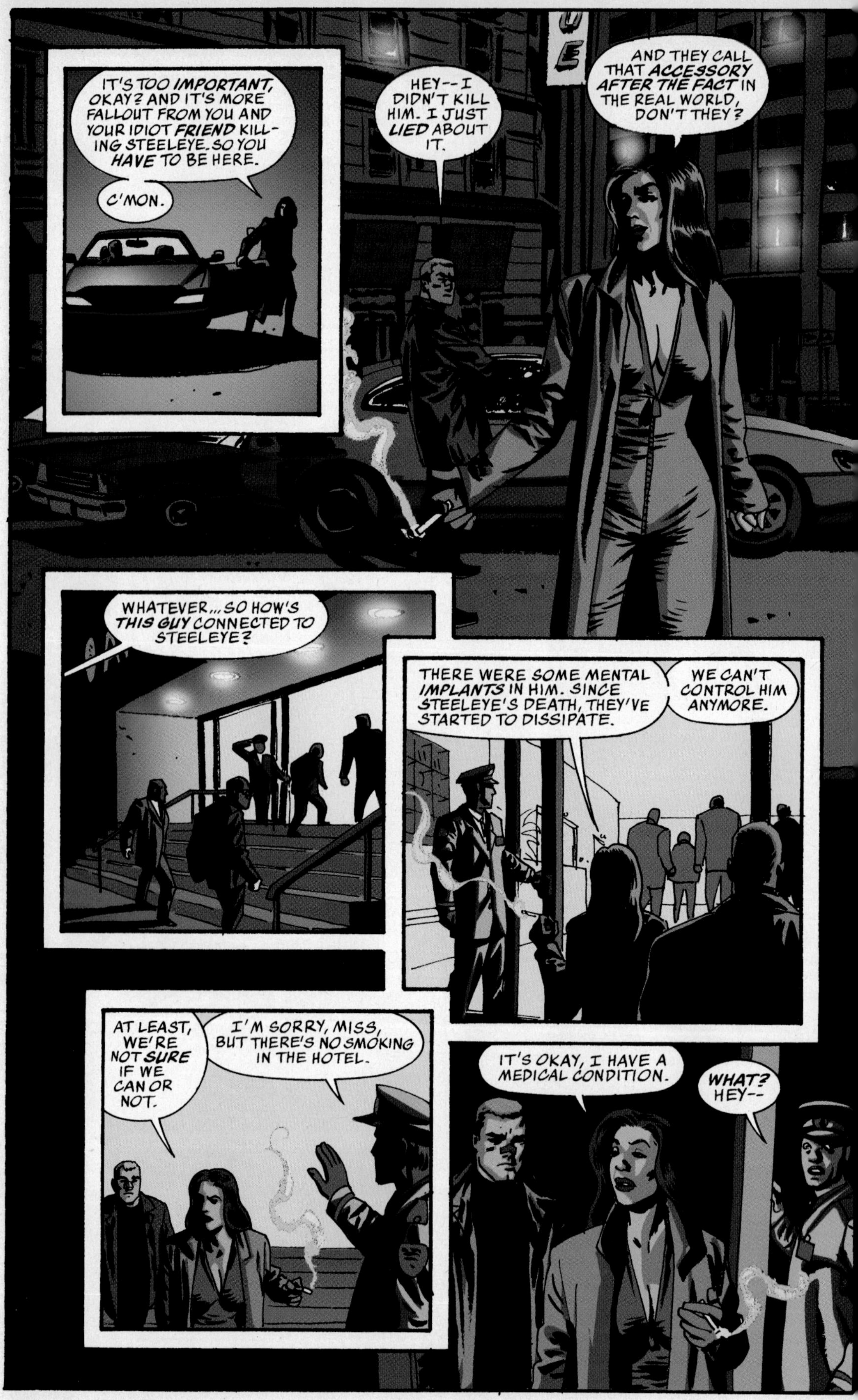
IT'S TOO IMPORTANT, OKAY? AND IT'S MORE FALLOUT FROM YOU AND YOUR IDIOT FRIEND KILLING STEELEYE. SO YOU HAVE TO BE HERE.
C'MON.
HEY-- I DIDN'T KILL HIM. I JUST LIED ABOUT IT.
AND THEY CALL THAT ACCESSORY AFTER THE FACT IN THE REAL WORLD, DON'T THEY?
WHATEVER... SO HOW'S THIS GUY CONNECTED TO STEELEYE?
THERE WERE SOME MENTAL IMPLANTS IN HIM. SINCE STEELEYE'S DEATH, THEY'VE STARTED TO DISSIPATE.
WE CAN'T CONTROL HIM ANYMORE.
AT LEAST, WE'RE NOT SURE IF WE CAN OR NOT.
I'M SORRY, MISS, BUT THERE'S NO SMOKING IN THE HOTEL.
IT'S OKAY, I HAVE A MEDICAL CONDITION.
WHAT? HEY--

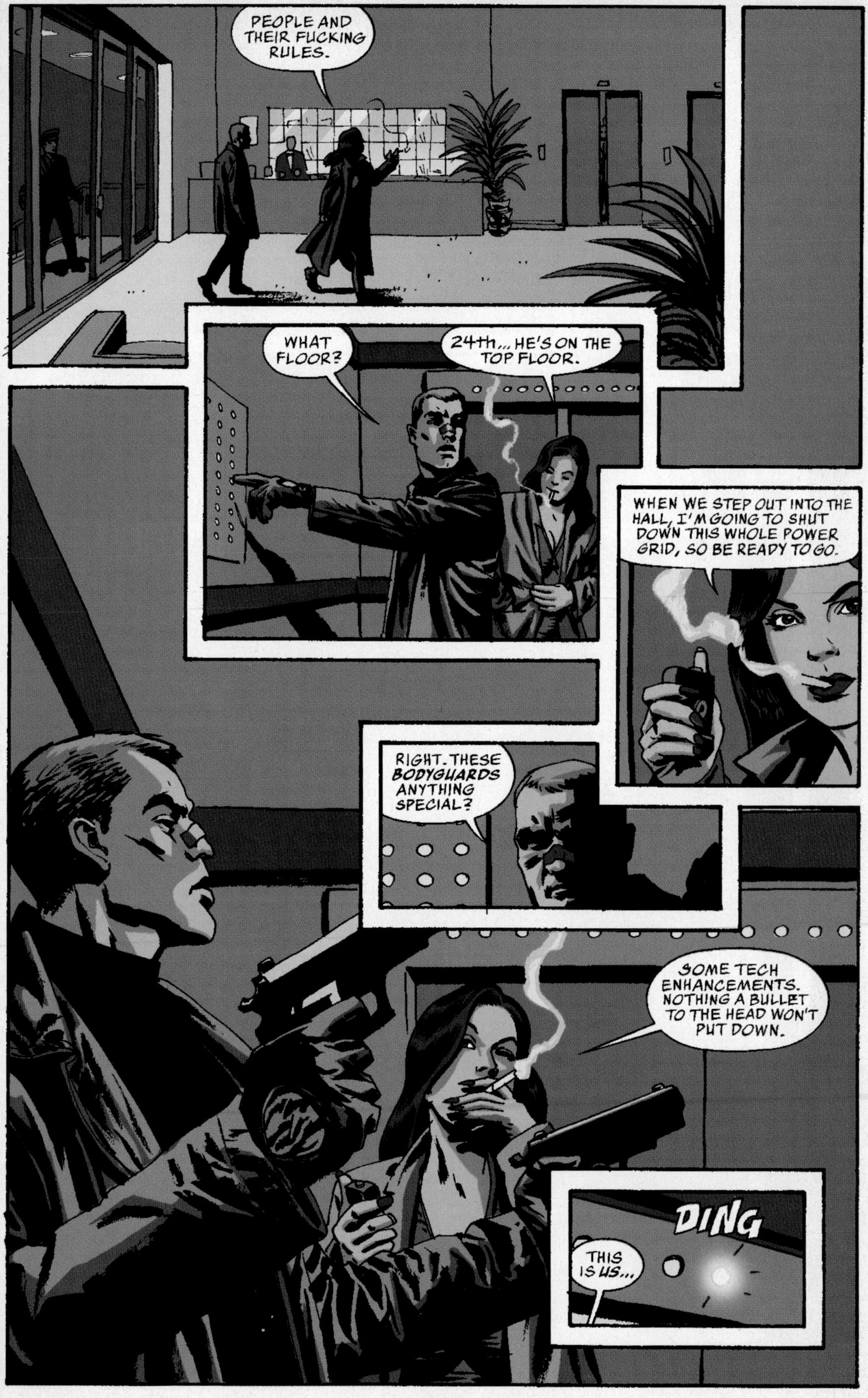
PEOPLE AND THEIR FUCKING RULES.
WHAT FLOOR?
24th... HE'S ON THE TOP FLOOR.
WHEN WE STEP OUT INTO THE HALL, I'M GOING TO SHUT DOWN THIS WHOLE POWER GRID, SO BE READY TO GO.
RIGHT. THESE BODYGUARDS ANYTHING SPECIAL?
SOME TECH ENHANCEMENTS. NOTHING A BULLET TO THE HEAD WON'T PUT DOWN.
DING
THIS IS US...

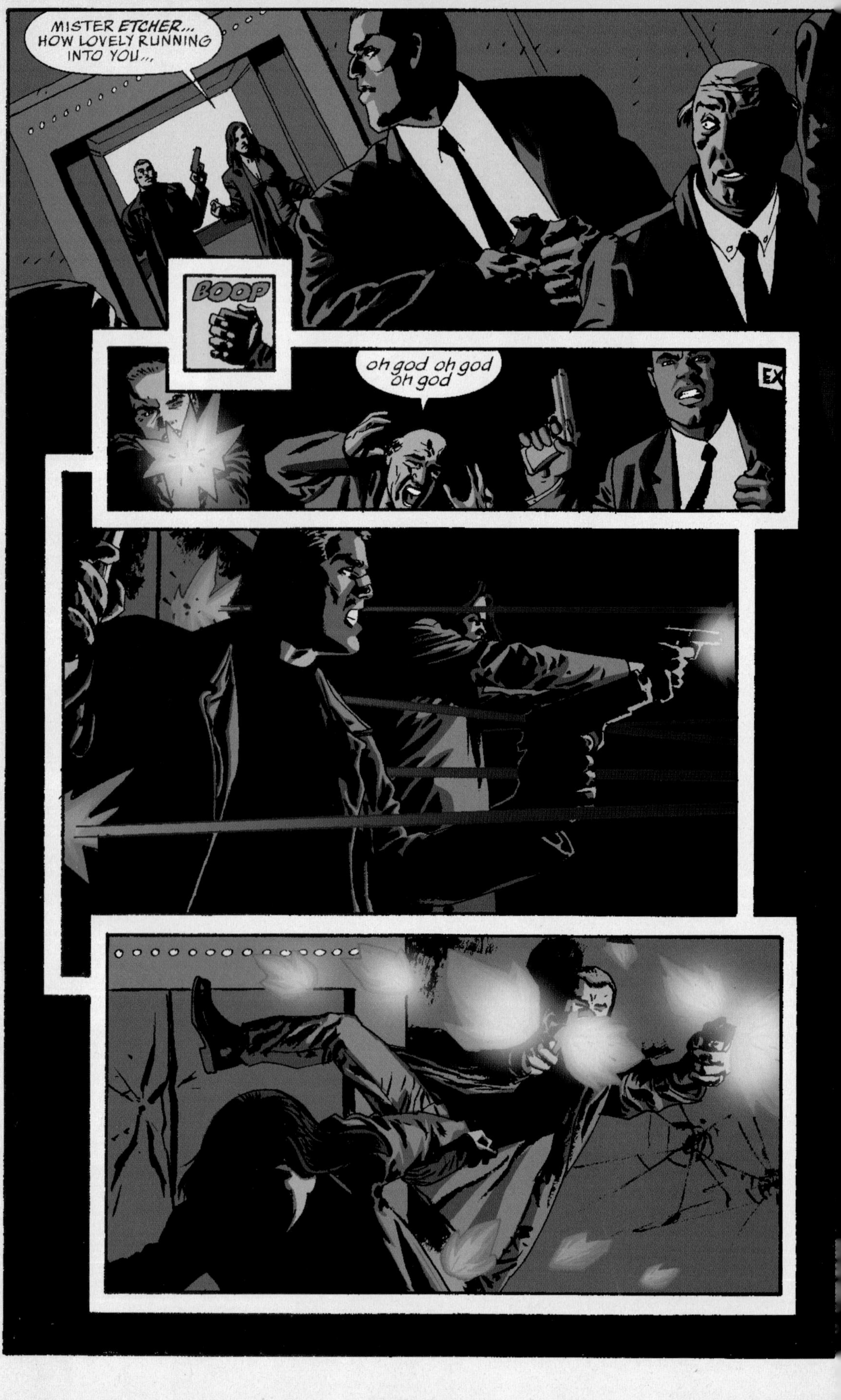
MISTER ETCHER... HOW LOVELY RUNNING INTO YOU...
BOOP
oh god oh god oh god
EX

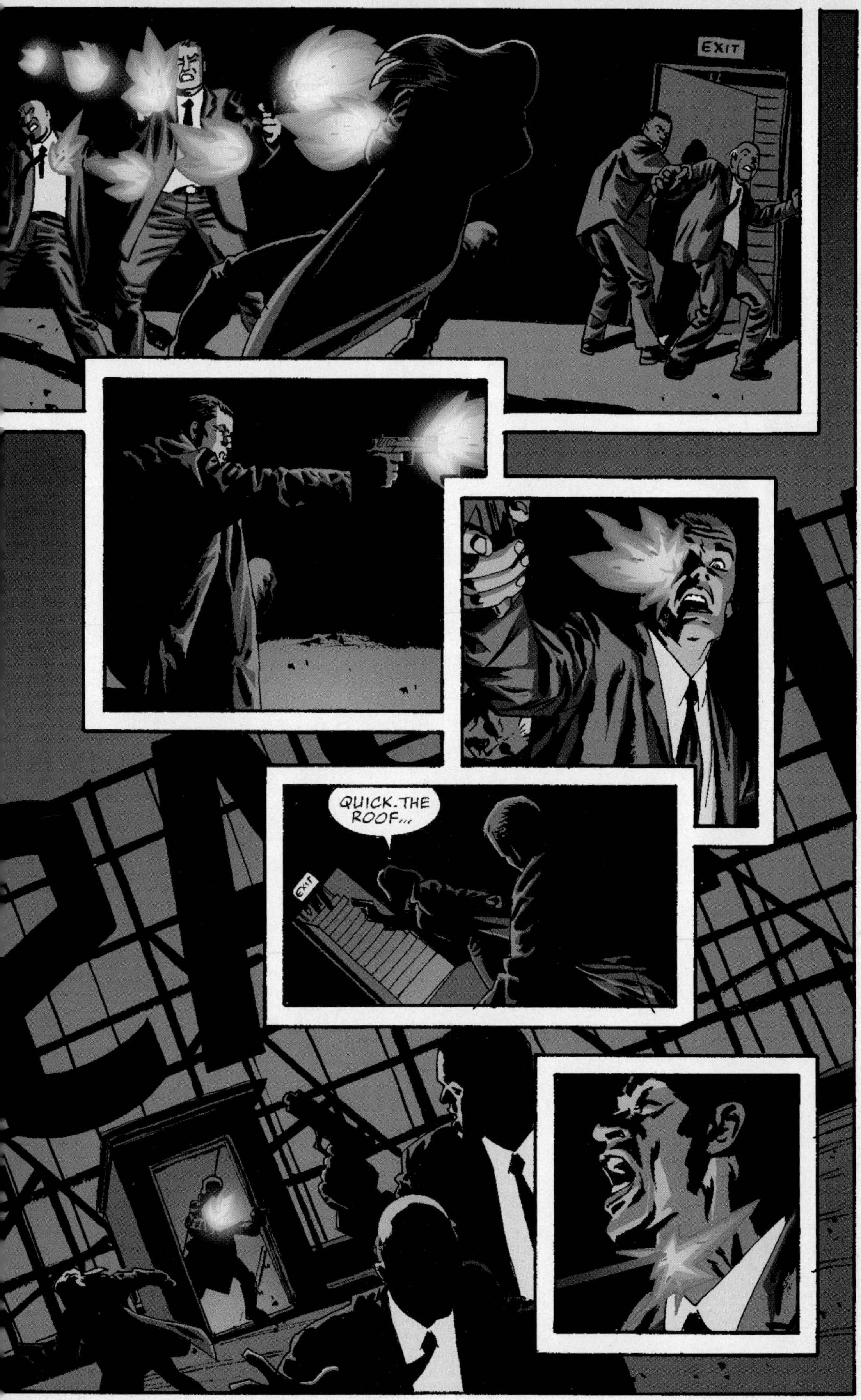
EXIT
QUICK. THE ROOF...
EXIT

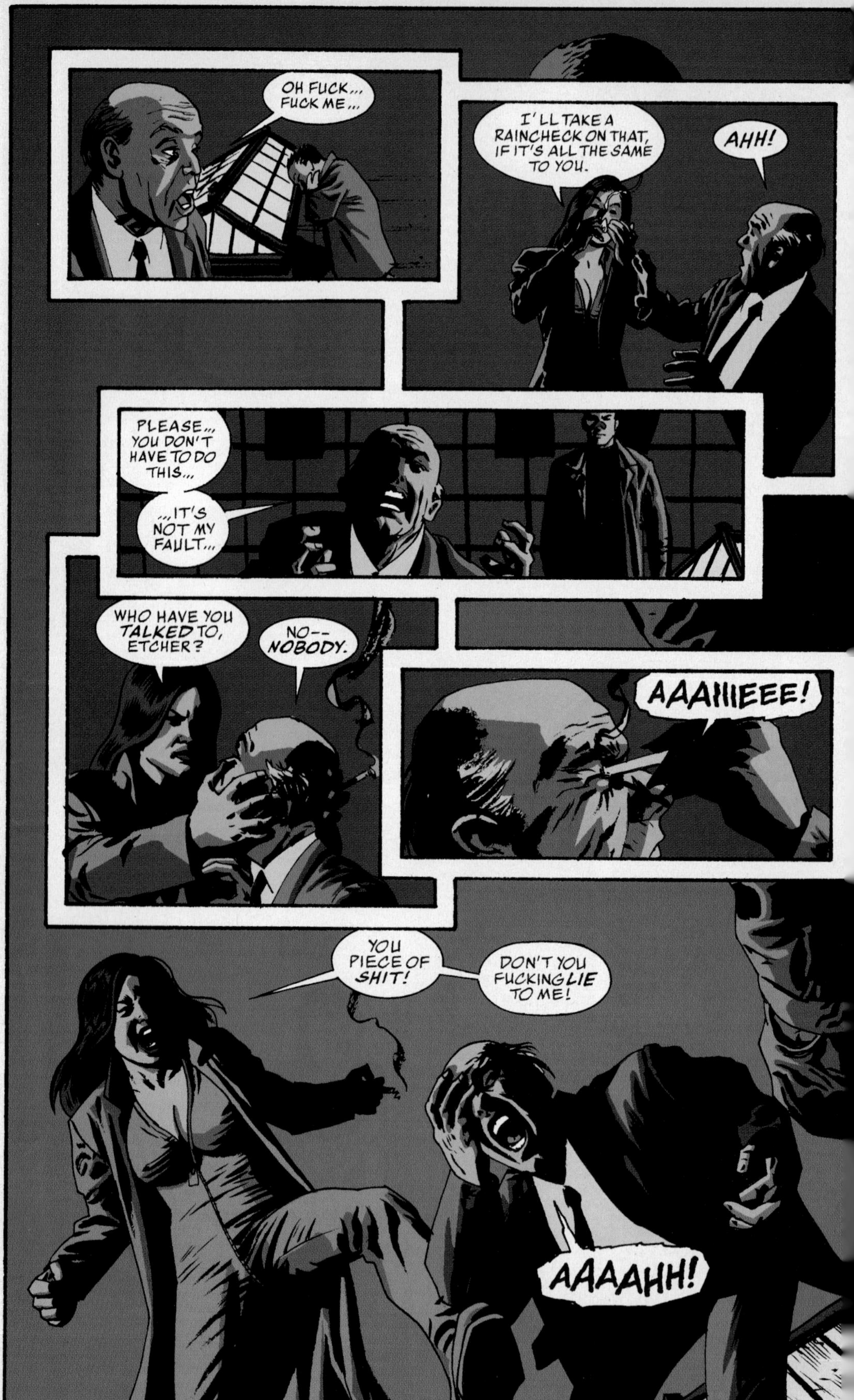
OH FUCK... FUCK ME...
I'LL TAKE A RAINCHECK ON THAT, IF IT'S ALL THE SAME TO YOU.
AHH!
PLEASE... YOU DON'T HAVE TO DO THIS...
...IT'S NOT MY FAULT...
WHO HAVE YOU TALKED TO, ETCHER?
NO-- NOBODY.
AAAIIIEEE!
YOU PIECE OF SHIT!
DON'T YOU FUCKING LIE TO ME!
AAAAHH!

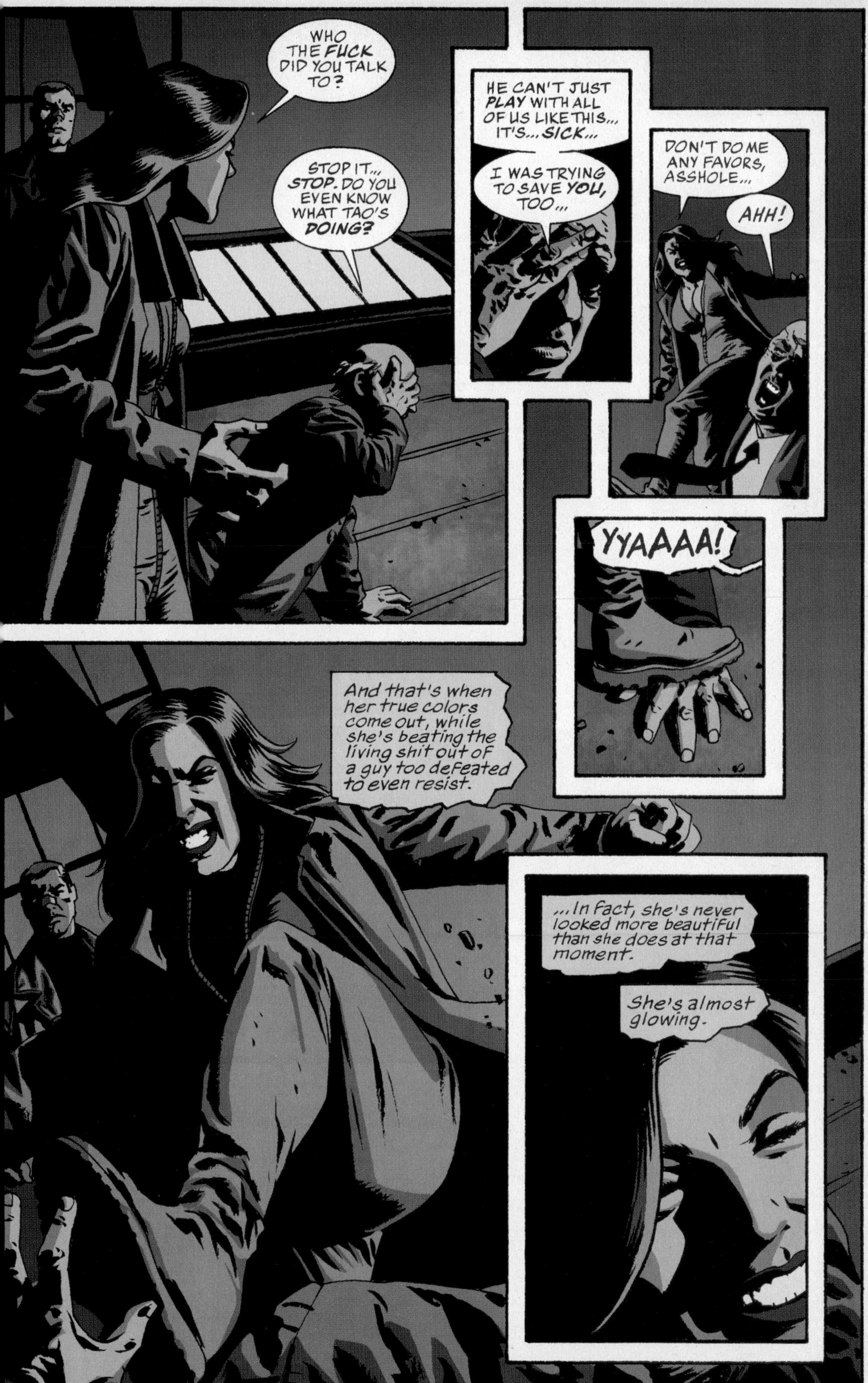
WHO THE FUCK DID YOU TALK TO?
STOP IT... STOP. DO YOU EVEN KNOW WHAT TAO'S DOING?
HE CAN'T JUST PLAY WITH ALL OF US LIKE THIS... IT'S... SICK...
I WAS TRYING TO SAVE YOU, TOO...
DON'T DO ME ANY FAVORS, ASSHOLE...
AHH!
YYAAAA!
And that's when her true colors come out, while she's beating the living shit out of a guy too defeated to even resist.
...In fact, she's never looked more beautiful than she does at that moment.
She's almost glowing.

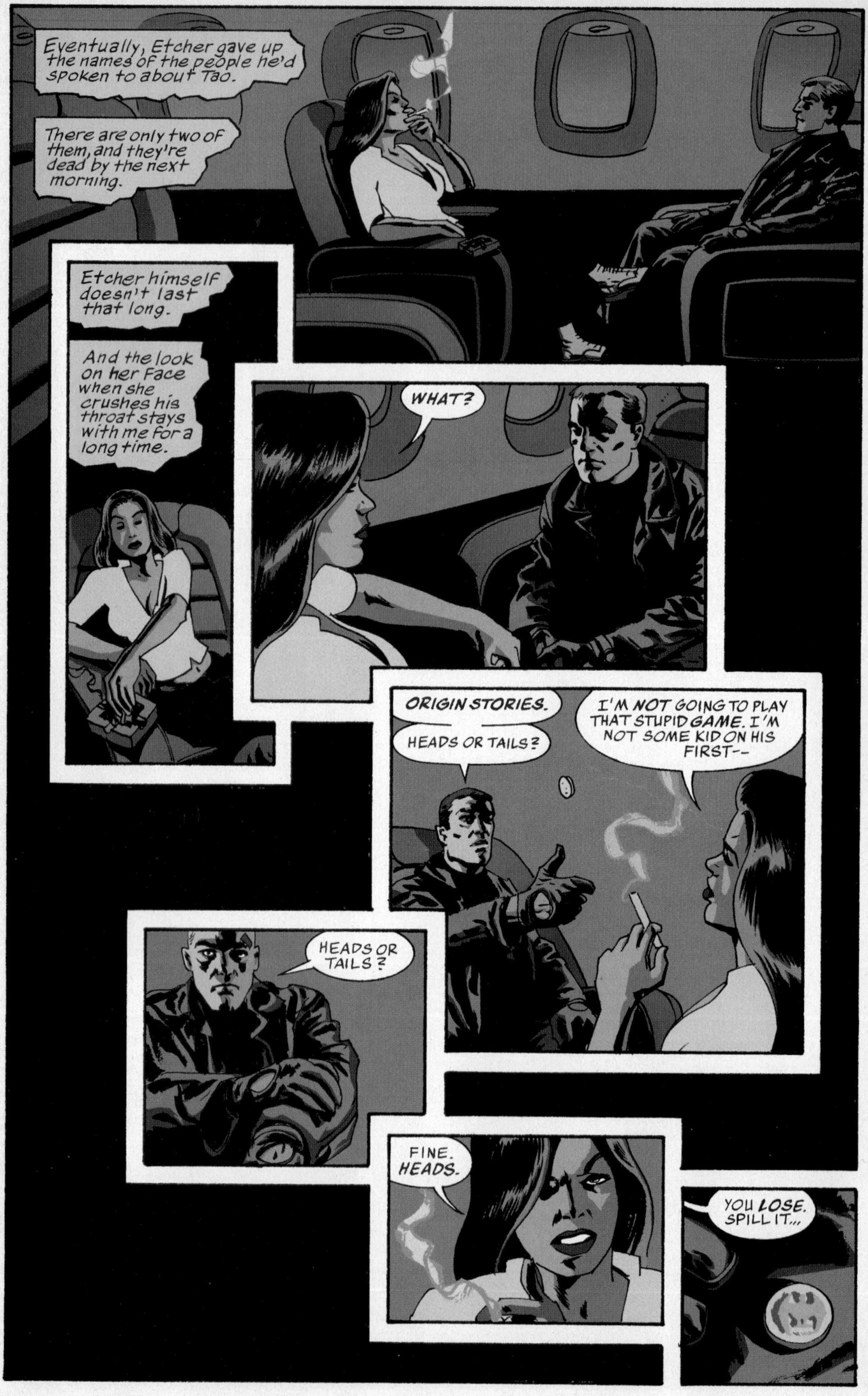
Eventually, Etcher gave up the names of the people he'd spoken to about Tao.
There are only two of them, and they're dead by the next morning.
Etcher himself doesn't last that long.
And the look on her face when she crushes his throat stays with me for a long time.
WHAT?
ORIGIN STORIES.
HEADS OR TAILS?
I'M NOT GOING TO PLAY THAT STUPID GAME. I'M NOT SOME KID ON HIS FIRST--
HEADS OR TAILS?
FINE. HEADS.
YOU LOSE. SPILL IT...

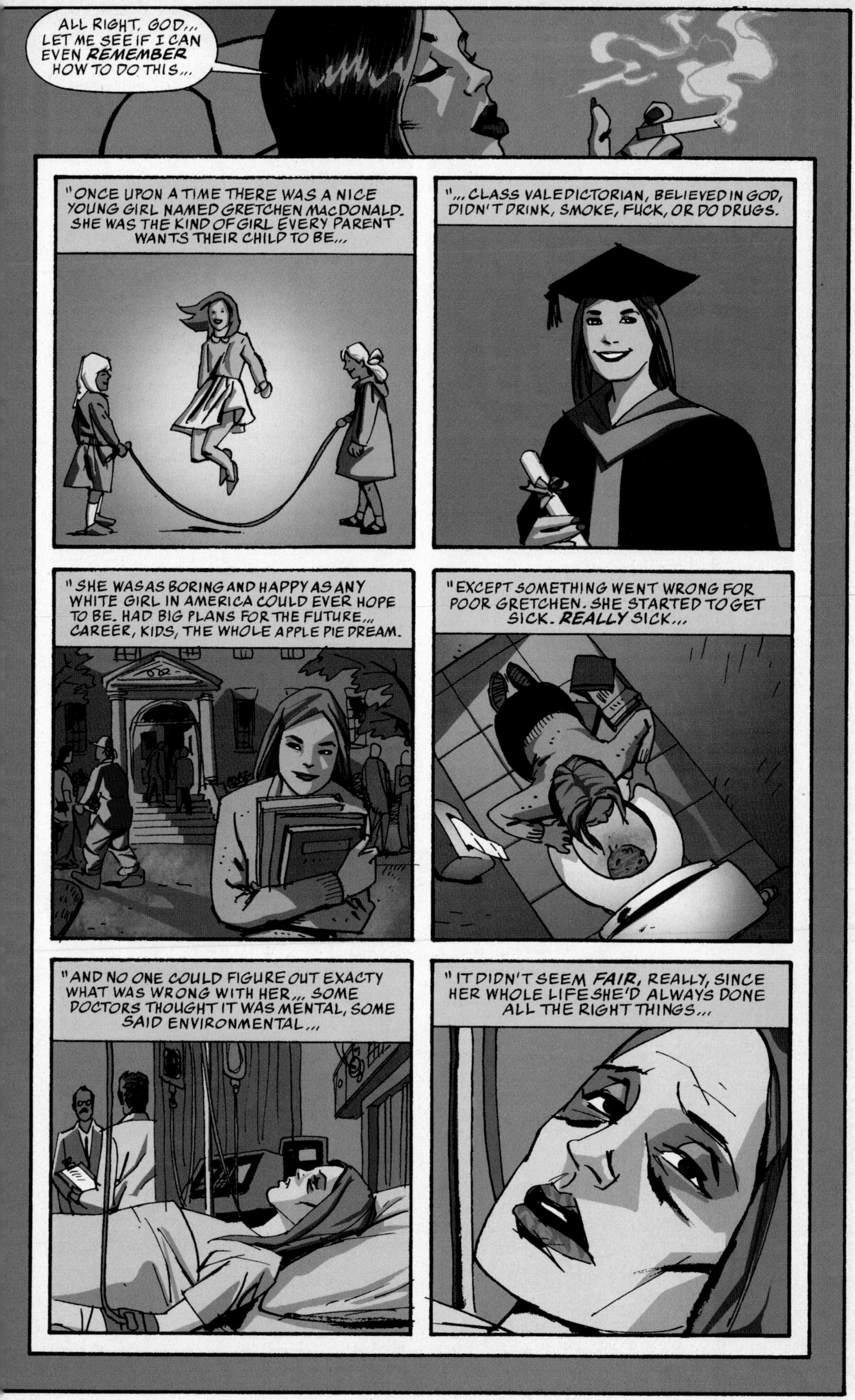
ALL RIGHT, GOD... LET ME SEE IF I CAN EVEN REMEMBER HOW TO DO THIS...
"ONCE UPON A TIME THERE WAS A NICE YOUNG GIRL NAMED GRETCHEN MACDONALD. SHE WAS THE KIND OF GIRL EVERY PARENT WANTS THEIR CHILD TO BE...
"...CLASS VALEDICTORIAN, BELIEVED IN GOD, DIDN'T DRINK, SMOKE, FUCK, OR DO DRUGS.
"SHE WAS AS BORING AND HAPPY AS ANY WHITE GIRL IN AMERICA COULD EVER HOPE TO BE. HAD BIG PLANS FOR THE FUTURE... CAREER, KIDS, THE WHOLE APPLE PIE DREAM.
"EXCEPT SOMETHING WENT WRONG FOR POOR GRETCHEN. SHE STARTED TO GET SICK. REALLY SICK...
"AND NO ONE COULD FIGURE OUT EXACTY WHAT WAS WRONG WITH HER... SOME DOCTORS THOUGHT IT WAS MENTAL, SOME SAID ENVIRONMENTAL...
"IT DIDN'T SEEM FAIR, REALLY, SINCE HER WHOLE LIFE SHE'D ALWAYS DONE ALL THE RIGHT THINGS...

"AND IT WENT ON FOR YEARS. SHE'D START TO GET BETTER, AND THINK EVERYTHING WAS GOING TO BE OKAY AGAIN...

"...THEN THE NEXT WEEK SHE'D BE WORSE THAN EVER. IT WAS LIKE HER WHOLE BODY WAS REJECTING ITSELF.

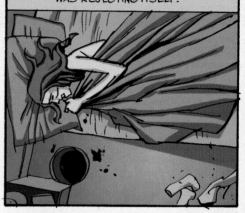

"FINALLY ONE DAY, AFTER ALMOST THREE YEARS OF HOSPITALS AND SKEPTICAL DOCTORS AND BLOOD TESTS AND EVERYTHING, SHE'D SIMPLY HAD ENOUGH...

"AN EMERGENCY ROOM INTERN SAID SOMETHING THOUGHTLESS, AND THE PERFECT GOOD LITTLE AMERICAN GIRL JUST SNAPPED...

"FOR THE FIRST TIME IN HER LIFE, SHE ACTUALLY STRUCK ANOTHER PERSON...

THAT MOMENT CHANGED EVERYTHING. IT WAS--

SORRY TO INTERRUPT, MA'AM, BUT WE'LL BE LANDING IN A MINUTE.

ALL RIGHT, WE'VE GOT SOME WORK TO DO NOW... WE CAN FINISH THIS LATER...

HEY, WE BETTER. IT'S JUST GETTING TO THE GOOD PART.

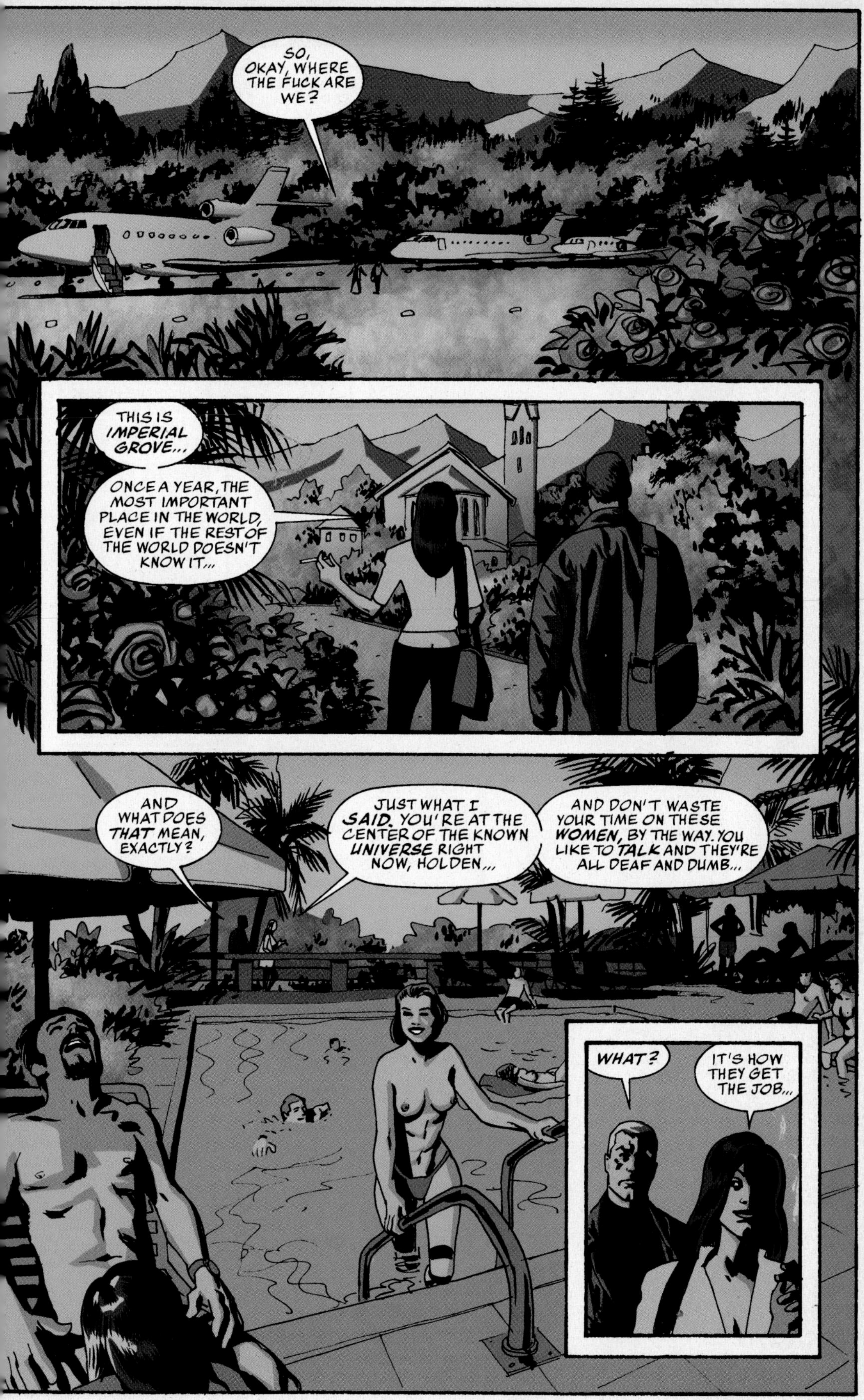
SO, OKAY, WHERE THE FUCK ARE WE?
THIS IS IMPERIAL GROVE...
ONCE A YEAR, THE MOST IMPORTANT PLACE IN THE WORLD, EVEN IF THE REST OF THE WORLD DOESN'T KNOW IT...
AND WHAT DOES THAT MEAN, EXACTLY?
JUST WHAT I SAID. YOU'RE AT THE CENTER OF THE KNOWN UNIVERSE RIGHT NOW, HOLDEN...
AND DON'T WASTE YOUR TIME ON THESE WOMEN, BY THE WAY. YOU LIKE TO TALK AND THEY'RE ALL DEAF AND DUMB...
WHAT?
IT'S HOW THEY GET THE JOB...

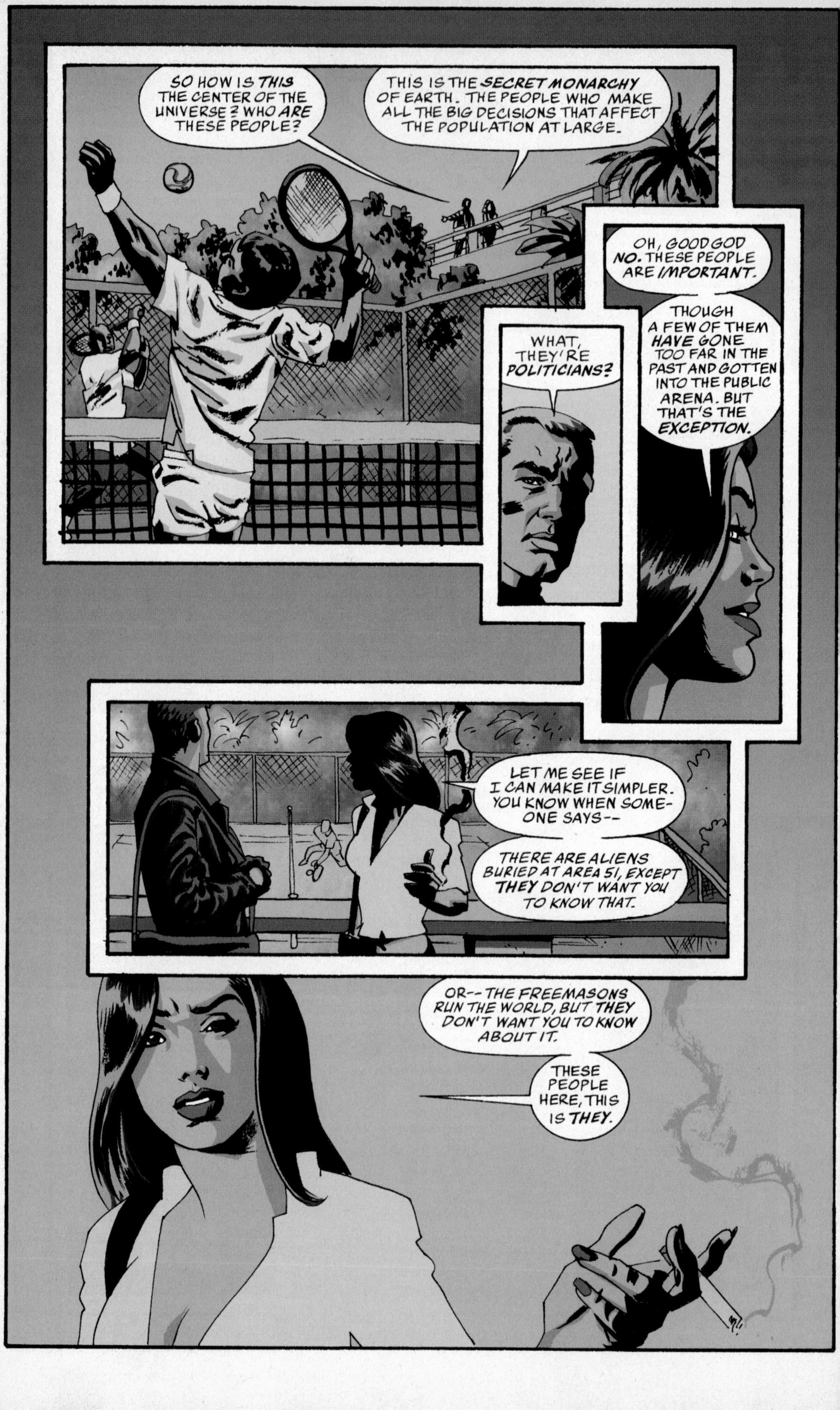
SO HOW IS THIS THE CENTER OF THE UNIVERSE? WHO ARE THESE PEOPLE?
THIS IS THE SECRET MONARCHY OF EARTH. THE PEOPLE WHO MAKE ALL THE BIG DECISIONS THAT AFFECT THE POPULATION AT LARGE.
WHAT, THEY'RE POLITICIANS?
OH, GOOD GOD NO. THESE PEOPLE ARE IMPORTANT.
THOUGH A FEW OF THEM HAVE GONE TOO FAR IN THE PAST AND GOTTEN INTO THE PUBLIC ARENA. BUT THAT'S THE EXCEPTION.
LET ME SEE IF I CAN MAKE IT SIMPLER. YOU KNOW WHEN SOME-ONE SAYS--
THERE ARE ALIENS BURIED AT AREA 51, EXCEPT THEY DON'T WANT YOU TO KNOW THAT.
OR--THE FREEMASONS RUN THE WORLD, BUT THEY DON'T WANT YOU TO KNOW ABOUT IT.
THESE PEOPLE HERE, THIS IS THEY.

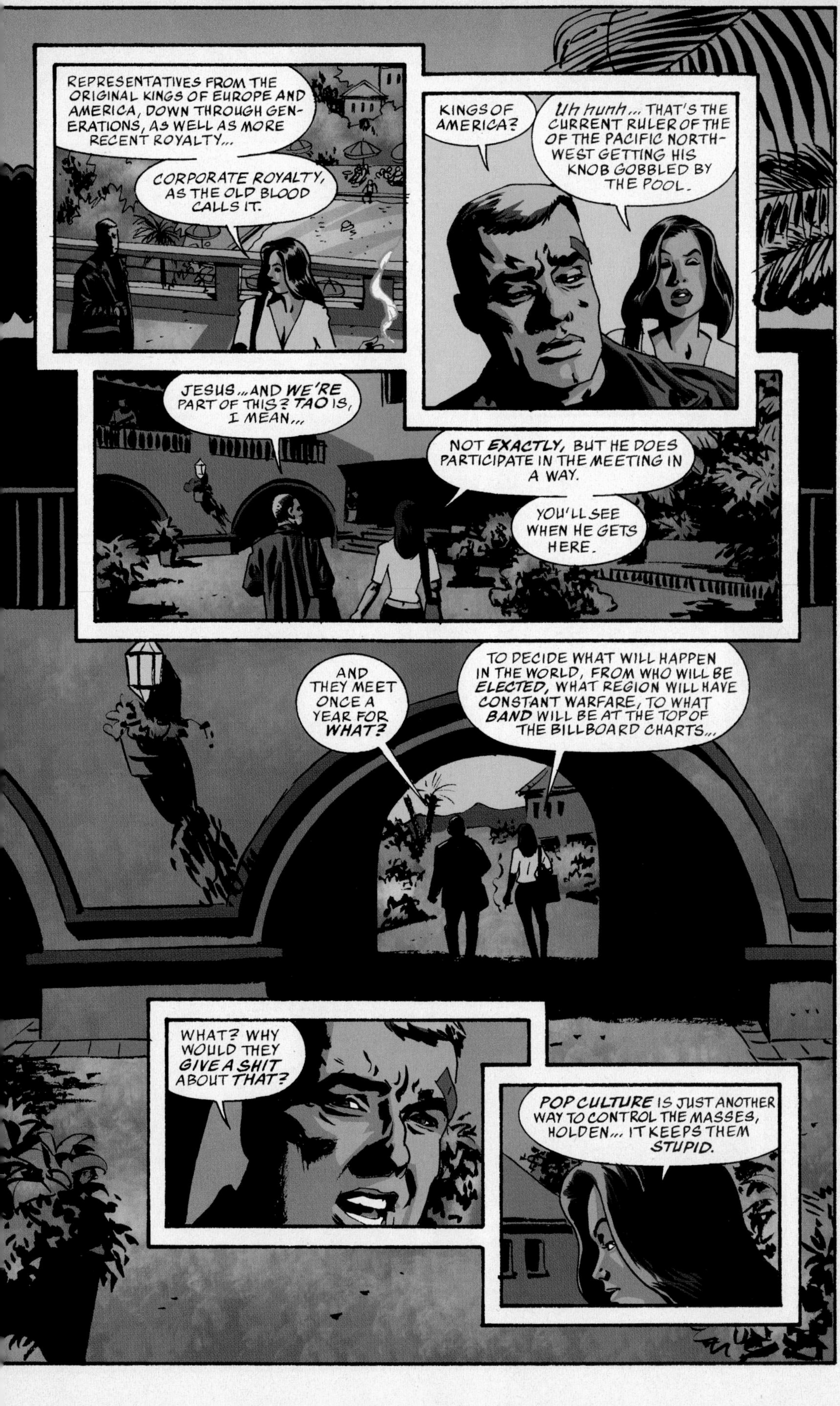
REPRESENTATIVES FROM THE ORIGINAL KINGS OF EUROPE AND AMERICA, DOWN THROUGH GENERATIONS, AS WELL AS MORE RECENT ROYALTY...
CORPORATE ROYALTY, AS THE OLD BLOOD CALLS IT.
KINGS OF AMERICA?
Uh hunh... THAT'S THE CURRENT RULER OF THE OF THE PACIFIC NORTHWEST GETTING HIS KNOB GOBBLED BY THE POOL.
JESUS...AND WE'RE PART OF THIS? TAO IS, I MEAN...
NOT EXACTLY, BUT HE DOES PARTICIPATE IN THE MEETING IN A WAY.
YOU'LL SEE WHEN HE GETS HERE.
AND THEY MEET ONCE A YEAR FOR WHAT?
TO DECIDE WHAT WILL HAPPEN IN THE WORLD, FROM WHO WILL BE ELECTED, WHAT REGION WILL HAVE CONSTANT WARFARE, TO WHAT BAND WILL BE AT THE TOP OF THE BILLBOARD CHARTS...
WHAT? WHY WOULD THEY GIVE A SHIT ABOUT THAT?
POP CULTURE IS JUST ANOTHER WAY TO CONTROL THE MASSES, HOLDEN... IT KEEPS THEM STUPID.

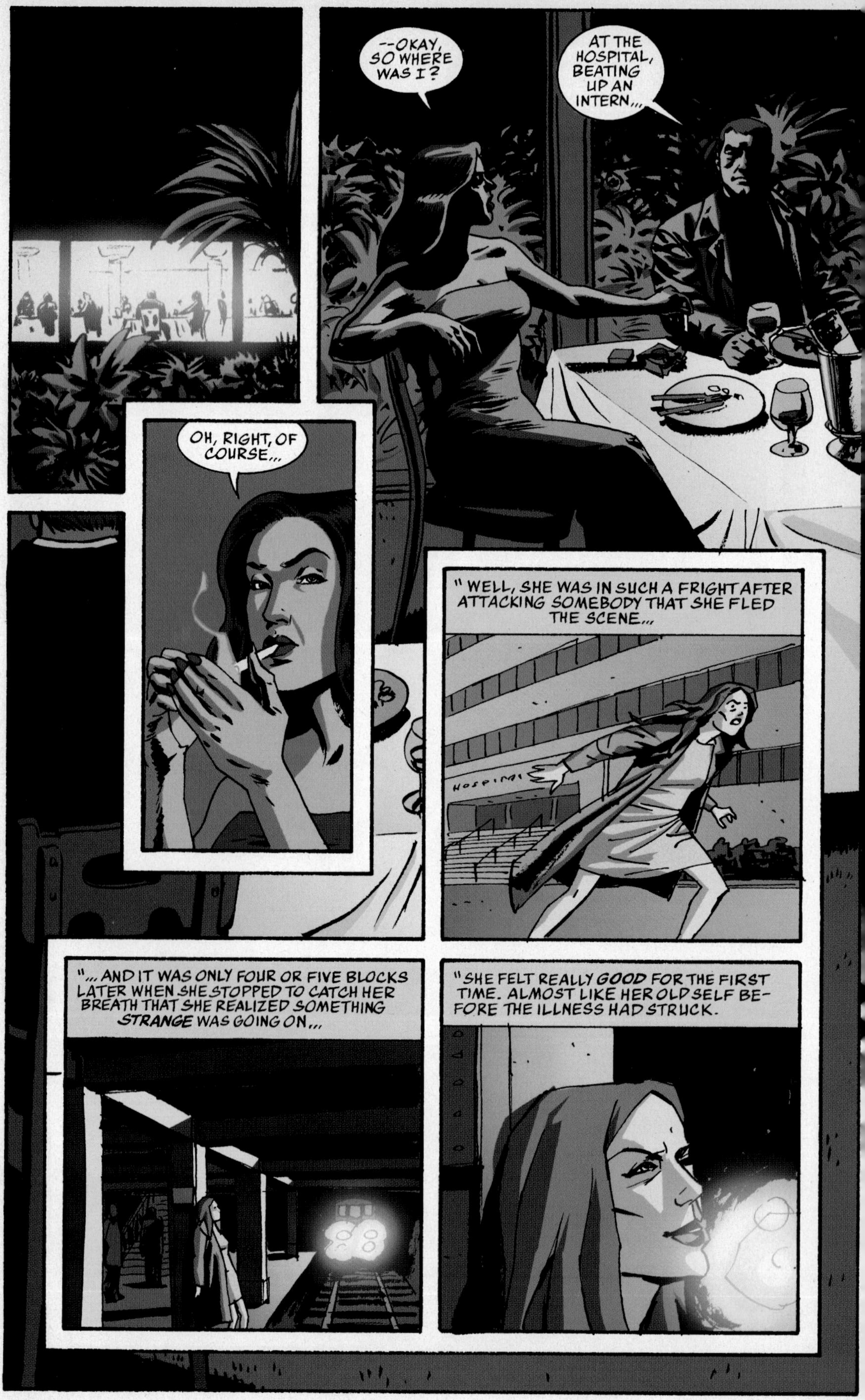
--OKAY, SO WHERE WAS I?
AT THE HOSPITAL, BEATING UP AN INTERN...
OH, RIGHT, OF COURSE...
"WELL, SHE WAS IN SUCH A FRIGHT AFTER ATTACKING SOMEBODY THAT SHE FLED THE SCENE...
"...AND IT WAS ONLY FOUR OR FIVE BLOCKS LATER WHEN SHE STOPPED TO CATCH HER BREATH THAT SHE REALIZED SOMETHING *STRANGE* WAS GOING ON...
"SHE FELT REALLY *GOOD* FOR THE FIRST TIME. ALMOST LIKE HER OLD SELF BEFORE THE ILLNESS HAD STRUCK.

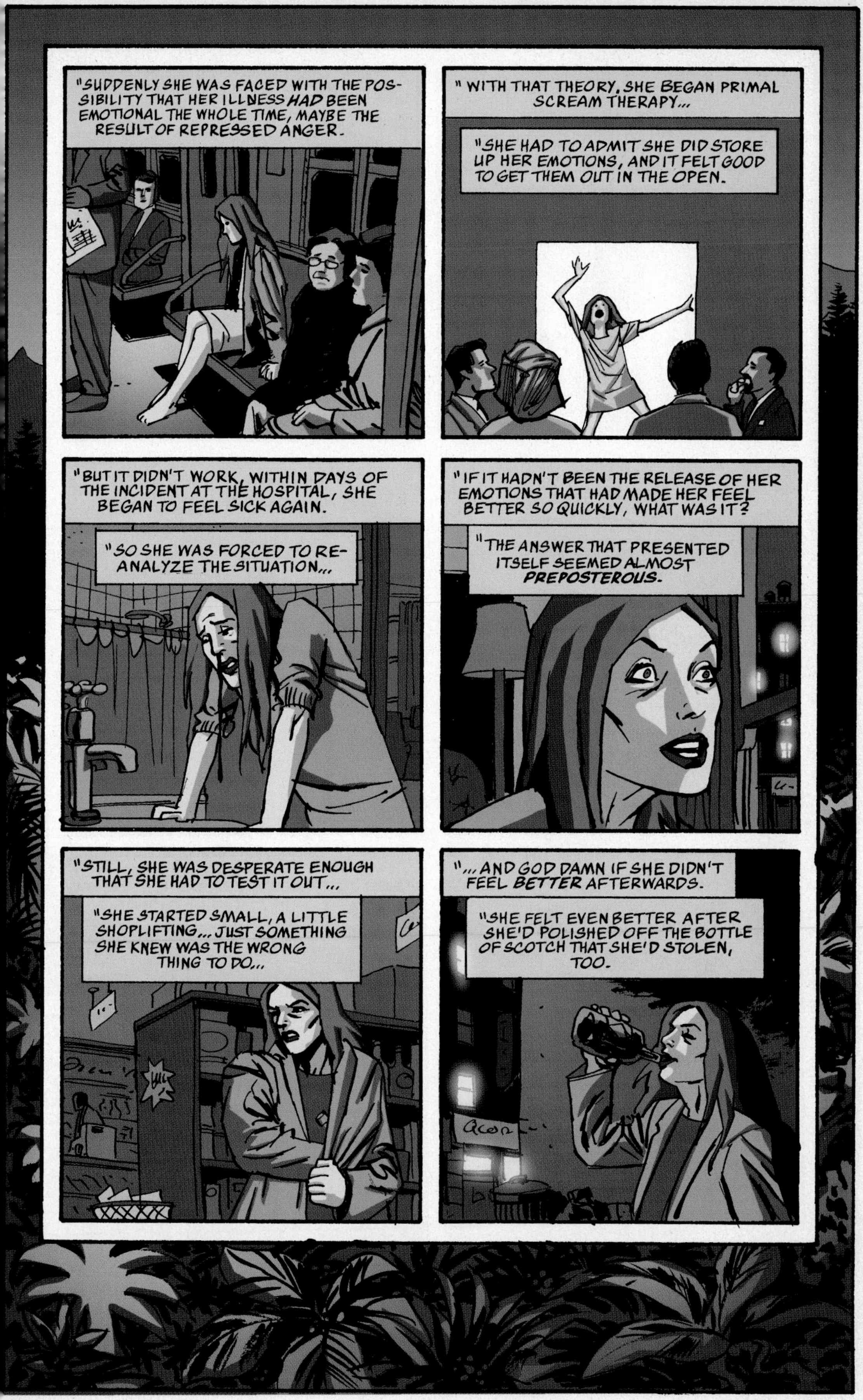
"SUDDENLY SHE WAS FACED WITH THE POSSIBILITY THAT HER ILLNESS HAD BEEN EMOTIONAL THE WHOLE TIME, MAYBE THE RESULT OF REPRESSED ANGER.
" WITH THAT THEORY, SHE BEGAN PRIMAL SCREAM THERAPY...
"SHE HAD TO ADMIT SHE DID STORE UP HER EMOTIONS, AND IT FELT GOOD TO GET THEM OUT IN THE OPEN.
"BUT IT DIDN'T WORK. WITHIN DAYS OF THE INCIDENT AT THE HOSPITAL, SHE BEGAN TO FEEL SICK AGAIN.
"SO SHE WAS FORCED TO RE-ANALYZE THE SITUATION...
"IF IT HADN'T BEEN THE RELEASE OF HER EMOTIONS THAT HAD MADE HER FEEL BETTER SO QUICKLY, WHAT WAS IT?
"THE ANSWER THAT PRESENTED ITSELF SEEMED ALMOST PREPOSTEROUS.
"STILL, SHE WAS DESPERATE ENOUGH THAT SHE HAD TO TEST IT OUT...
"SHE STARTED SMALL, A LITTLE SHOPLIFTING... JUST SOMETHING SHE KNEW WAS THE WRONG THING TO DO...
"... AND GOD DAMN IF SHE DIDN'T FEEL BETTER AFTERWARDS.
"SHE FELT EVEN BETTER AFTER SHE'D POLISHED OFF THE BOTTLE OF SCOTCH THAT SHE'D STOLEN, TOO.

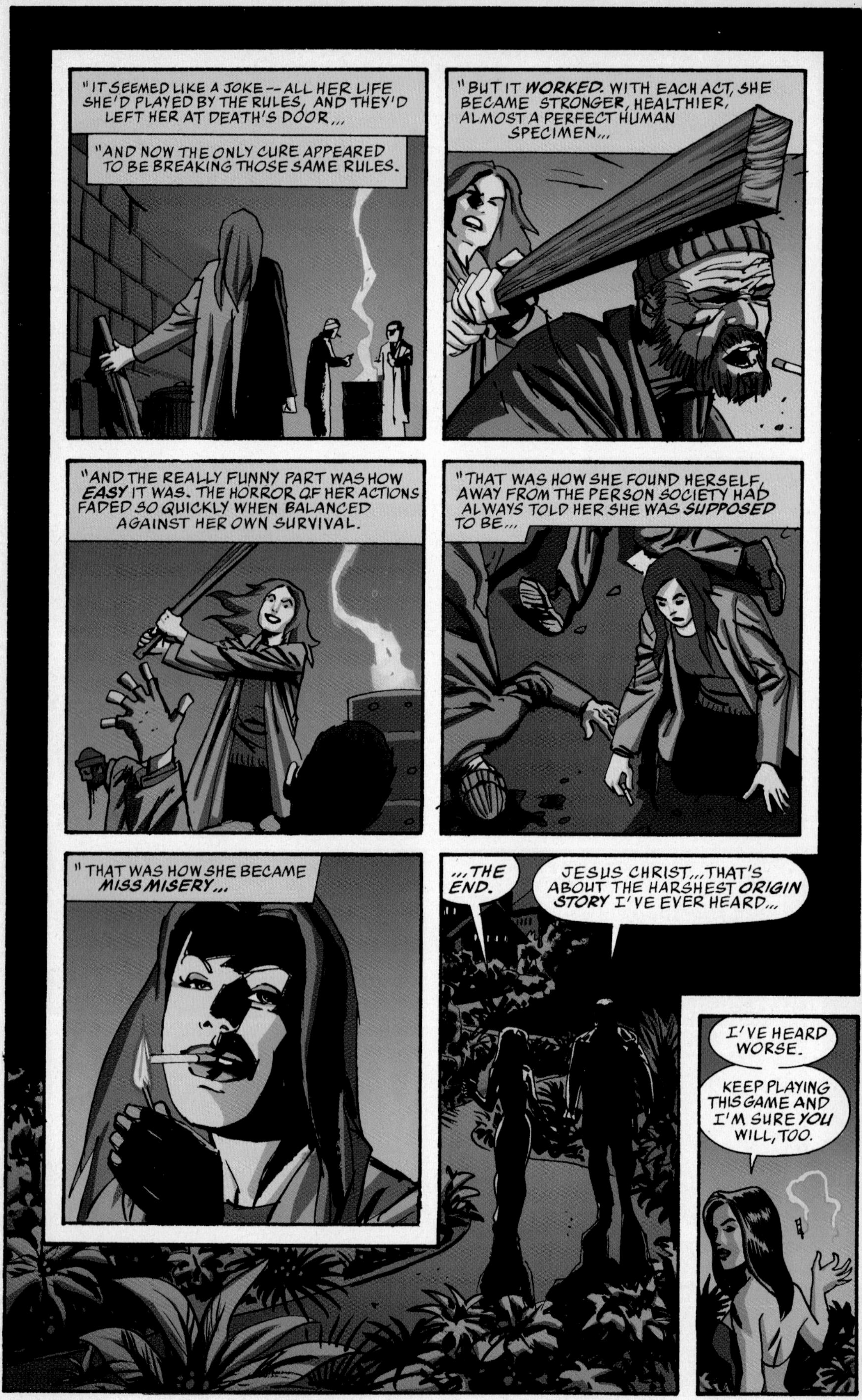
"IT SEEMED LIKE A JOKE--ALL HER LIFE SHE'D PLAYED BY THE RULES, AND THEY'D LEFT HER AT DEATH'S DOOR...
"AND NOW THE ONLY CURE APPEARED TO BE BREAKING THOSE SAME RULES.
"BUT IT WORKED. WITH EACH ACT, SHE BECAME STRONGER, HEALTHIER, ALMOST A PERFECT HUMAN SPECIMEN...
"AND THE REALLY FUNNY PART WAS HOW EASY IT WAS. THE HORROR OF HER ACTIONS FADED SO QUICKLY WHEN BALANCED AGAINST HER OWN SURVIVAL.
"THAT WAS HOW SHE FOUND HERSELF, AWAY FROM THE PERSON SOCIETY HAD ALWAYS TOLD HER SHE WAS SUPPOSED TO BE...
"THAT WAS HOW SHE BECAME MISS MISERY...
...THE END.
JESUS CHRIST... THAT'S ABOUT THE HARSHEST ORIGIN STORY I'VE EVER HEARD...
I'VE HEARD WORSE.
KEEP PLAYING THIS GAME AND I'M SURE YOU WILL, TOO.

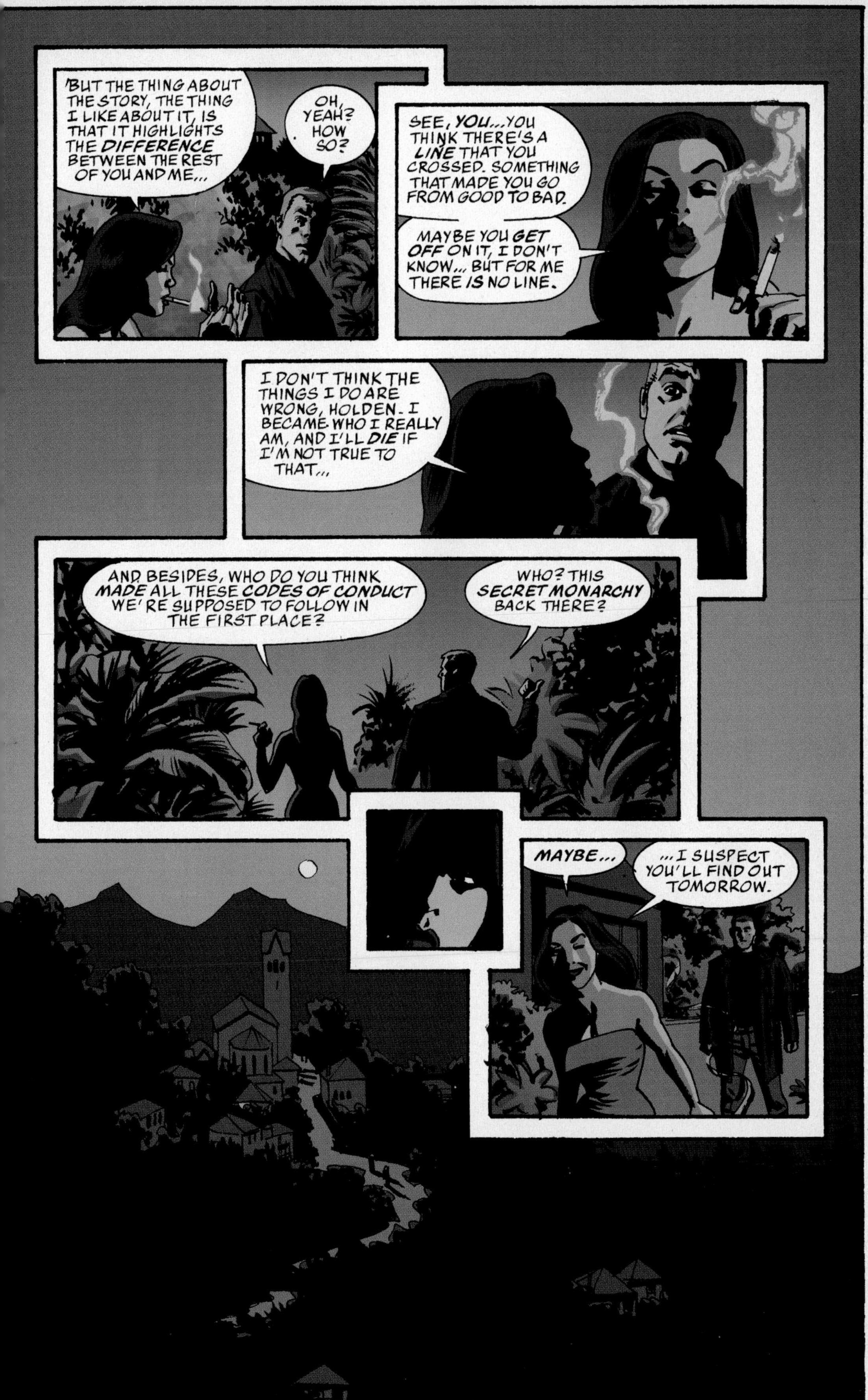
'BUT THE THING ABOUT THE STORY, THE THING I LIKE ABOUT IT, IS THAT IT HIGHLIGHTS THE DIFFERENCE BETWEEN THE REST OF YOU AND ME...
OH, YEAH? HOW SO?
SEE, YOU...YOU THINK THERE'S A LINE THAT YOU CROSSED. SOMETHING THAT MADE YOU GO FROM GOOD TO BAD.
MAYBE YOU GET OFF ON IT, I DON'T KNOW... BUT FOR ME THERE IS NO LINE.
I DON'T THINK THE THINGS I DO ARE WRONG, HOLDEN. I BECAME WHO I REALLY AM, AND I'LL DIE IF I'M NOT TRUE TO THAT...
AND BESIDES, WHO DO YOU THINK MADE ALL THESE CODES OF CONDUCT WE'RE SUPPOSED TO FOLLOW IN THE FIRST PLACE?
WHO? THIS SECRET MONARCHY BACK THERE?
MAYBE...
...I SUSPECT YOU'LL FIND OUT TOMORROW.

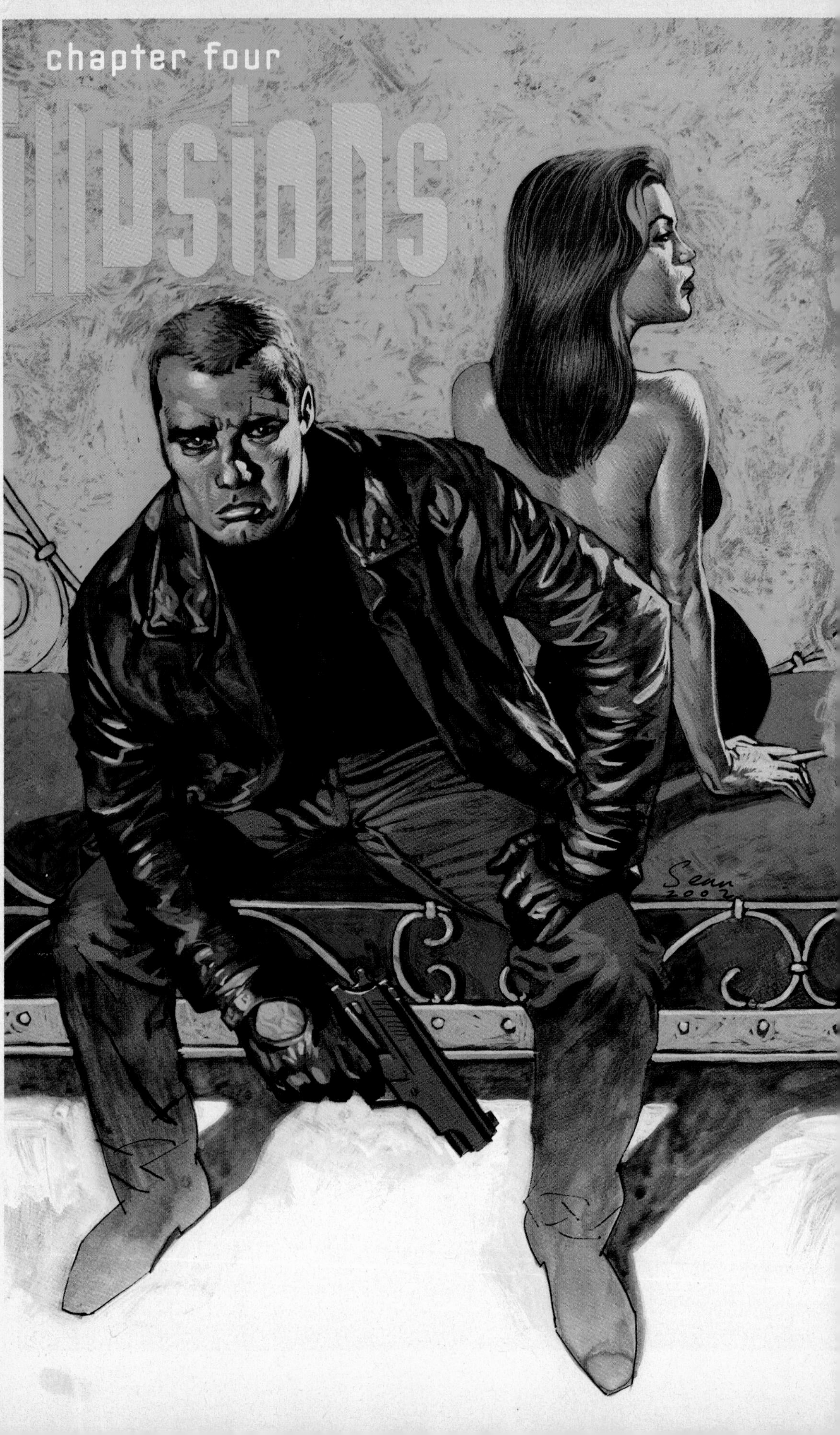
chapter four
Illusions
Sean 2002

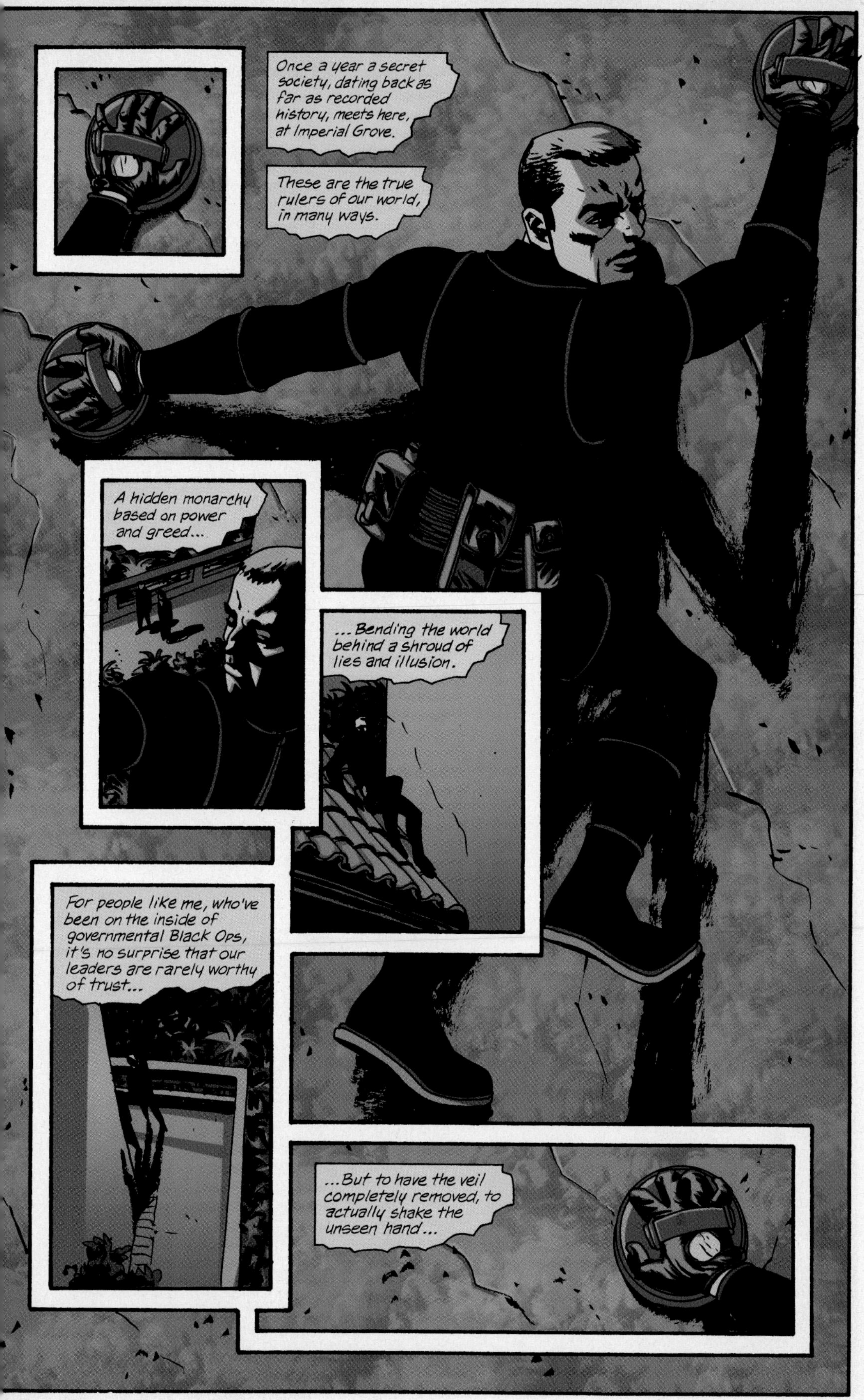
Once a year a secret society, dating back as far as recorded history, meets here, at Imperial Grove.
These are the true rulers of our world, in many ways.
A hidden monarchy based on power and greed...
...Bending the world behind a shroud of lies and illusion.
For people like me, who've been on the inside of governmental Black Ops, it's no surprise that our leaders are rarely worthy of trust...
...But to have the veil completely removed, to actually shake the unseen hand...

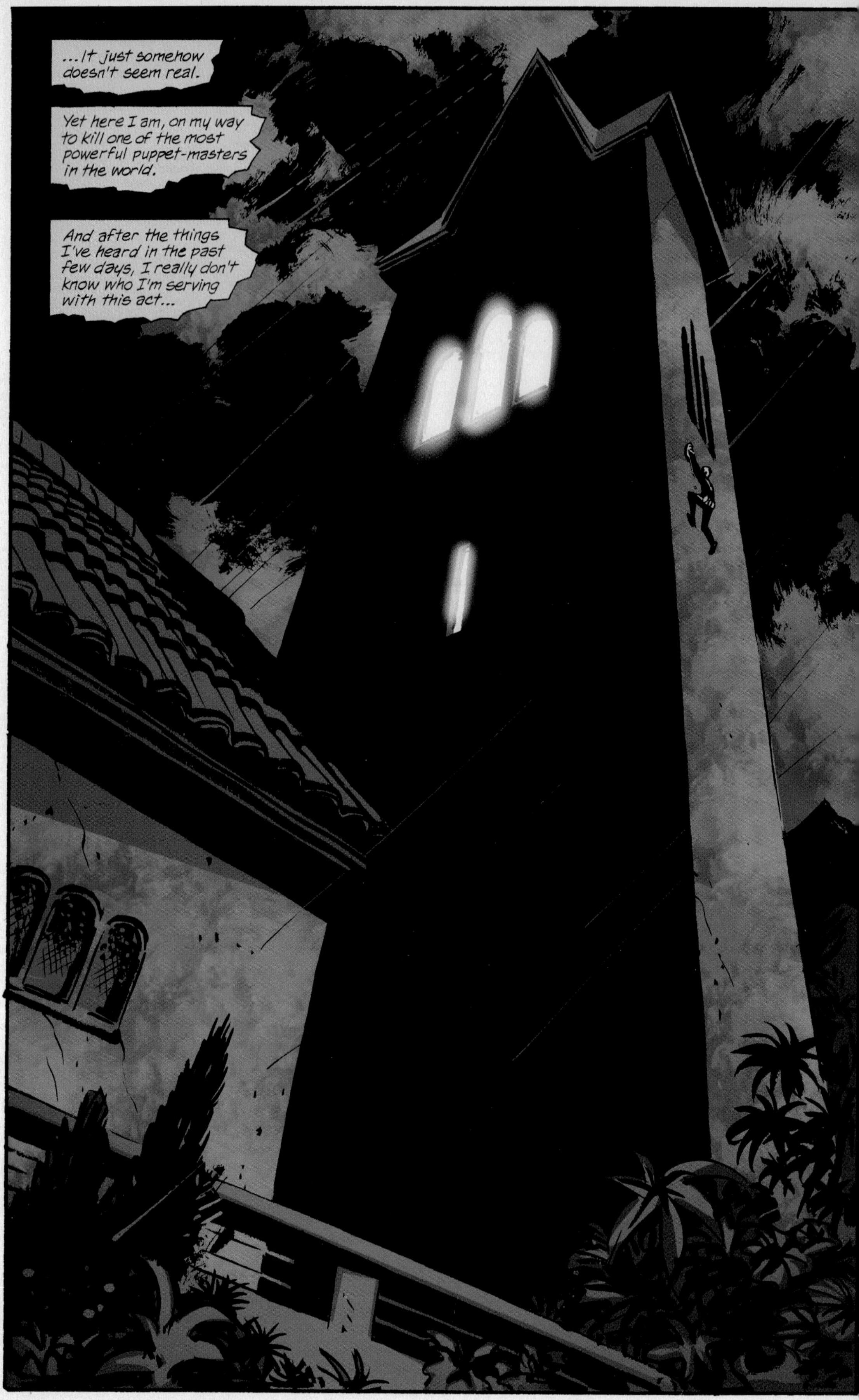
...It just somehow doesn't seem real.
Yet here I am, on my way to kill one of the most powerful puppet-masters in the world.
And after the things I've heard in the past few days, I really don't know who I'm serving with this act...

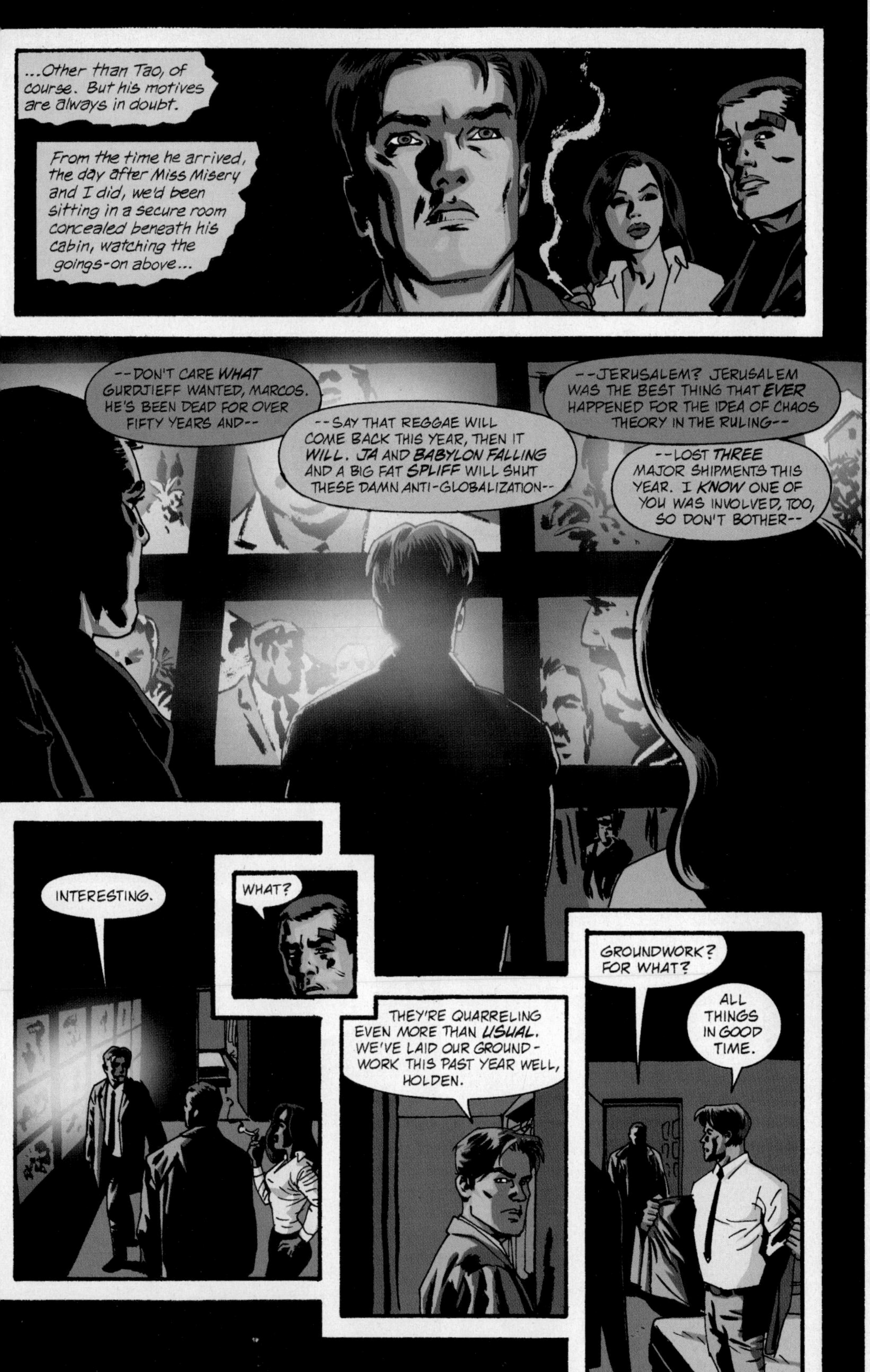
...Other than Tao, of course. But his motives are always in doubt.
From the time he arrived, the day after Miss Misery and I did, we'd been sitting in a secure room concealed beneath his cabin, watching the goings-on above...
--DON'T CARE WHAT GURDJIEFF WANTED, MARCOS. HE'S BEEN DEAD FOR OVER FIFTY YEARS AND--
--SAY THAT REGGAE WILL COME BACK THIS YEAR, THEN IT WILL. JA AND BABYLON FALLING AND A BIG FAT SPLIFF WILL SHUT THESE DAMN ANTI-GLOBALIZATION--
--JERUSALEM? JERUSALEM WAS THE BEST THING THAT EVER HAPPENED FOR THE IDEA OF CHAOS THEORY IN THE RULING--
--LOST THREE MAJOR SHIPMENTS THIS YEAR. I KNOW ONE OF YOU WAS INVOLVED, TOO, SO DON'T BOTHER--
INTERESTING.
WHAT?
THEY'RE QUARRELING EVEN MORE THAN USUAL. WE'VE LAID OUR GROUND-WORK THIS PAST YEAR WELL, HOLDEN.
GROUNDWORK? FOR WHAT?
ALL THINGS IN GOOD TIME.

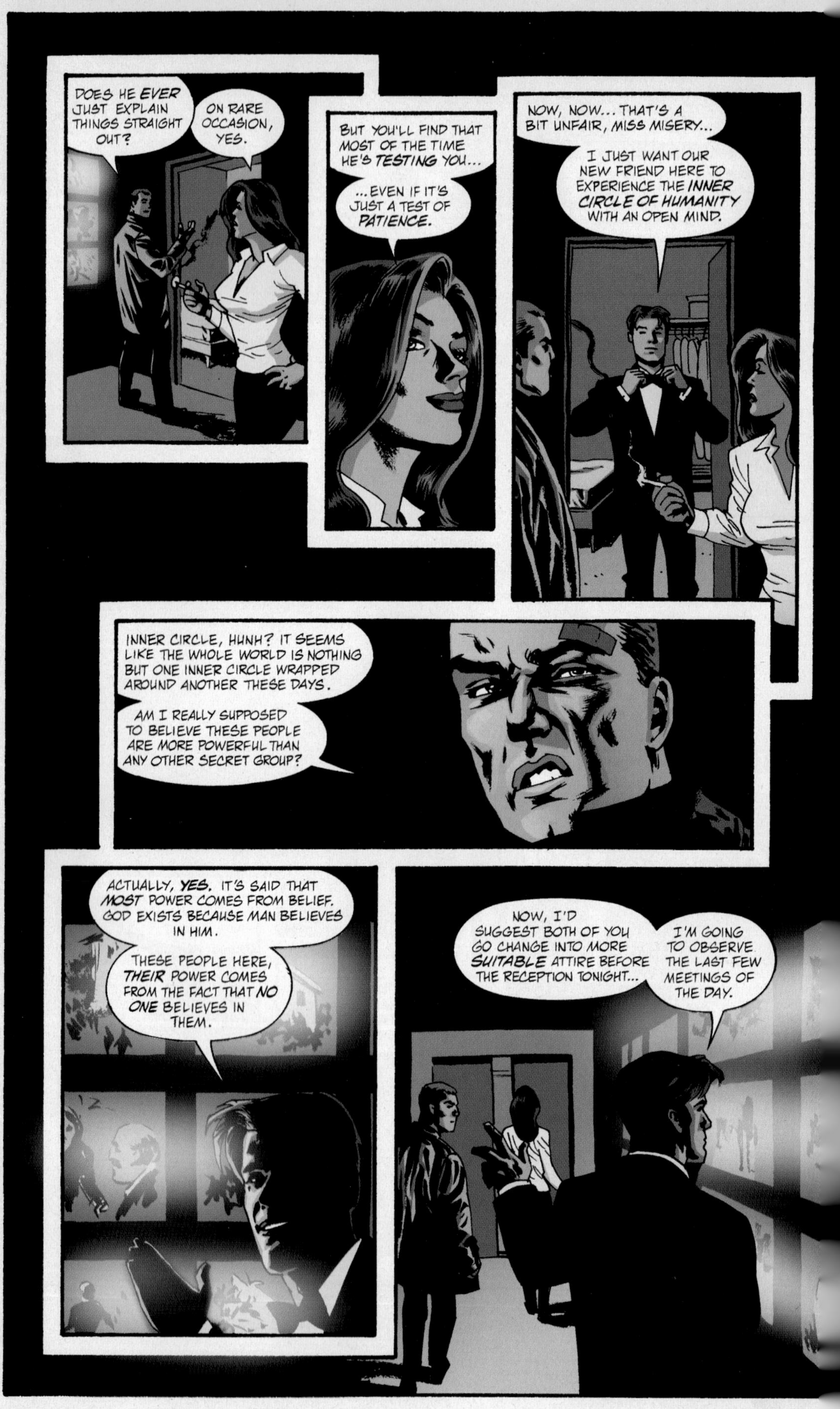
DOES HE EVER JUST EXPLAIN THINGS STRAIGHT OUT?
ON RARE OCCASION, YES.
BUT YOU'LL FIND THAT MOST OF THE TIME HE'S TESTING YOU...
...EVEN IF IT'S JUST A TEST OF PATIENCE.
NOW, NOW... THAT'S A BIT UNFAIR, MISS MISERY...
I JUST WANT OUR NEW FRIEND HERE TO EXPERIENCE THE INNER CIRCLE OF HUMANITY WITH AN OPEN MIND.
INNER CIRCLE, HUNH? IT SEEMS LIKE THE WHOLE WORLD IS NOTHING BUT ONE INNER CIRCLE WRAPPED AROUND ANOTHER THESE DAYS.
AM I REALLY SUPPOSED TO BELIEVE THESE PEOPLE ARE MORE POWERFUL THAN ANY OTHER SECRET GROUP?
ACTUALLY, YES. IT'S SAID THAT MOST POWER COMES FROM BELIEF. GOD EXISTS BECAUSE MAN BELIEVES IN HIM.
THESE PEOPLE HERE, THEIR POWER COMES FROM THE FACT THAT NO ONE BELIEVES IN THEM.
NOW, I'D SUGGEST BOTH OF YOU GO CHANGE INTO MORE SUITABLE ATTIRE BEFORE THE RECEPTION TONIGHT...
I'M GOING TO OBSERVE THE LAST FEW MEETINGS OF THE DAY.

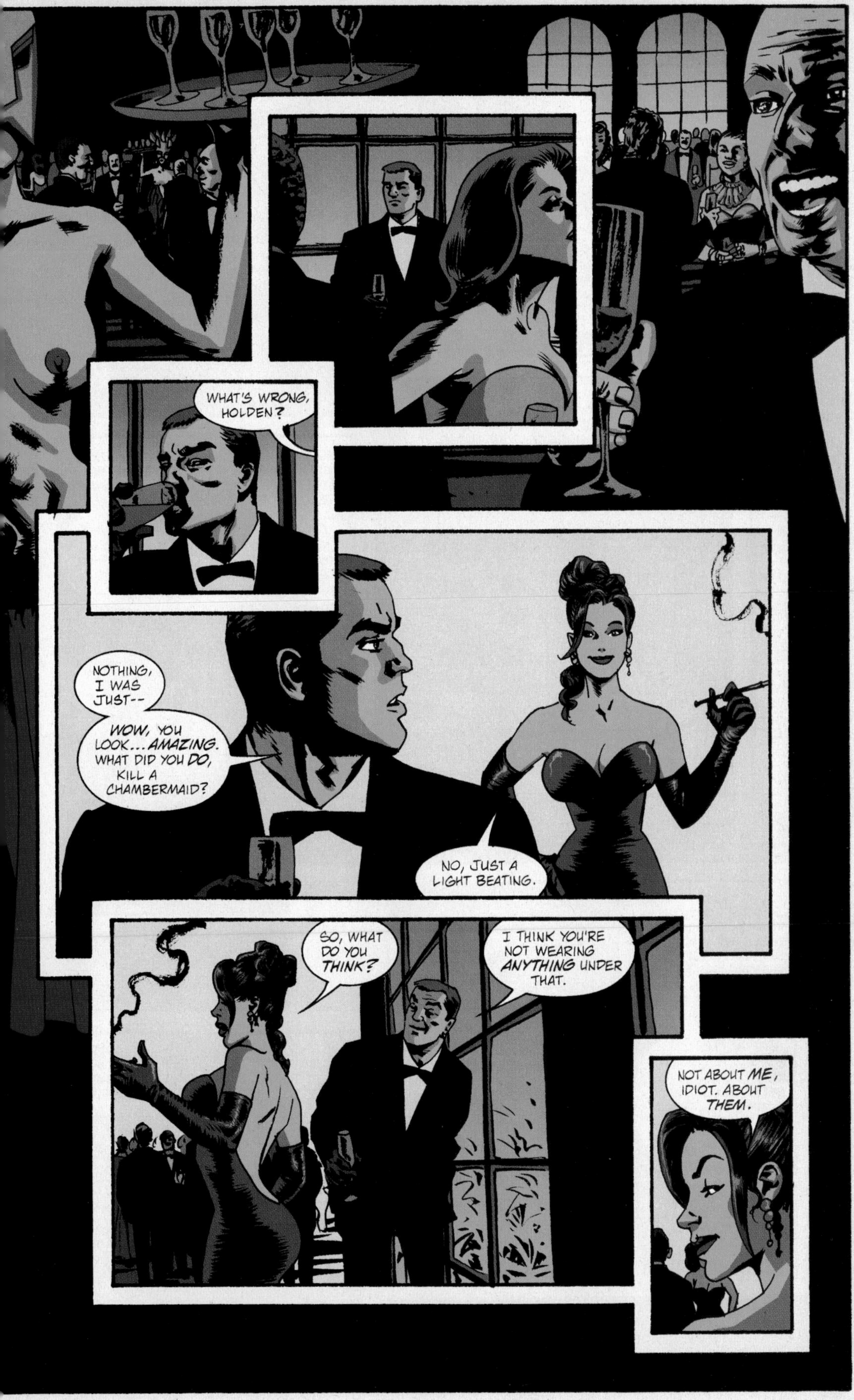
WHAT'S WRONG, HOLDEN?
NOTHING, I WAS JUST--
WOW, YOU LOOK... AMAZING. WHAT DID YOU DO, KILL A CHAMBERMAID?
NO, JUST A LIGHT BEATING.
SO, WHAT DO YOU THINK?
I THINK YOU'RE NOT WEARING ANYTHING UNDER THAT.
NOT ABOUT ME, IDIOT. ABOUT THEM.

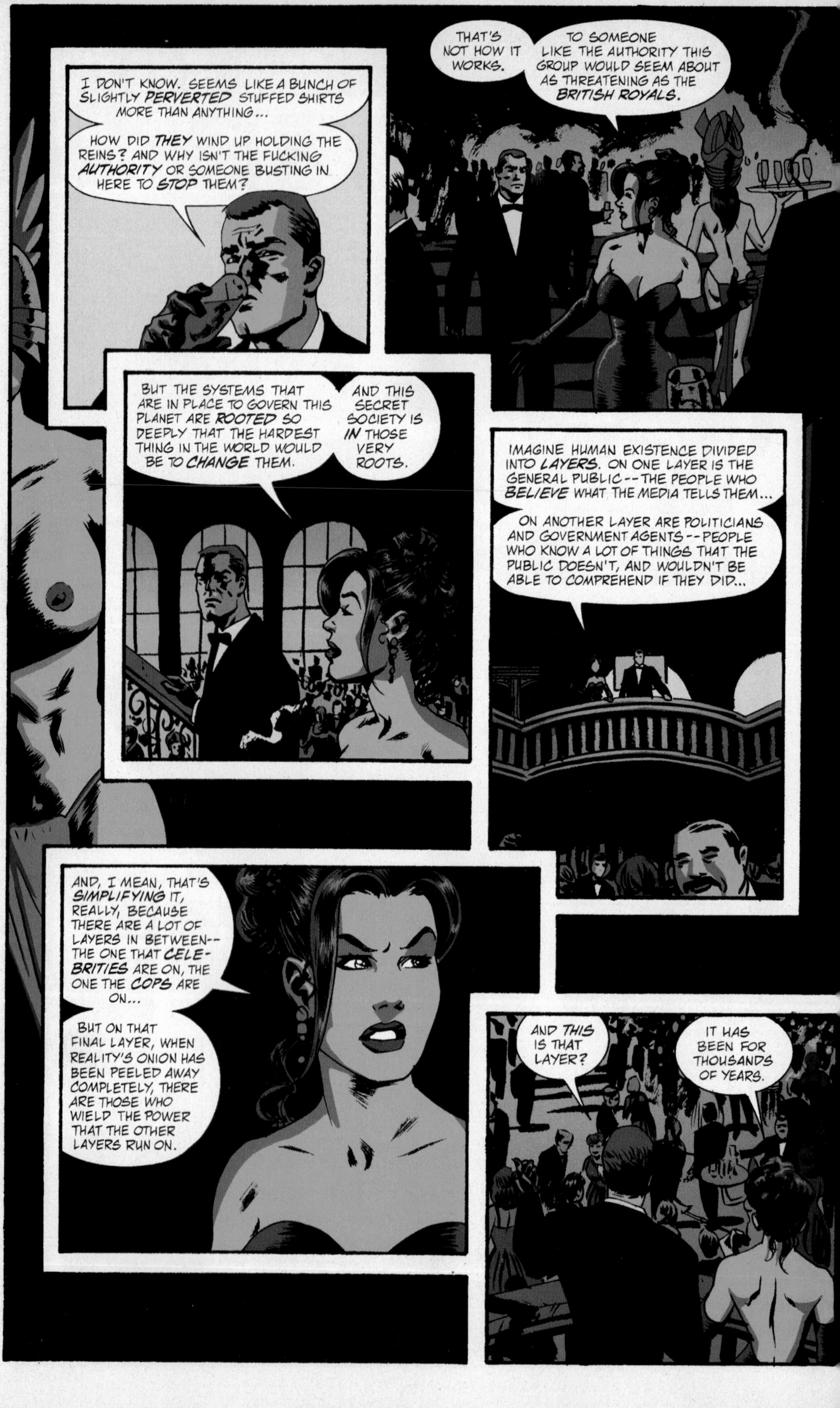
I DON'T KNOW. SEEMS LIKE A BUNCH OF SLIGHTLY PERVERTED STUFFED SHIRTS MORE THAN ANYTHING...
HOW DID THEY WIND UP HOLDING THE REINS? AND WHY ISN'T THE FUCKING AUTHORITY OR SOMEONE BUSTING IN HERE TO STOP THEM?
THAT'S NOT HOW IT WORKS.
TO SOMEONE LIKE THE AUTHORITY THIS GROUP WOULD SEEM ABOUT AS THREATENING AS THE BRITISH ROYALS.
BUT THE SYSTEMS THAT ARE IN PLACE TO GOVERN THIS PLANET ARE ROOTED SO DEEPLY THAT THE HARDEST THING IN THE WORLD WOULD BE TO CHANGE THEM.
AND THIS SECRET SOCIETY IS IN THOSE VERY ROOTS.
IMAGINE HUMAN EXISTENCE DIVIDED INTO LAYERS. ON ONE LAYER IS THE GENERAL PUBLIC--THE PEOPLE WHO BELIEVE WHAT THE MEDIA TELLS THEM...
ON ANOTHER LAYER ARE POLITICIANS AND GOVERNMENT AGENTS--PEOPLE WHO KNOW A LOT OF THINGS THAT THE PUBLIC DOESN'T, AND WOULDN'T BE ABLE TO COMPREHEND IF THEY DID...
AND, I MEAN, THAT'S SIMPLIFYING IT, REALLY, BECAUSE THERE ARE A LOT OF LAYERS IN BETWEEN--THE ONE THAT CELEBRITIES ARE ON, THE ONE THE COPS ARE ON...
BUT ON THAT FINAL LAYER, WHEN REALITY'S ONION HAS BEEN PEELED AWAY COMPLETELY, THERE ARE THOSE WHO WIELD THE POWER THAT THE OTHER LAYERS RUN ON.
AND THIS IS THAT LAYER?
IT HAS BEEN FOR THOUSANDS OF YEARS.

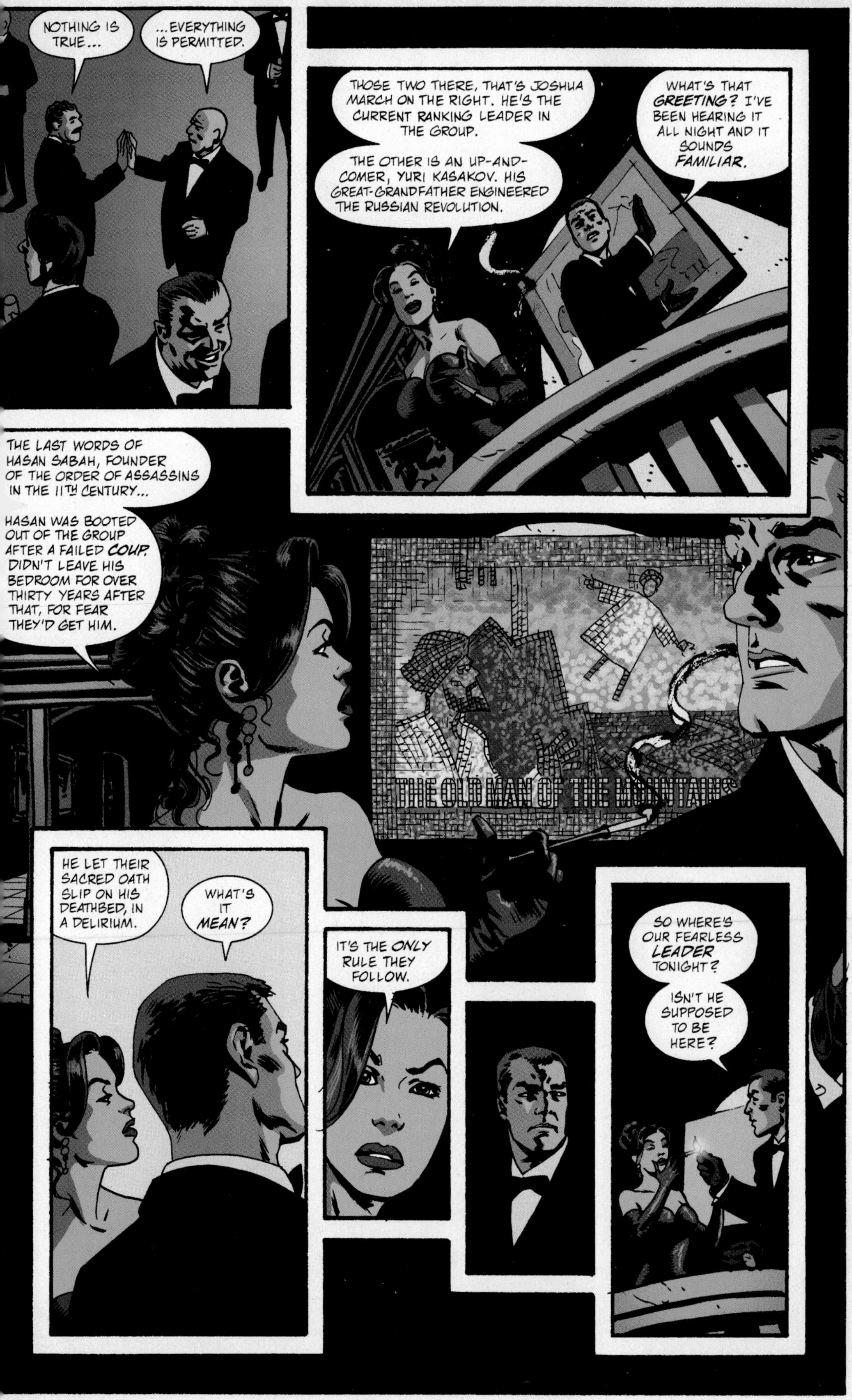

NOTHING IS TRUE...
...EVERYTHING IS PERMITTED.
THOSE TWO THERE, THAT'S JOSHUA MARCH ON THE RIGHT. HE'S THE CURRENT RANKING LEADER IN THE GROUP.
THE OTHER IS AN UP-AND-COMER, YURI KASAKOV. HIS GREAT-GRANDFATHER ENGINEERED THE RUSSIAN REVOLUTION.
WHAT'S THAT GREETING? I'VE BEEN HEARING IT ALL NIGHT AND IT SOUNDS FAMILIAR.
THE LAST WORDS OF HASAN SABAH, FOUNDER OF THE ORDER OF ASSASSINS IN THE 11TH CENTURY...
HASAN WAS BOOTED OUT OF THE GROUP AFTER A FAILED COUP. DIDN'T LEAVE HIS BEDROOM FOR OVER THIRTY YEARS AFTER THAT, FOR FEAR THEY'D GET HIM.
THE OLD MAN OF THE MOUNTAINS
HE LET THEIR SACRED OATH SLIP ON HIS DEATHBED, IN A DELIRIUM.
WHAT'S IT MEAN?
IT'S THE ONLY RULE THEY FOLLOW.
SO WHERE'S OUR FEARLESS LEADER TONIGHT?
ISN'T HE SUPPOSED TO BE HERE?

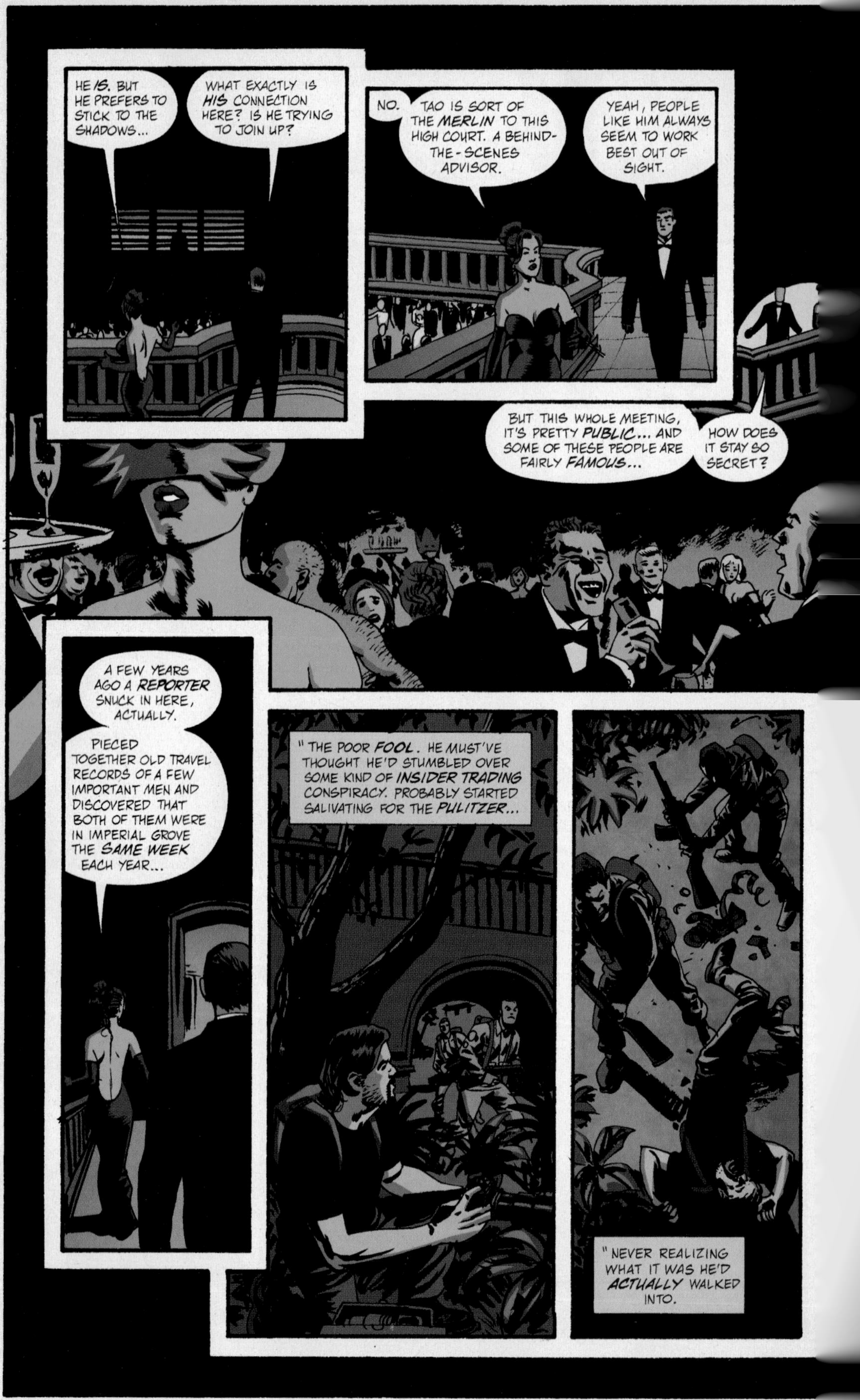
HE IS. BUT HE PREFERS TO STICK TO THE SHADOWS...
WHAT EXACTLY IS HIS CONNECTION HERE? IS HE TRYING TO JOIN UP?
NO.
TAO IS SORT OF THE MERLIN TO THIS HIGH COURT. A BEHIND-THE-SCENES ADVISOR.
YEAH, PEOPLE LIKE HIM ALWAYS SEEM TO WORK BEST OUT OF SIGHT.
BUT THIS WHOLE MEETING, IT'S PRETTY PUBLIC... AND SOME OF THESE PEOPLE ARE FAIRLY FAMOUS...
HOW DOES IT STAY SO SECRET?
A FEW YEARS AGO A REPORTER SNUCK IN HERE, ACTUALLY.
PIECED TOGETHER OLD TRAVEL RECORDS OF A FEW IMPORTANT MEN AND DISCOVERED THAT BOTH OF THEM WERE IN IMPERIAL GROVE THE SAME WEEK EACH YEAR...
"THE POOR FOOL. HE MUST'VE THOUGHT HE'D STUMBLED OVER SOME KIND OF INSIDER TRADING CONSPIRACY. PROBABLY STARTED SALIVATING FOR THE PULITZER...
"NEVER REALIZING WHAT IT WAS HE'D ACTUALLY WALKED INTO.

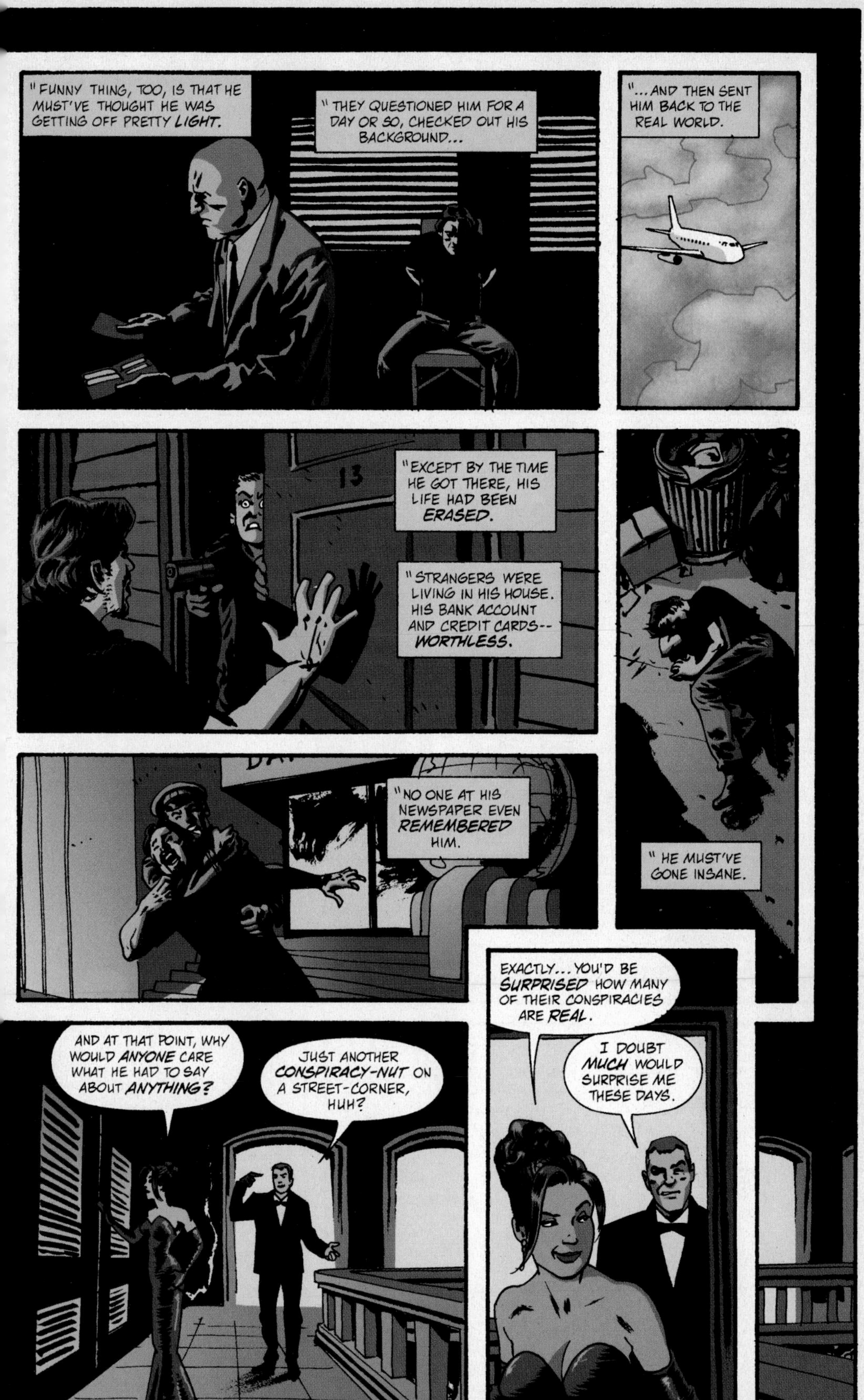
"FUNNY THING, TOO, IS THAT HE MUST'VE THOUGHT HE WAS GETTING OFF PRETTY LIGHT.
"THEY QUESTIONED HIM FOR A DAY OR SO, CHECKED OUT HIS BACKGROUND...
"...AND THEN SENT HIM BACK TO THE REAL WORLD.
13
"EXCEPT BY THE TIME HE GOT THERE, HIS LIFE HAD BEEN ERASED.
"STRANGERS WERE LIVING IN HIS HOUSE. HIS BANK ACCOUNT AND CREDIT CARDS-- WORTHLESS.
"NO ONE AT HIS NEWSPAPER EVEN REMEMBERED HIM.
"HE MUST'VE GONE INSANE.
AND AT THAT POINT, WHY WOULD ANYONE CARE WHAT HE HAD TO SAY ABOUT ANYTHING?
JUST ANOTHER CONSPIRACY-NUT ON A STREET-CORNER, HUH?
EXACTLY... YOU'D BE SURPRISED HOW MANY OF THEIR CONSPIRACIES ARE REAL.
I DOUBT MUCH WOULD SURPRISE ME THESE DAYS.

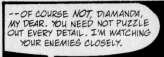
--OF COURSE *NOT*, DIAMANDA, MY DEAR. YOU NEED NOT PUZZLE OUT EVERY DETAIL. I'M WATCHING YOUR ENEMIES CLOSELY.

I'M SURE YOU *ARE*, TAO, BUT WHO IS WATCHING *YOU?*

YOU WOUND ME. MY INVITATION STILL STANDS AND YOU KNOW IT.

ALLOW ME TO INTRODUCE MY NEWEST *PRODIGAL*, HOLDEN CARVER... THIS IS DIAMANDA M'BATU, QUEEN OF EGYPT, AND MONARCH OF NEARLY ALL OF AFRICA...

IT'S AN *HONOR*, YOUR MAJESTY.

JUST MAKE SURE MARCH VOTES IN *MY FAVOR* TOMORROW, DARLING, AND WE'LL *SEE* ABOUT THE REST.

AS ALWAYS, I'M AT YOUR SERVICE.

YOU'RE TRAINING THEM WELL THIS YEAR. THE LAST ONE WAS BARELY *HOUSE-BROKEN.*

NICELY *DONE*, HOLDEN.

IS EVERYTHING TAKEN CARE OF, MISS?

YES, YOU SHOULD BE A *VERY* BUSY BEE FOR THE NEXT FEW HOURS. WHAT WOULD YOU LIKE US TO *DO* NOW?

YOU'LL NEED TO GET STARTED ON THAT *OTHER* THING, BUT I WANT HOLDEN TO STAY...

YOU'LL BE FINE ON YOUR OWN?

I'M *SURE*...

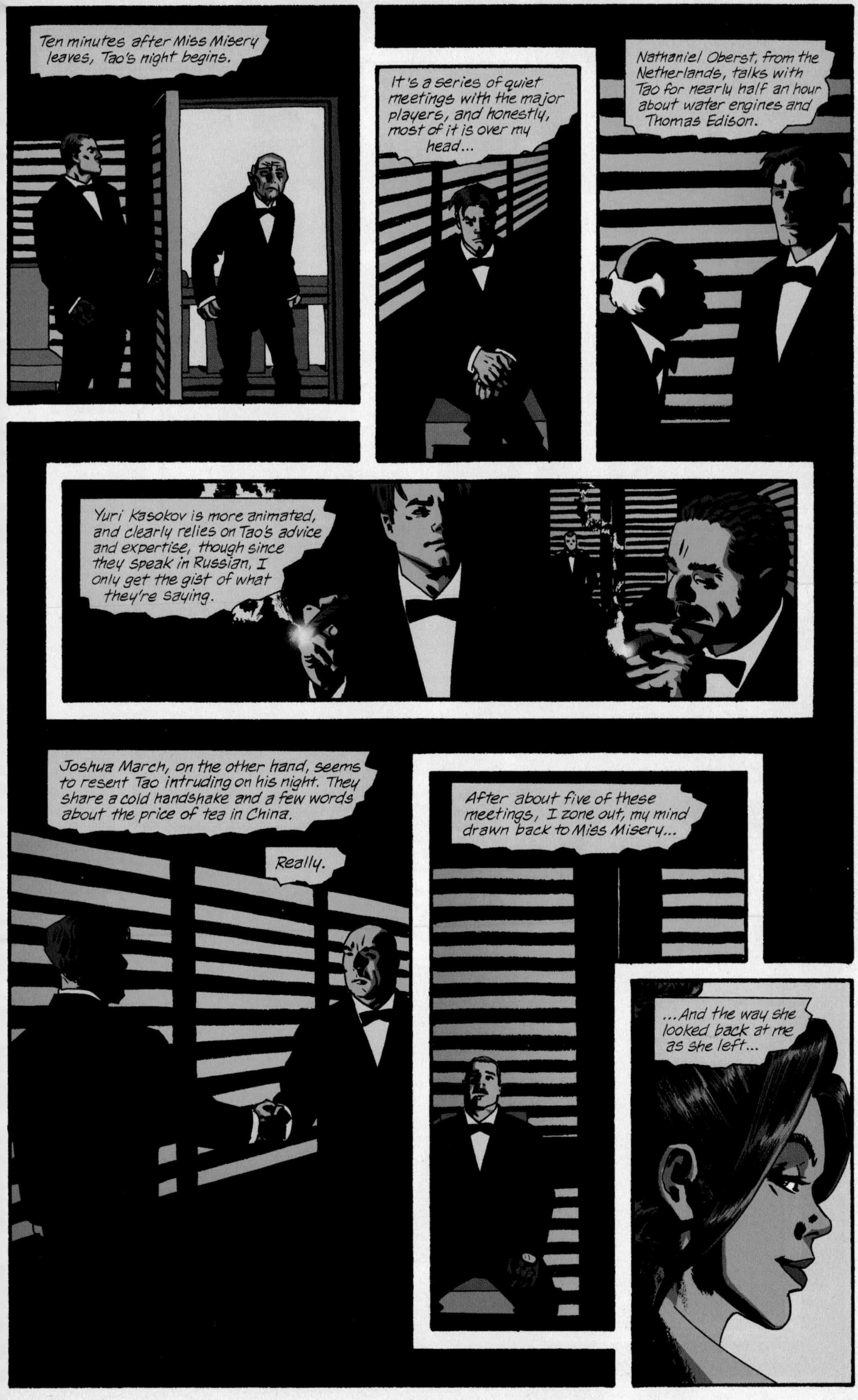
Ten minutes after Miss Misery leaves, Tao's night begins.
It's a series of quiet meetings with the major players, and honestly, most of it is over my head...
Nathaniel Oberst, from the Netherlands, talks with Tao for nearly half an hour about water engines and Thomas Edison.
Yuri Kasokov is more animated, and clearly relies on Tao's advice and expertise, though since they speak in Russian, I only get the gist of what they're saying.
Joshua March, on the other hand, seems to resent Tao intruding on his night. They share a cold handshake and a few words about the price of tea in China.
Really.
After about five of these meetings, I zone out, my mind drawn back to Miss Misery...
...And the way she looked back at me as she left...

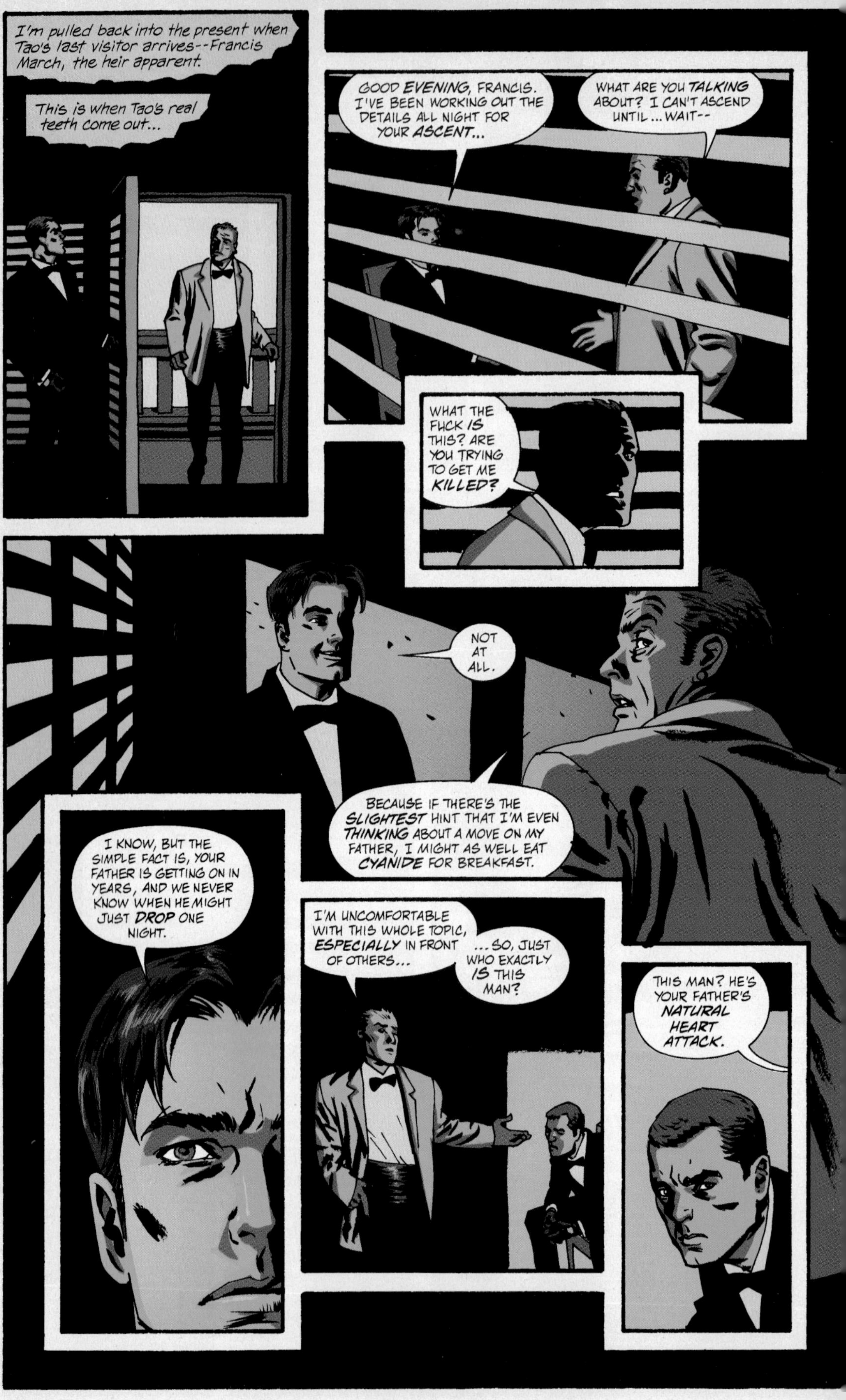
I'm pulled back into the present when Tao's last visitor arrives--Francis March, the heir apparent.
This is when Tao's real teeth come out...
GOOD EVENING, FRANCIS. I'VE BEEN WORKING OUT THE DETAILS ALL NIGHT FOR YOUR ASCENT...
WHAT ARE YOU TALKING ABOUT? I CAN'T ASCEND UNTIL ... WAIT--
WHAT THE FUCK IS THIS? ARE YOU TRYING TO GET ME KILLED?
NOT AT ALL.
BECAUSE IF THERE'S THE SLIGHTEST HINT THAT I'M EVEN THINKING ABOUT A MOVE ON MY FATHER, I MIGHT AS WELL EAT CYANIDE FOR BREAKFAST.
I KNOW, BUT THE SIMPLE FACT IS, YOUR FATHER IS GETTING ON IN YEARS, AND WE NEVER KNOW WHEN HE MIGHT JUST DROP ONE NIGHT.
I'M UNCOMFORTABLE WITH THIS WHOLE TOPIC, ESPECIALLY IN FRONT OF OTHERS...
...SO, JUST WHO EXACTLY IS THIS MAN?
THIS MAN? HE'S YOUR FATHER'S NATURAL HEART ATTACK.

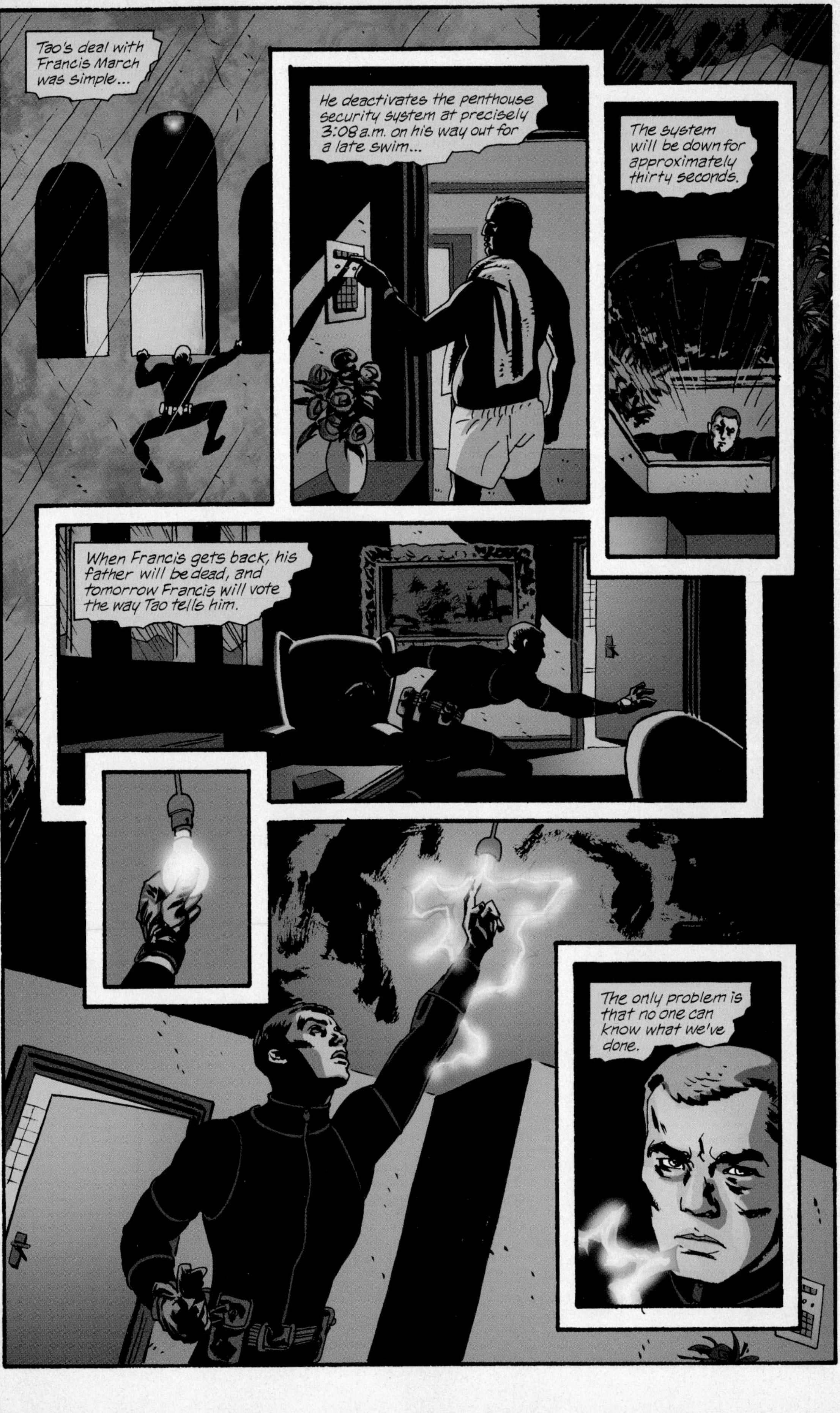
Tao's deal with Francis March was simple...
He deactivates the penthouse security system at precisely 3:08 a.m. on his way out for a late swim...
The system will be down for approximately thirty seconds.
When Francis gets back, his father will be dead, and tomorrow Francis will vote the way Tao tells him.
The only problem is that no one can know what we've done.

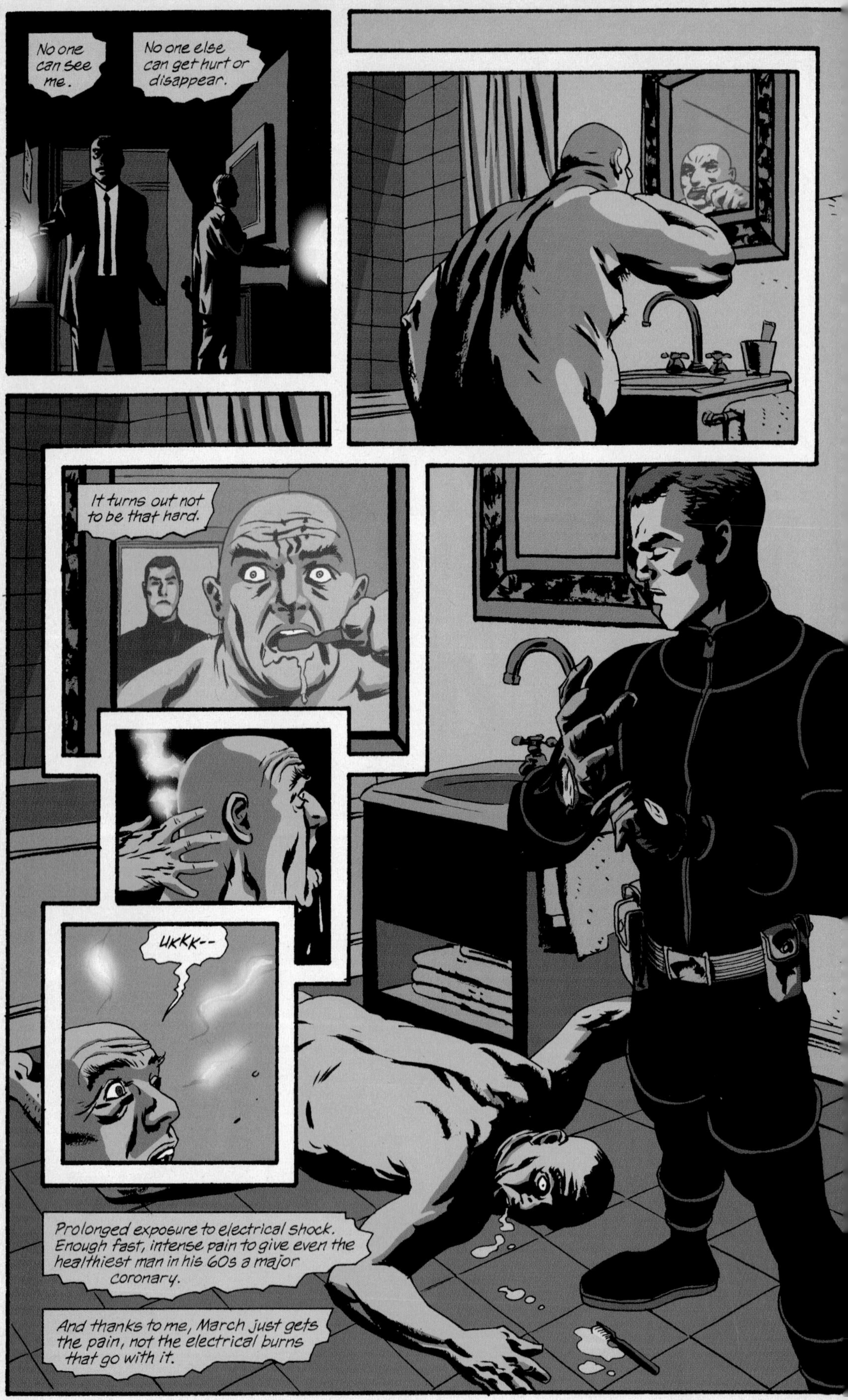
No one can see me.
No one else can get hurt or disappear.
It turns out not to be that hard.
UKKK--
Prolonged exposure to electrical shock. Enough fast, intense pain to give even the healthiest man in his 60s a major coronary.
And thanks to me, March just gets the pain, not the electrical burns that go with it.

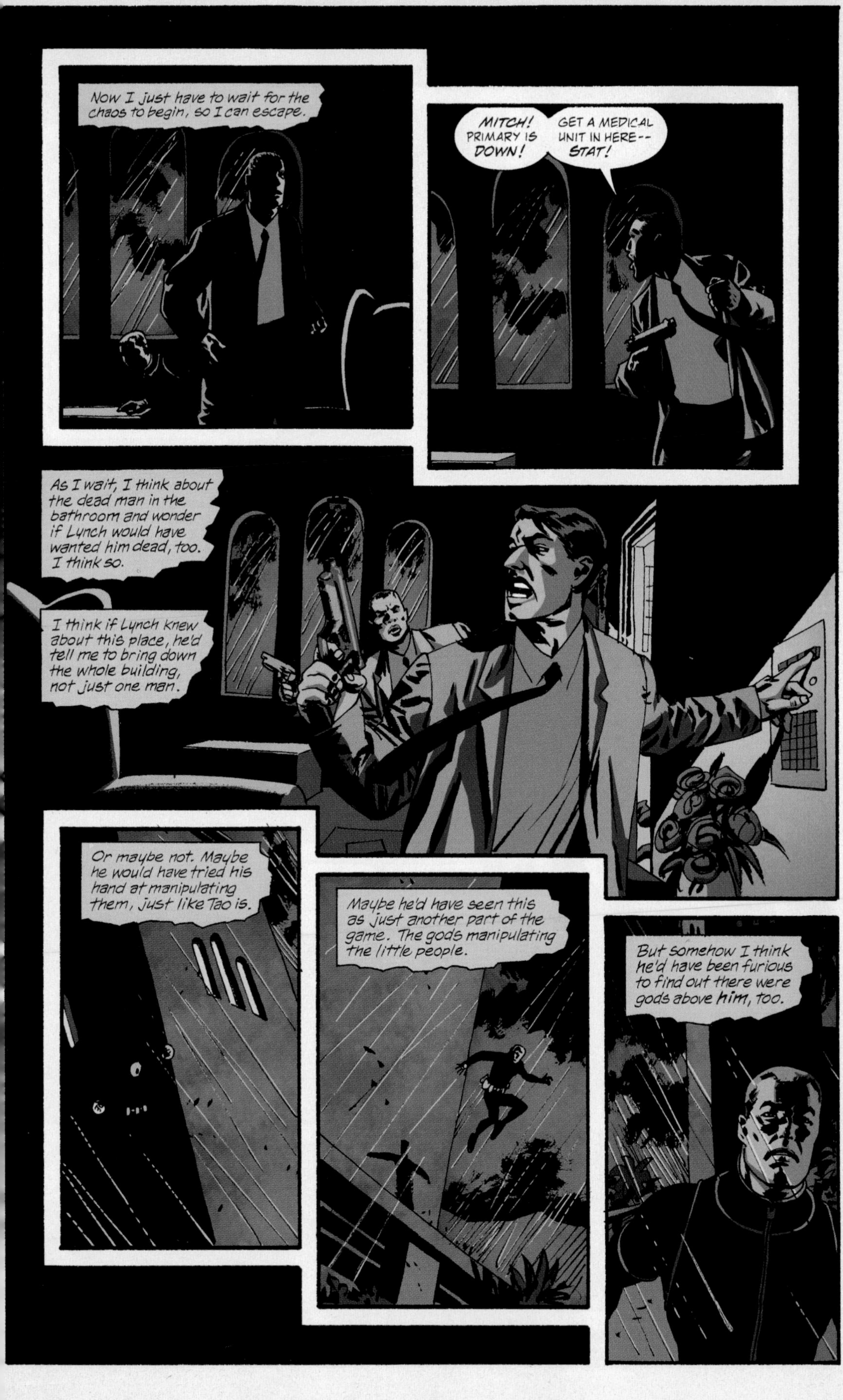
Now I just have to wait for the chaos to begin, so I can escape.
MITCH! PRIMARY IS DOWN!
GET A MEDICAL UNIT IN HERE-- STAT!
As I wait, I think about the dead man in the bathroom and wonder if Lynch would have wanted him dead, too. I think so.
I think if Lynch knew about this place, he'd tell me to bring down the whole building, not just one man.
Or maybe not. Maybe he would have tried his hand at manipulating them, just like Tao is.
Maybe he'd have seen this as just another part of the game. The gods manipulating the little people.
But somehow I think he'd have been furious to find out there were gods above him, too.

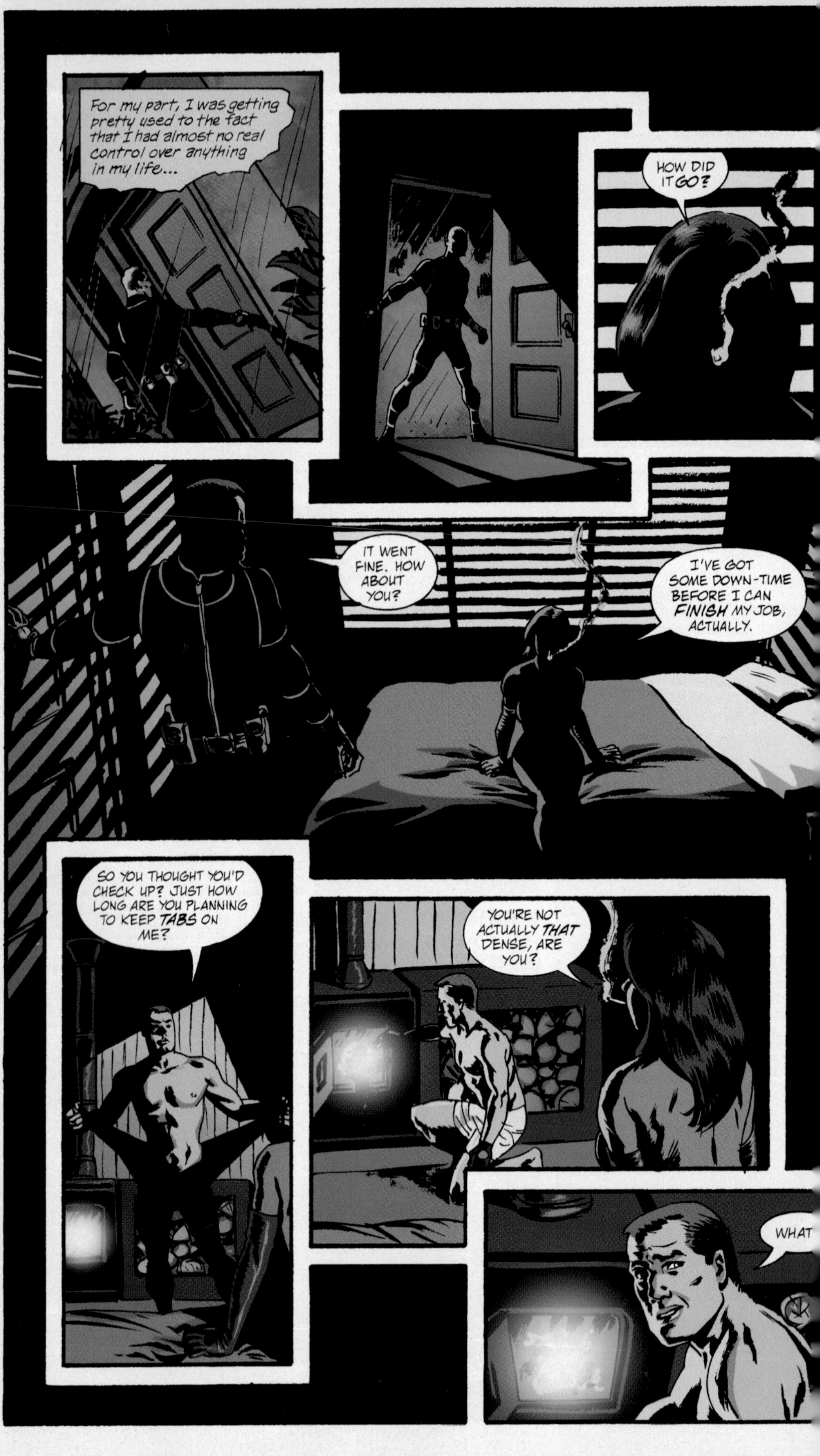
For my part, I was getting pretty used to the fact that I had almost no real control over anything in my life...
HOW DID IT GO?
IT WENT FINE. HOW ABOUT YOU?
I'VE GOT SOME DOWN-TIME BEFORE I CAN FINISH MY JOB, ACTUALLY.
SO YOU THOUGHT YOU'D CHECK UP? JUST HOW LONG ARE YOU PLANNING TO KEEP TABS ON ME?
YOU'RE NOT ACTUALLY THAT DENSE, ARE YOU?
WHAT

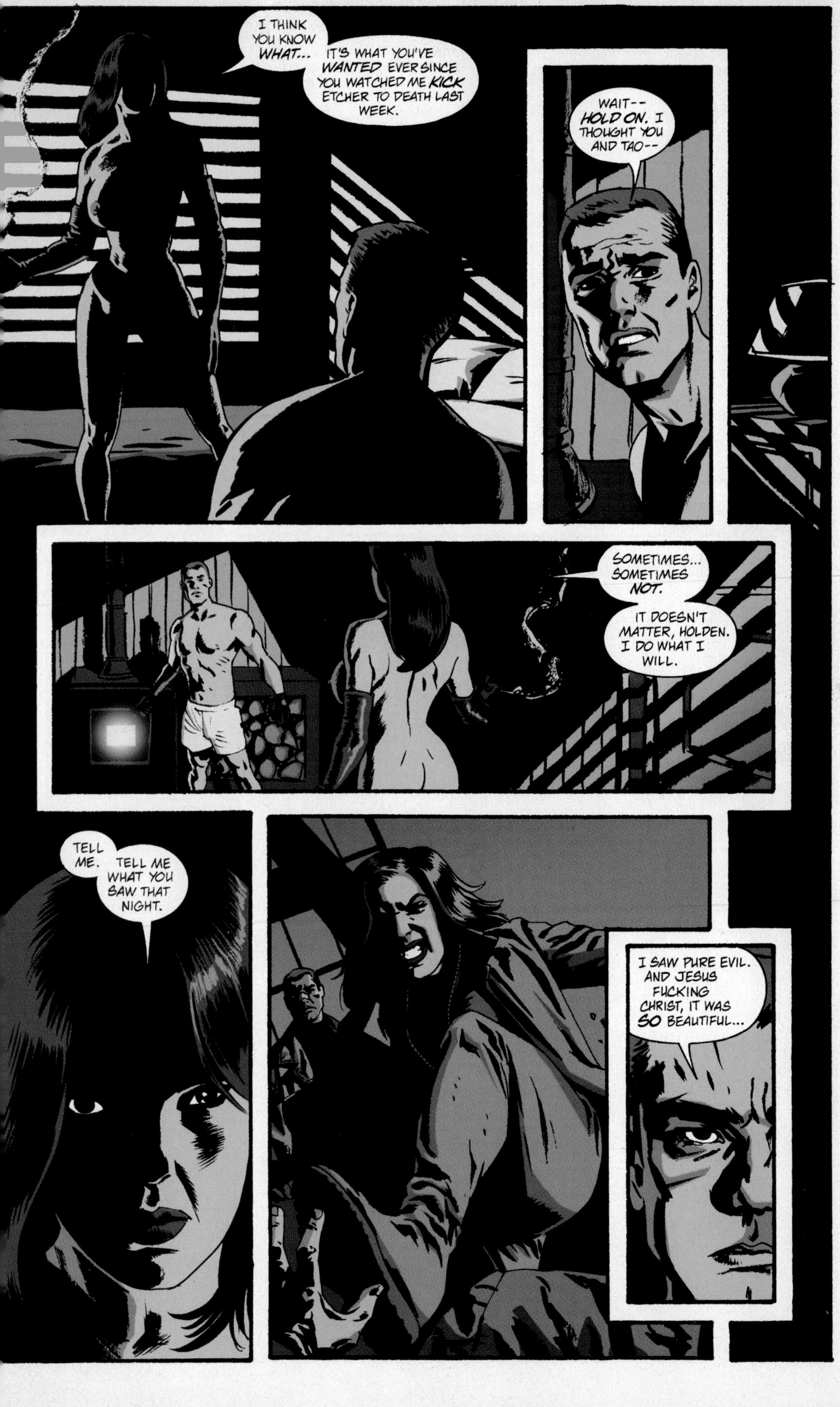

I THINK YOU KNOW WHAT...
IT'S WHAT YOU'VE WANTED EVER SINCE YOU WATCHED ME KICK ETCHER TO DEATH LAST WEEK.
WAIT-- HOLD ON. I THOUGHT YOU AND TAO--
SOMETIMES... SOMETIMES NOT.
IT DOESN'T MATTER, HOLDEN. I DO WHAT I WILL.
TELL ME.
TELL ME WHAT YOU SAW THAT NIGHT.
I SAW PURE EVIL. AND JESUS FUCKING CHRIST, IT WAS SO BEAUTIFUL...

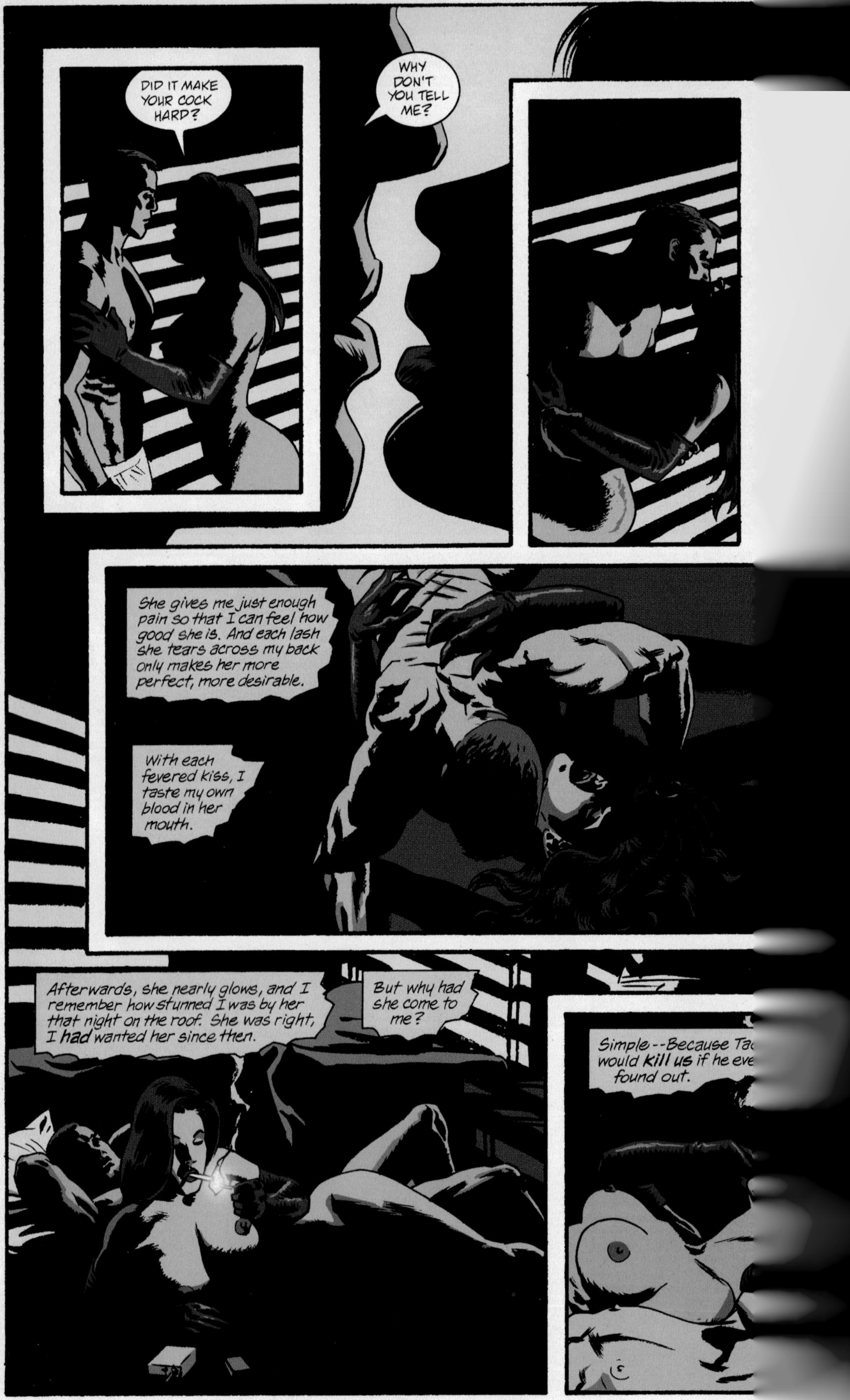
DID IT MAKE YOUR COCK HARD?
WHY DON'T YOU TELL ME?
She gives me just enough pain so that I can feel how good she is. And each lash she tears across my back only makes her more perfect, more desirable.
With each fevered kiss, I taste my own blood in her mouth.
Afterwards, she nearly glows, and I remember how stunned I was by her that night on the roof. She was right, I had wanted her since then.
But why had she come to me?
Simple--Because Tac
would kill us if he eve
found out.

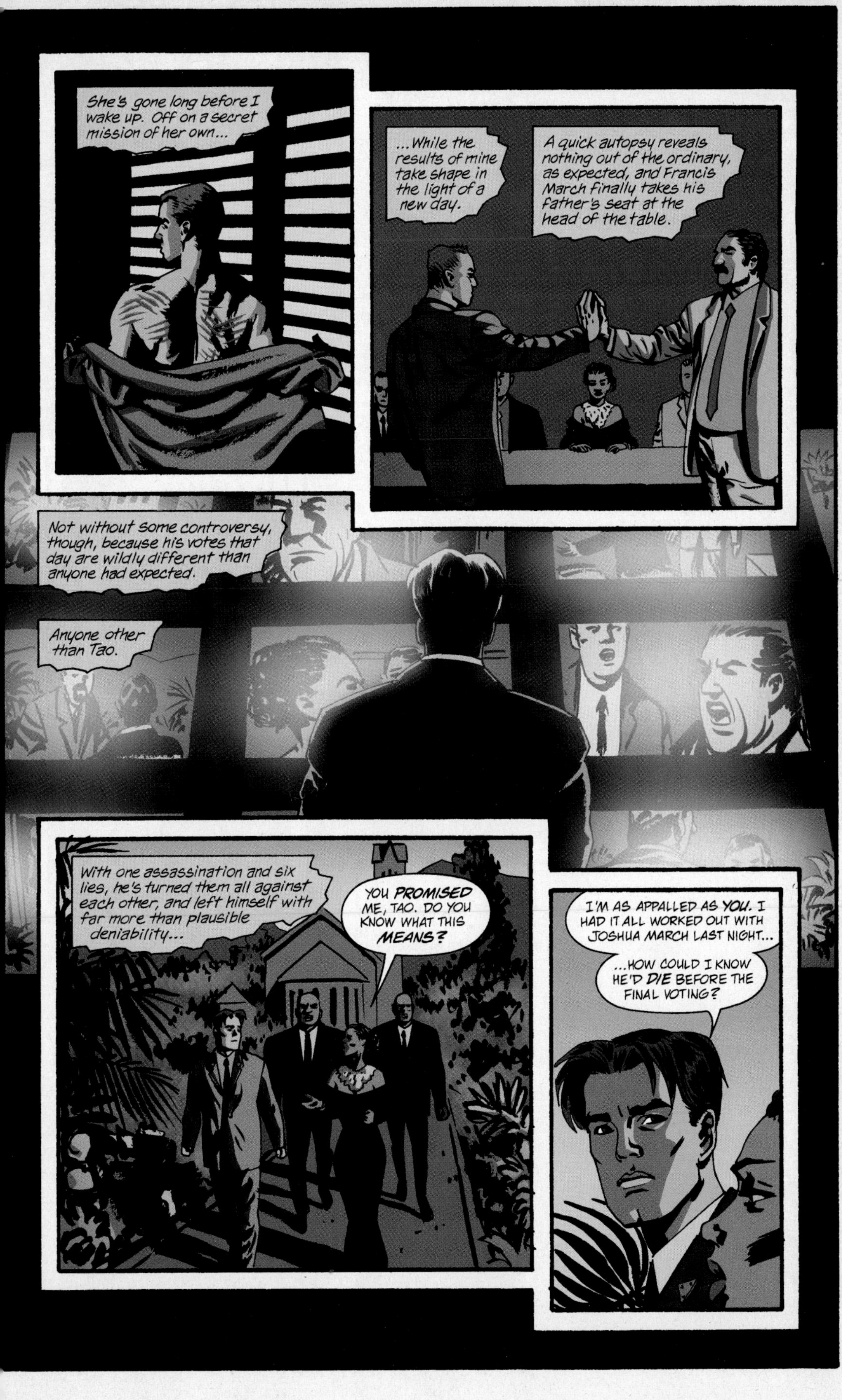
She's gone long before I wake up. Off on a secret mission of her own...
...While the results of mine take shape in the light of a new day.
A quick autopsy reveals nothing out of the ordinary, as expected, and Francis March finally takes his father's seat at the head of the table.
Not without some controversy, though, because his votes that day are wildly different than anyone had expected.
Anyone other than Tao.
With one assassination and six lies, he's turned them all against each other, and left himself with far more than plausible deniability...
YOU PROMISED ME, TAO. DO YOU KNOW WHAT THIS MEANS?
I'M AS APPALLED AS YOU. I HAD IT ALL WORKED OUT WITH JOSHUA MARCH LAST NIGHT...
...HOW COULD I KNOW HE'D DIE BEFORE THE FINAL VOTING?

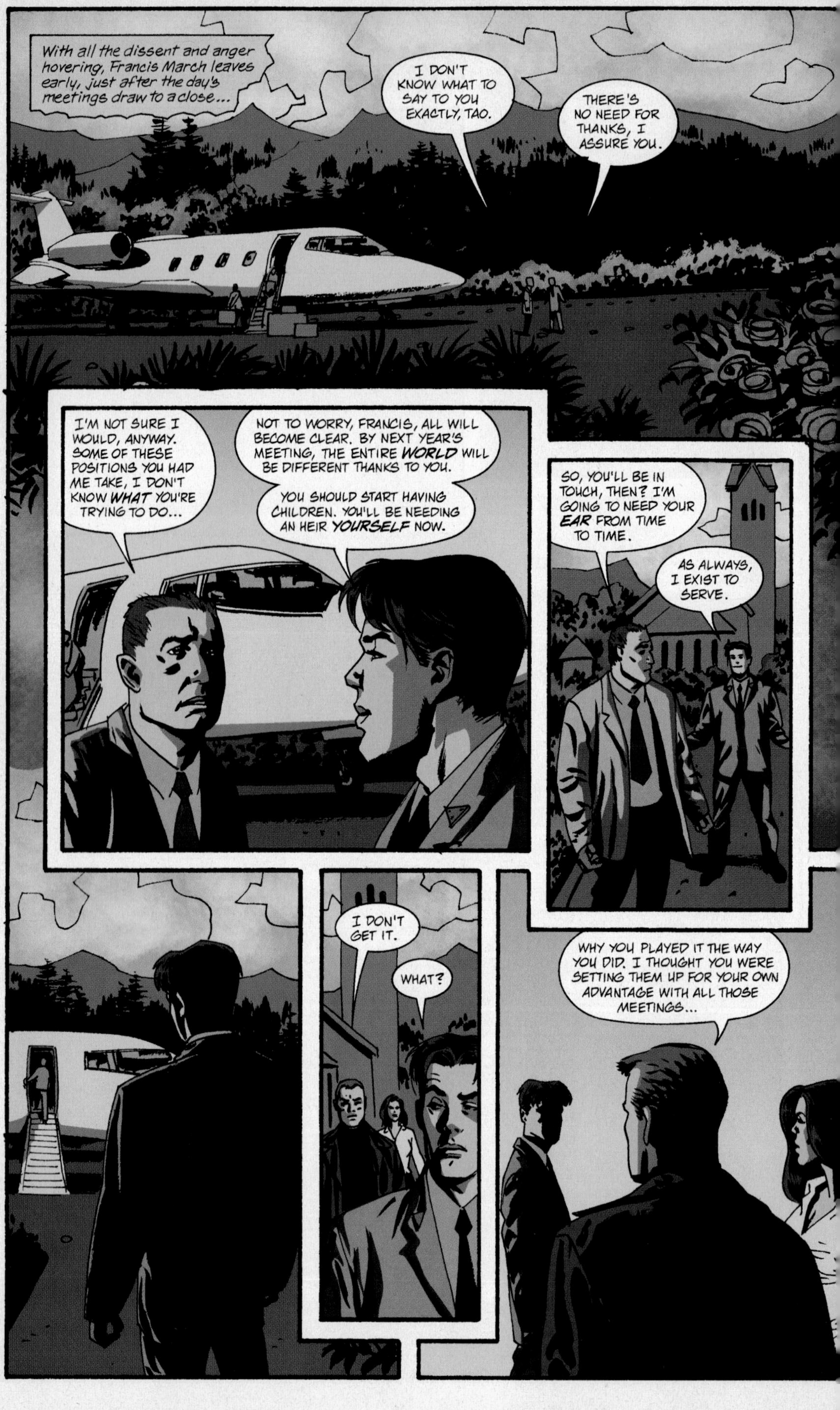
With all the dissent and anger hovering, Francis March leaves early, just after the day's meetings draw to a close...
I DON'T KNOW WHAT TO SAY TO YOU EXACTLY, TAO.
THERE'S NO NEED FOR THANKS, I ASSURE YOU.
I'M NOT SURE I WOULD, ANYWAY. SOME OF THESE POSITIONS YOU HAD ME TAKE, I DON'T KNOW WHAT YOU'RE TRYING TO DO...
NOT TO WORRY, FRANCIS, ALL WILL BECOME CLEAR. BY NEXT YEAR'S MEETING, THE ENTIRE WORLD WILL BE DIFFERENT THANKS TO YOU.
YOU SHOULD START HAVING CHILDREN. YOU'LL BE NEEDING AN HEIR YOURSELF NOW.
SO, YOU'LL BE IN TOUCH, THEN? I'M GOING TO NEED YOUR EAR FROM TIME TO TIME.
AS ALWAYS, I EXIST TO SERVE.
I DON'T GET IT.
WHAT?
WHY YOU PLAYED IT THE WAY YOU DID. I THOUGHT YOU WERE SETTING THEM UP FOR YOUR OWN ADVANTAGE WITH ALL THOSE MEETINGS...

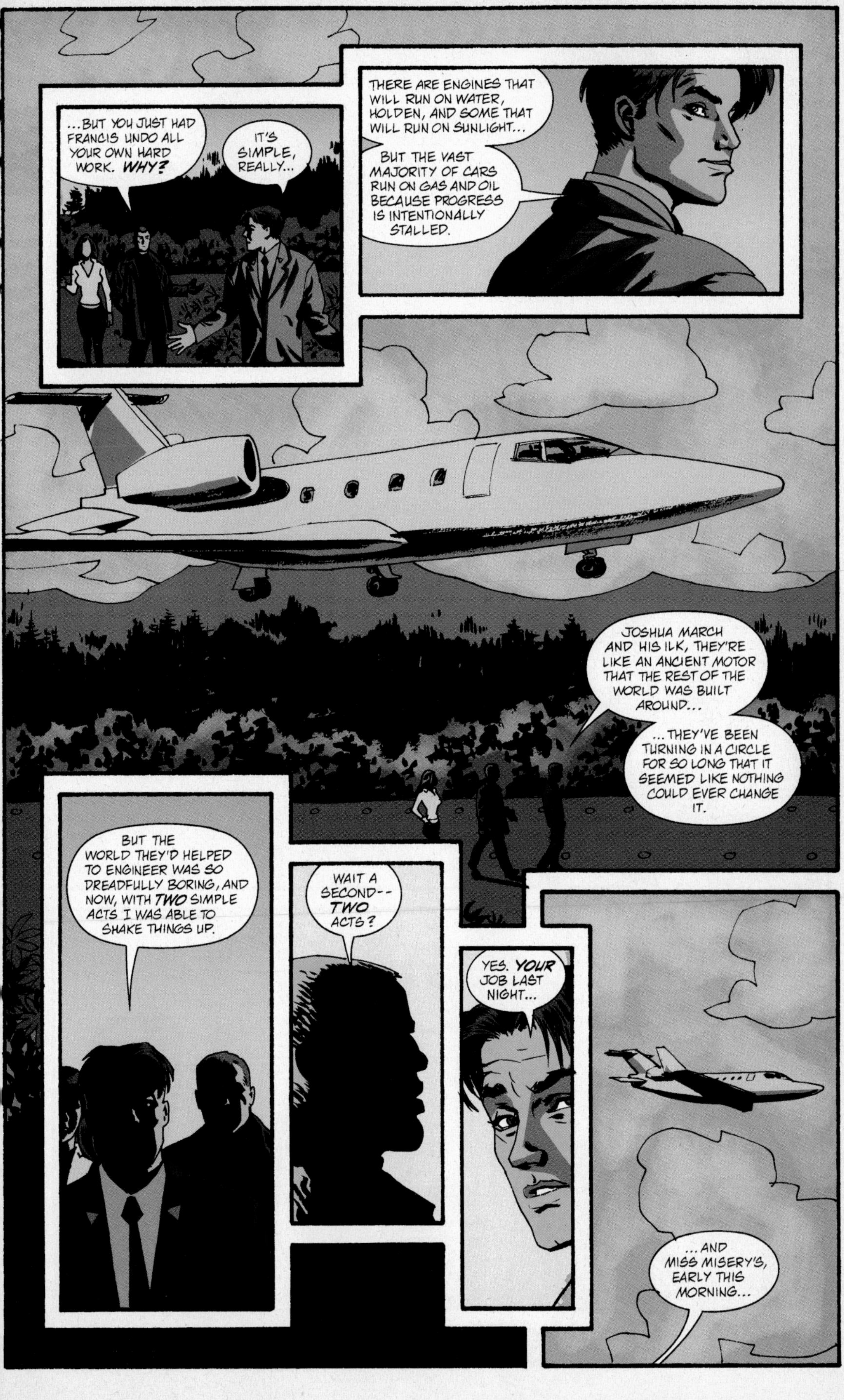
...BUT YOU JUST HAD FRANCIS UNDO ALL YOUR OWN HARD WORK. WHY?
IT'S SIMPLE, REALLY...
THERE ARE ENGINES THAT WILL RUN ON WATER, HOLDEN, AND SOME THAT WILL RUN ON SUNLIGHT...
BUT THE VAST MAJORITY OF CARS RUN ON GAS AND OIL BECAUSE PROGRESS IS INTENTIONALLY STALLED.
JOSHUA MARCH AND HIS ILK, THEY'RE LIKE AN ANCIENT MOTOR THAT THE REST OF THE WORLD WAS BUILT AROUND...
...THEY'VE BEEN TURNING IN A CIRCLE FOR SO LONG THAT IT SEEMED LIKE NOTHING COULD EVER CHANGE IT.
BUT THE WORLD THEY'D HELPED TO ENGINEER WAS SO DREADFULLY BORING, AND NOW, WITH TWO SIMPLE ACTS I WAS ABLE TO SHAKE THINGS UP.
WAIT A SECOND-- TWO ACTS?
YES. YOUR JOB LAST NIGHT...
...AND MISS MISERY'S, EARLY THIS MORNING...

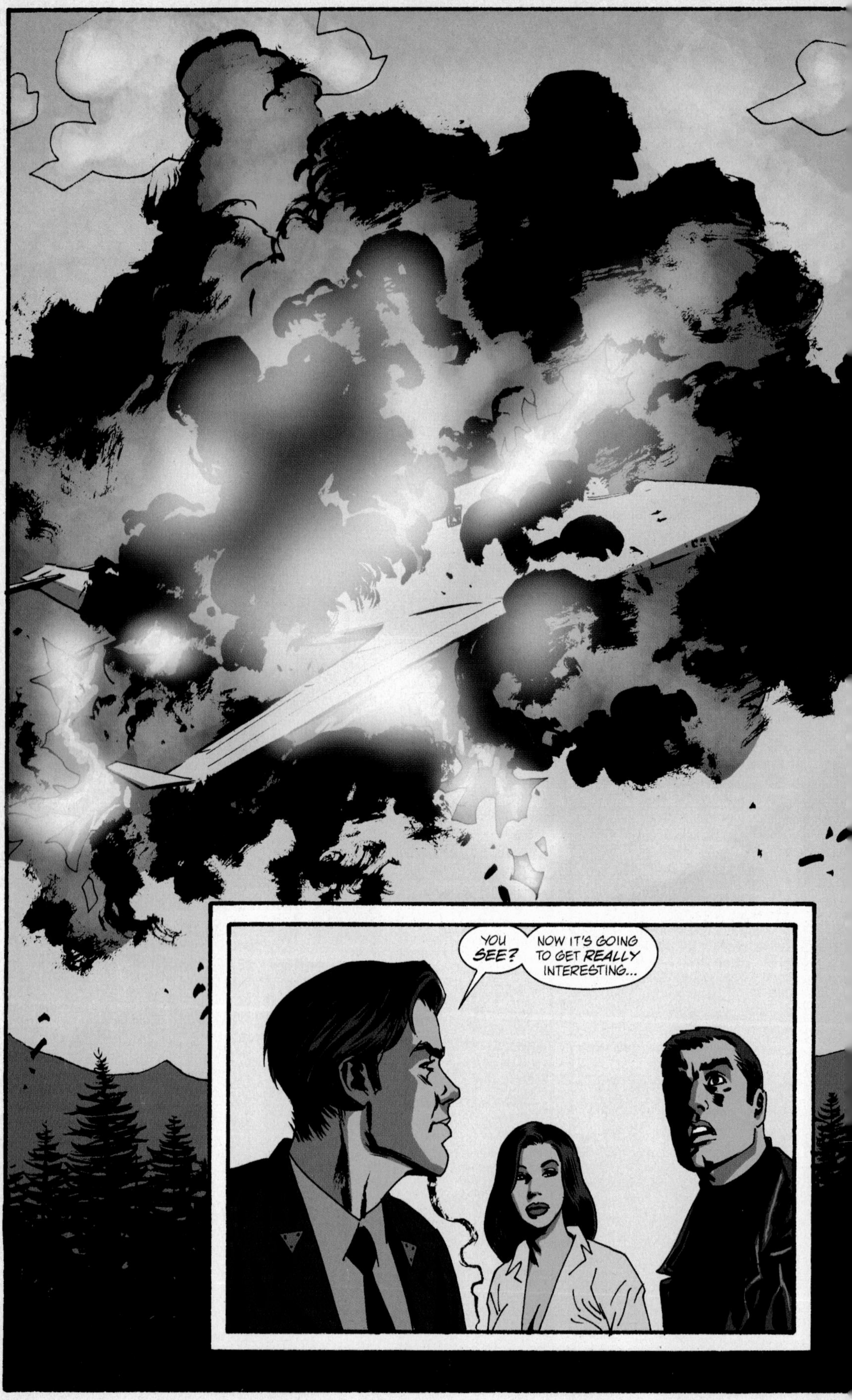
YOU SEE?
NOW IT'S GOING TO GET REALLY INTERESTING...

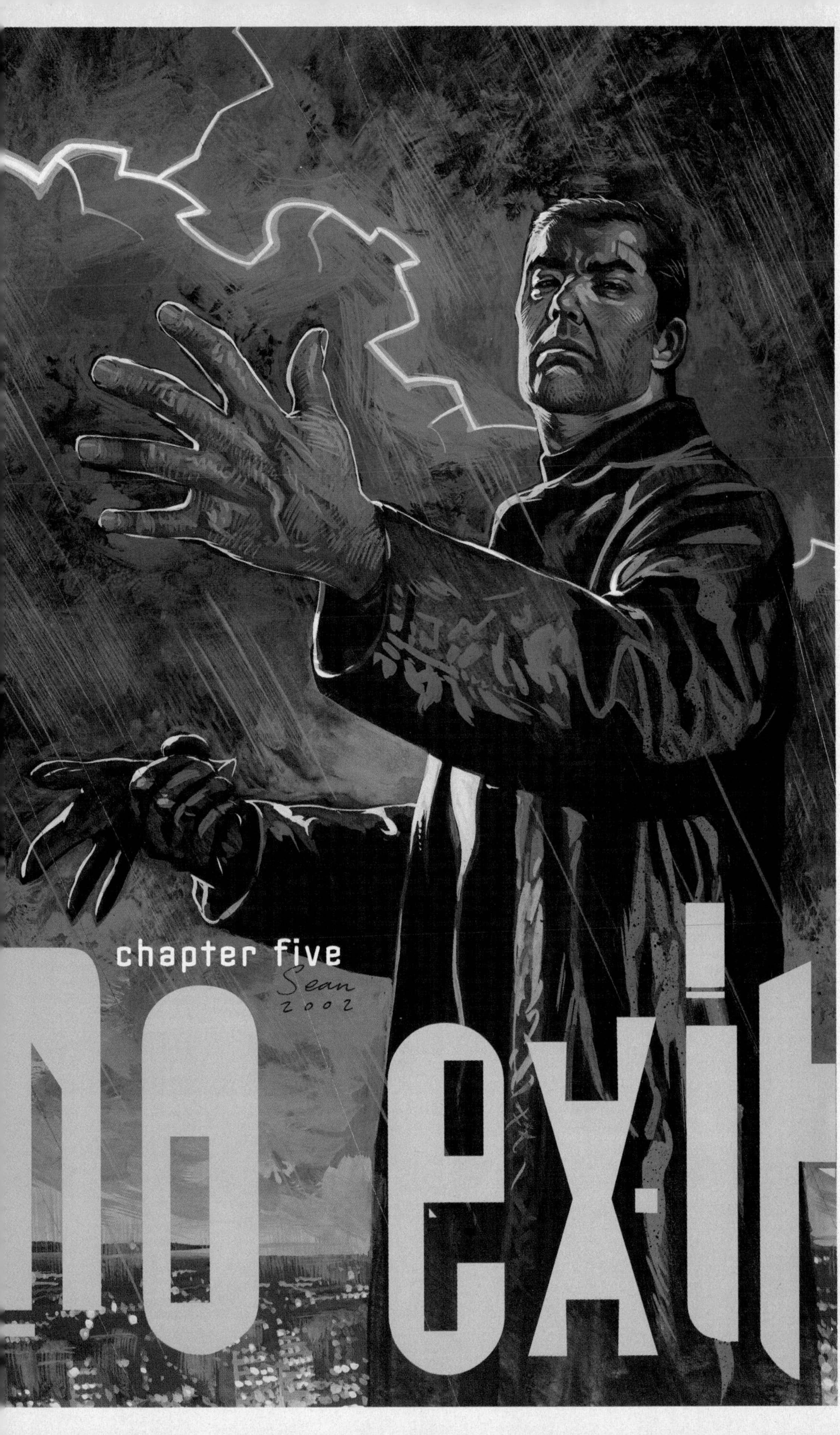
chapter five
Sean
2002
no exit

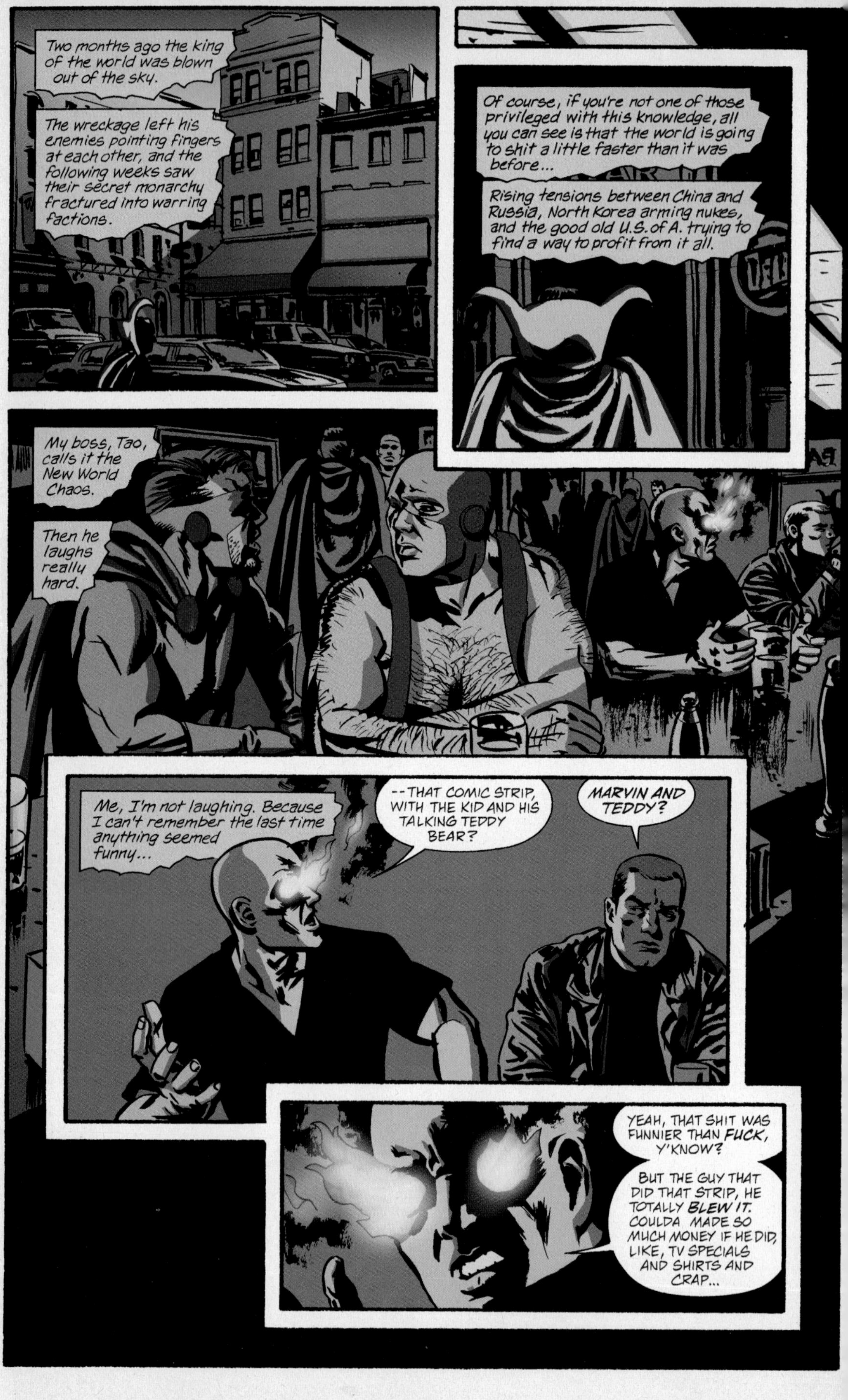

Two months ago the king of the world was blown out of the sky.
The wreckage left his enemies pointing fingers at each other, and the following weeks saw their secret monarchy fractured into warring factions.
Of course, if you're not one of those privileged with this knowledge, all you can see is that the world is going to shit a little faster than it was before...
Rising tensions between China and Russia, North Korea arming nukes, and the good old U.S. of A. trying to find a way to profit from it all.
My boss, Tao, calls it the New World Chaos.
Then he laughs really hard.
Me, I'm not laughing. Because I can't remember the last time anything seemed funny...
--THAT COMIC STRIP, WITH THE KID AND HIS TALKING TEDDY BEAR?
MARVIN AND TEDDY?
YEAH, THAT SHIT WAS FUNNIER THAN FUCK, Y'KNOW?
BUT THE GUY THAT DID THAT STRIP, HE TOTALLY BLEW IT. COULDA MADE SO MUCH MONEY IF HE DID, LIKE, TV SPECIALS AND SHIRTS AND CRAP...

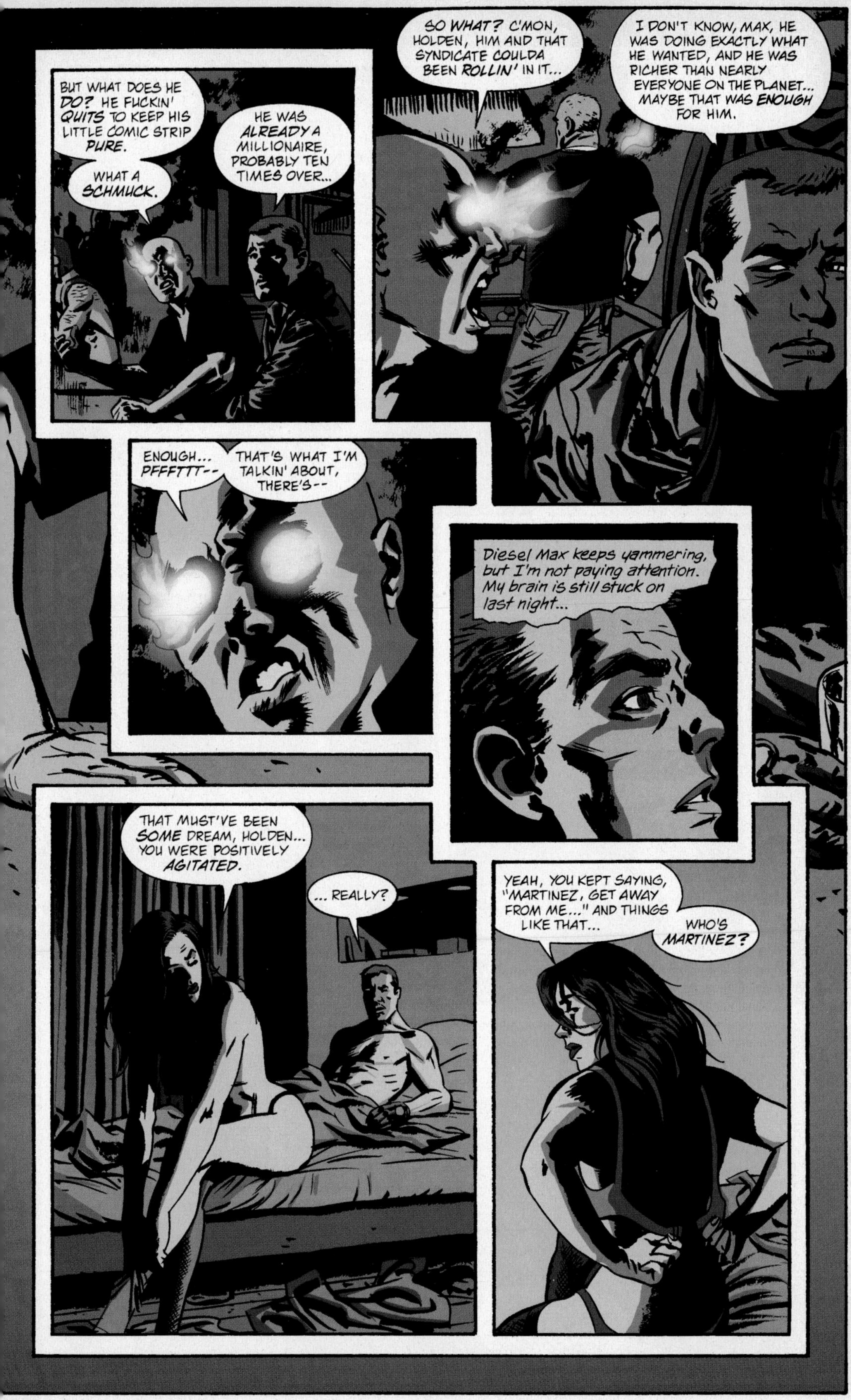
BUT WHAT DOES HE DO? HE FUCKIN' QUITS TO KEEP HIS LITTLE COMIC STRIP PURE.
WHAT A SCHMUCK.
HE WAS ALREADY A MILLIONAIRE, PROBABLY TEN TIMES OVER...
SO WHAT? C'MON, HOLDEN, HIM AND THAT SYNDICATE COULDA BEEN ROLLIN' IN IT...
I DON'T KNOW, MAX, HE WAS DOING EXACTLY WHAT HE WANTED, AND HE WAS RICHER THAN NEARLY EVERYONE ON THE PLANET... MAYBE THAT WAS ENOUGH FOR HIM.
ENOUGH... PFFFTTT--
THAT'S WHAT I'M TALKIN' ABOUT, THERE'S--
Diesel Max keeps yammering, but I'm not paying attention. My brain is still stuck on last night...
THAT MUST'VE BEEN SOME DREAM, HOLDEN... YOU WERE POSITIVELY AGITATED.
...REALLY?
YEAH, YOU KEPT SAYING, "MARTINEZ, GET AWAY FROM ME..." AND THINGS LIKE THAT...
WHO'S MARTINEZ?

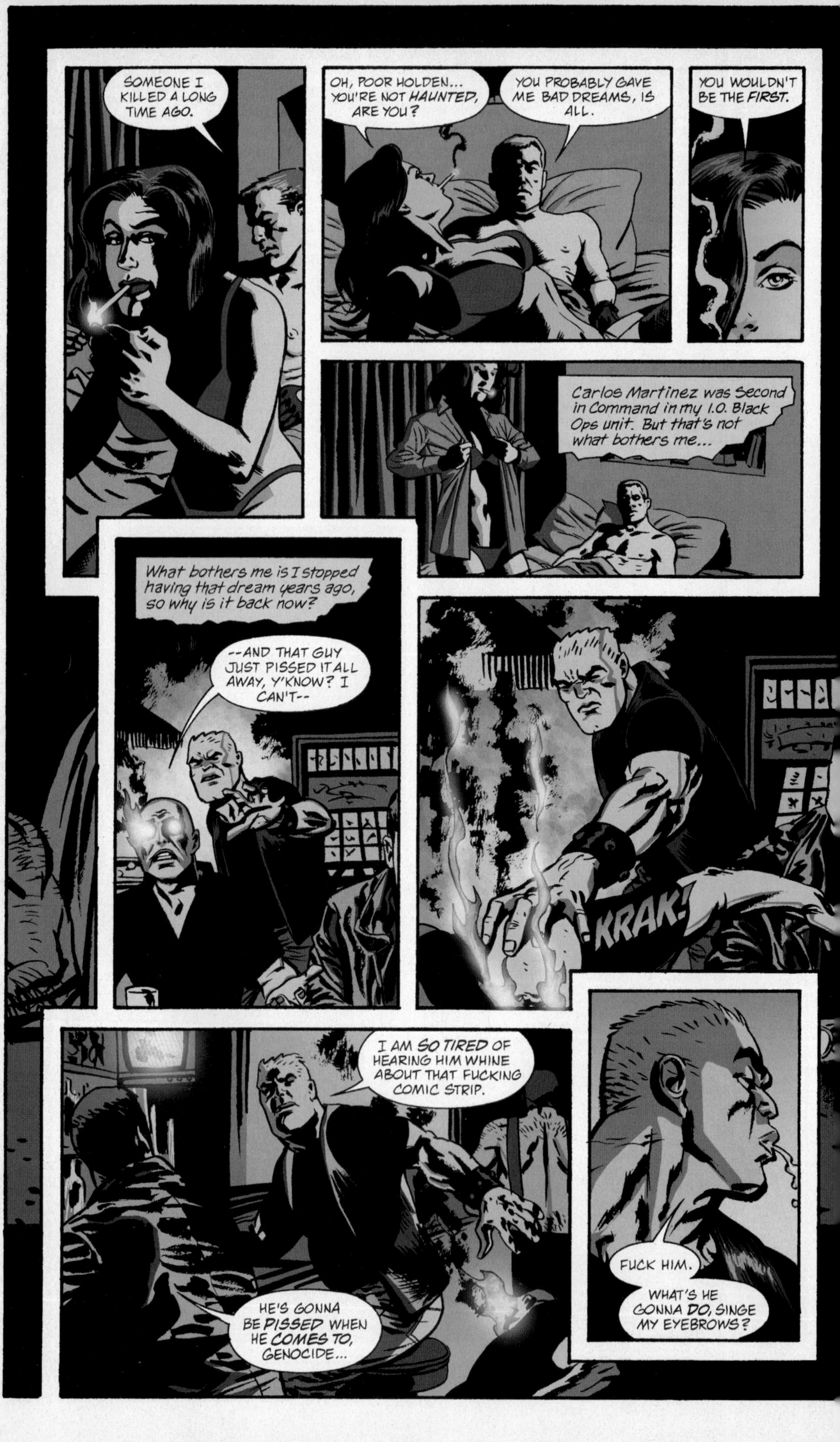
SOMEONE I KILLED A LONG TIME AGO.
OH, POOR HOLDEN... YOU'RE NOT HAUNTED, ARE YOU?
YOU PROBABLY GAVE ME BAD DREAMS, IS ALL.
YOU WOULDN'T BE THE FIRST.
Carlos Martinez was Second in Command in my I.O. Black Ops unit. But that's not what bothers me...
What bothers me is I stopped having that dream years ago, so why is it back now?
--AND THAT GUY JUST PISSED IT ALL AWAY, Y'KNOW? I CAN'T--
KRAK!
I AM SO TIRED OF HEARING HIM WHINE ABOUT THAT FUCKING COMIC STRIP.
HE'S GONNA BE PISSED WHEN HE COMES TO, GENOCIDE...
FUCK HIM.
WHAT'S HE GONNA DO, SINGE MY EYEBROWS?

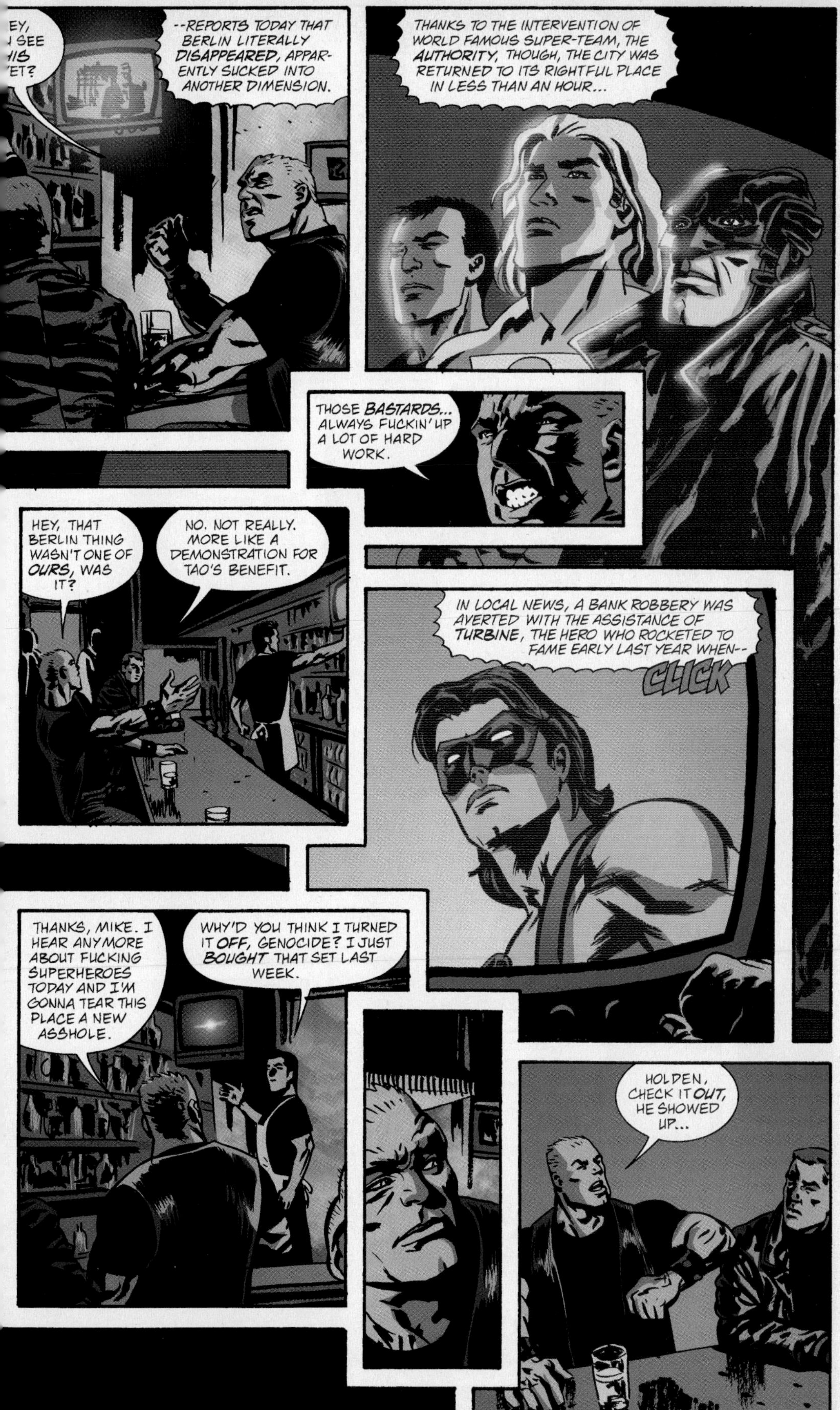
--REPORTS TODAY THAT BERLIN LITERALLY DISAPPEARED, APPARENTLY SUCKED INTO ANOTHER DIMENSION.
THANKS TO THE INTERVENTION OF WORLD FAMOUS SUPER-TEAM, THE AUTHORITY, THOUGH, THE CITY WAS RETURNED TO ITS RIGHTFUL PLACE IN LESS THAN AN HOUR...
THOSE BASTARDS... ALWAYS FUCKIN' UP A LOT OF HARD WORK.
HEY, THAT BERLIN THING WASN'T ONE OF OURS, WAS IT?
NO. NOT REALLY. MORE LIKE A DEMONSTRATION FOR TAO'S BENEFIT.
IN LOCAL NEWS, A BANK ROBBERY WAS AVERTED WITH THE ASSISTANCE OF TURBINE, THE HERO WHO ROCKETED TO FAME EARLY LAST YEAR WHEN--
CLICK
THANKS, MIKE. I HEAR ANYMORE ABOUT FUCKING SUPERHEROES TODAY AND I'M GONNA TEAR THIS PLACE A NEW ASSHOLE.
WHY'D YOU THINK I TURNED IT OFF, GENOCIDE? I JUST BOUGHT THAT SET LAST WEEK.
HOLDEN, CHECK IT OUT, HE SHOWED UP...

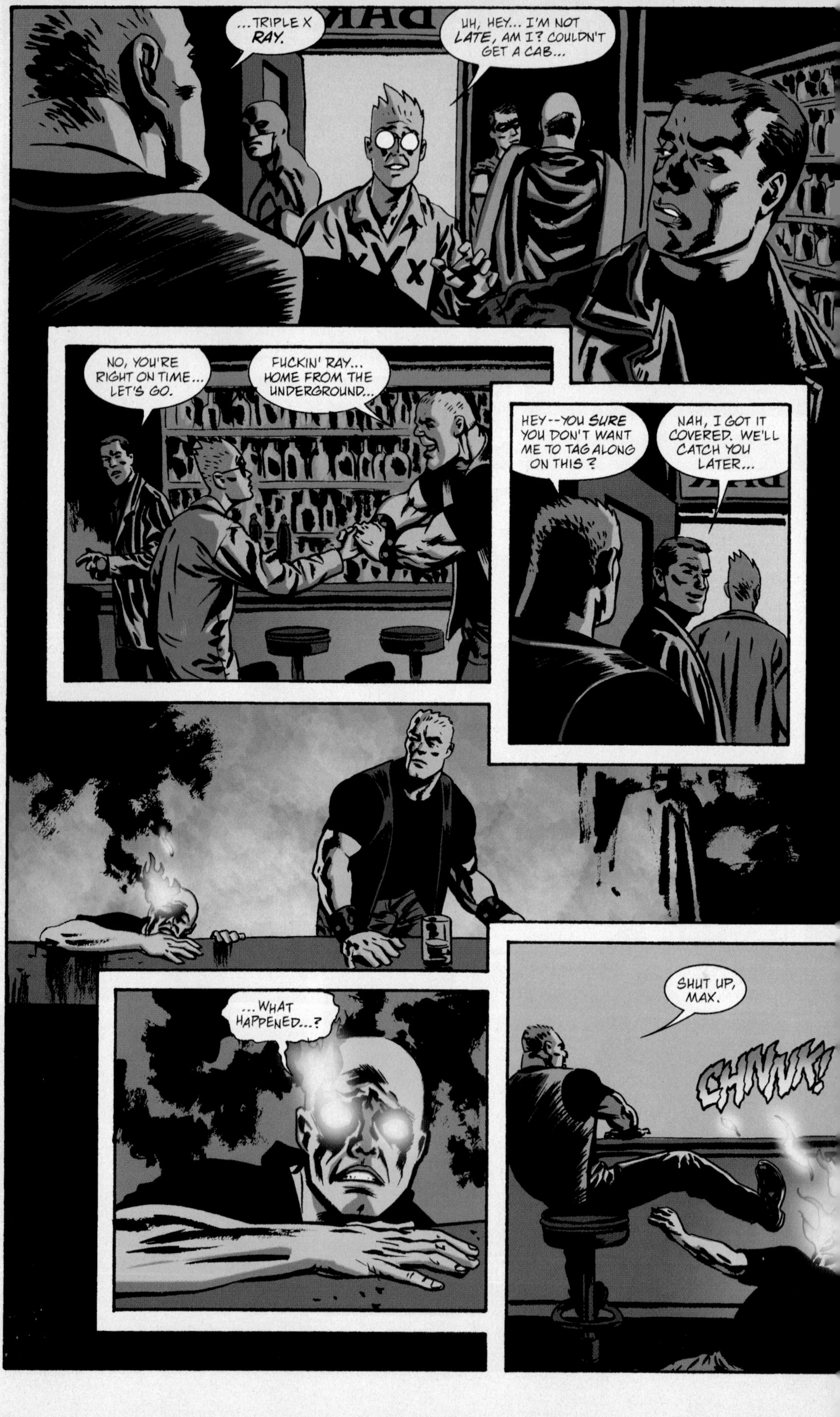
...TRIPLE X RAY.
UH, HEY... I'M NOT LATE, AM I? COULDN'T GET A CAB...
NO, YOU'RE RIGHT ON TIME... LET'S GO.
FUCKIN' RAY... HOME FROM THE UNDERGROUND...
HEY--YOU SURE YOU DON'T WANT ME TO TAG ALONG ON THIS?
NAH, I GOT IT COVERED. WE'LL CATCH YOU LATER...
...WHAT HAPPENED...?
SHUT UP, MAX.
CHNNK!

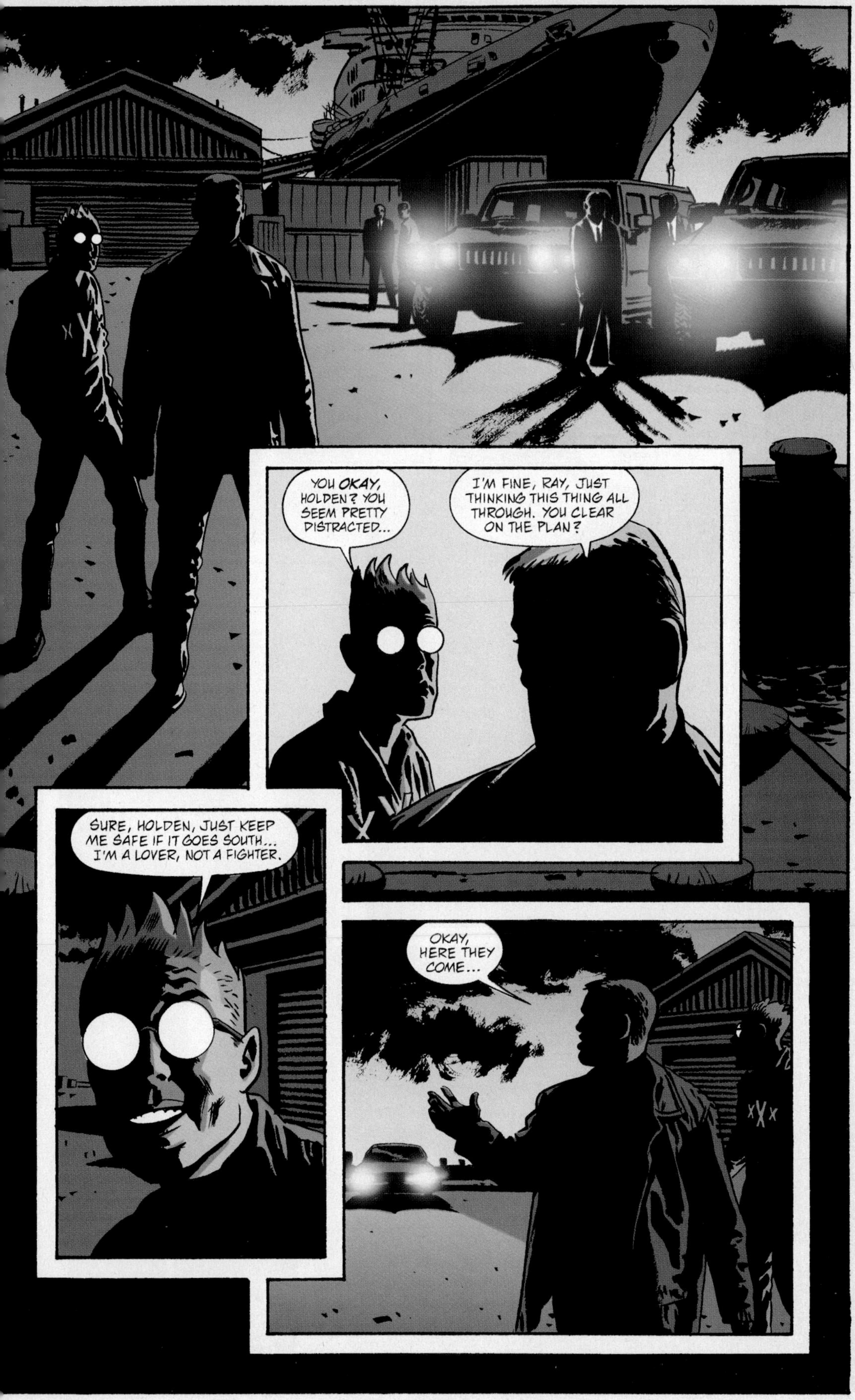
YOU OKAY, HOLDEN? YOU SEEM PRETTY DISTRACTED...
I'M FINE, RAY, JUST THINKING THIS THING ALL THROUGH. YOU CLEAR ON THE PLAN?
SURE, HOLDEN, JUST KEEP ME SAFE IF IT GOES SOUTH... I'M A LOVER, NOT A FIGHTER.
OKAY, HERE THEY COME...

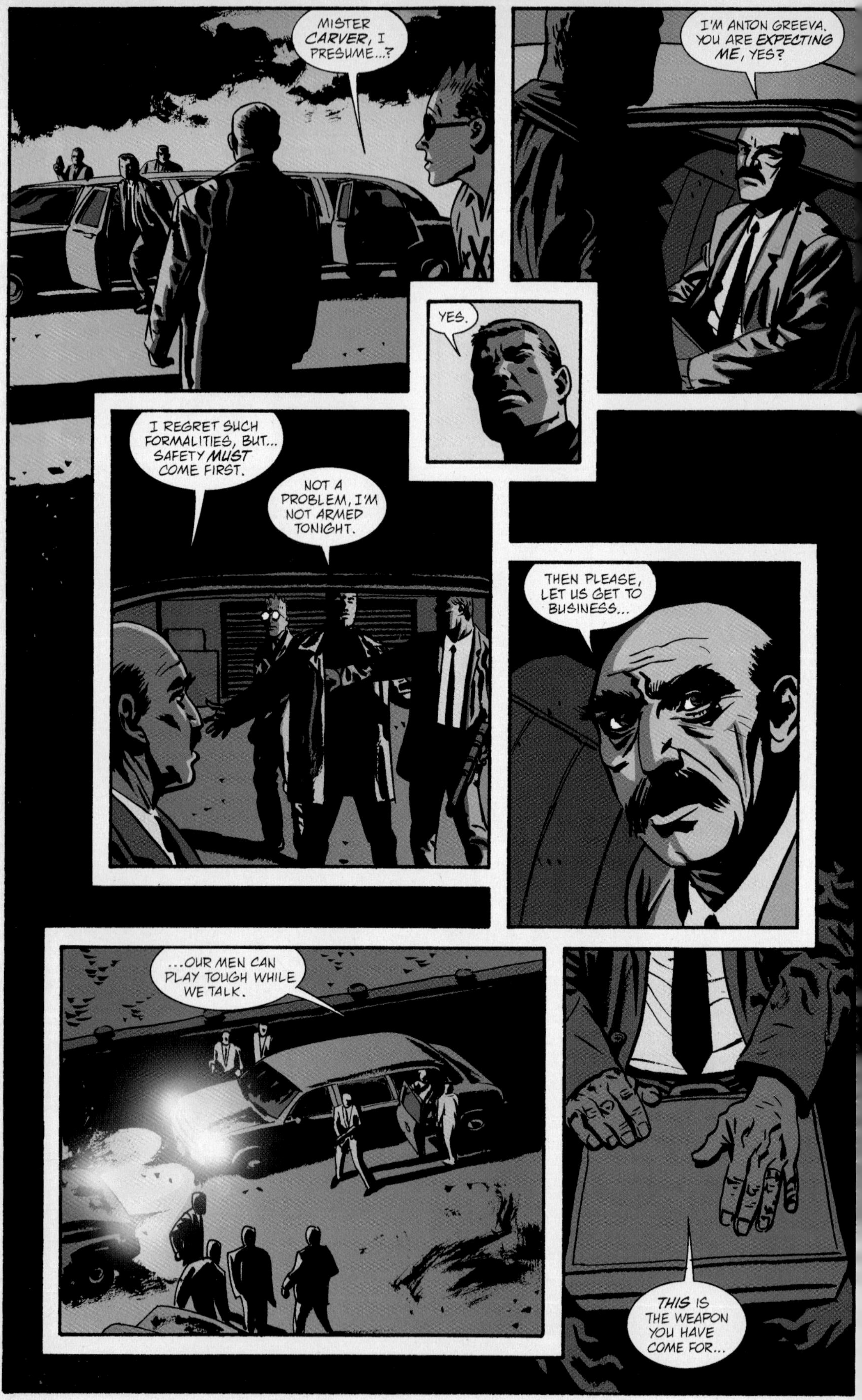
MISTER *CARVER*, I PRESUME...?
I'M ANTON GREEVA. YOU ARE *EXPECTING ME*, YES?
YES.
I REGRET SUCH FORMALITIES, BUT... SAFETY *MUST* COME FIRST.
NOT A PROBLEM, I'M NOT ARMED TONIGHT.
THEN PLEASE, LET US GET TO BUSINESS...
...OUR MEN CAN PLAY TOUGH WHILE WE TALK.
THIS IS THE WEAPON YOU HAVE COME FOR...

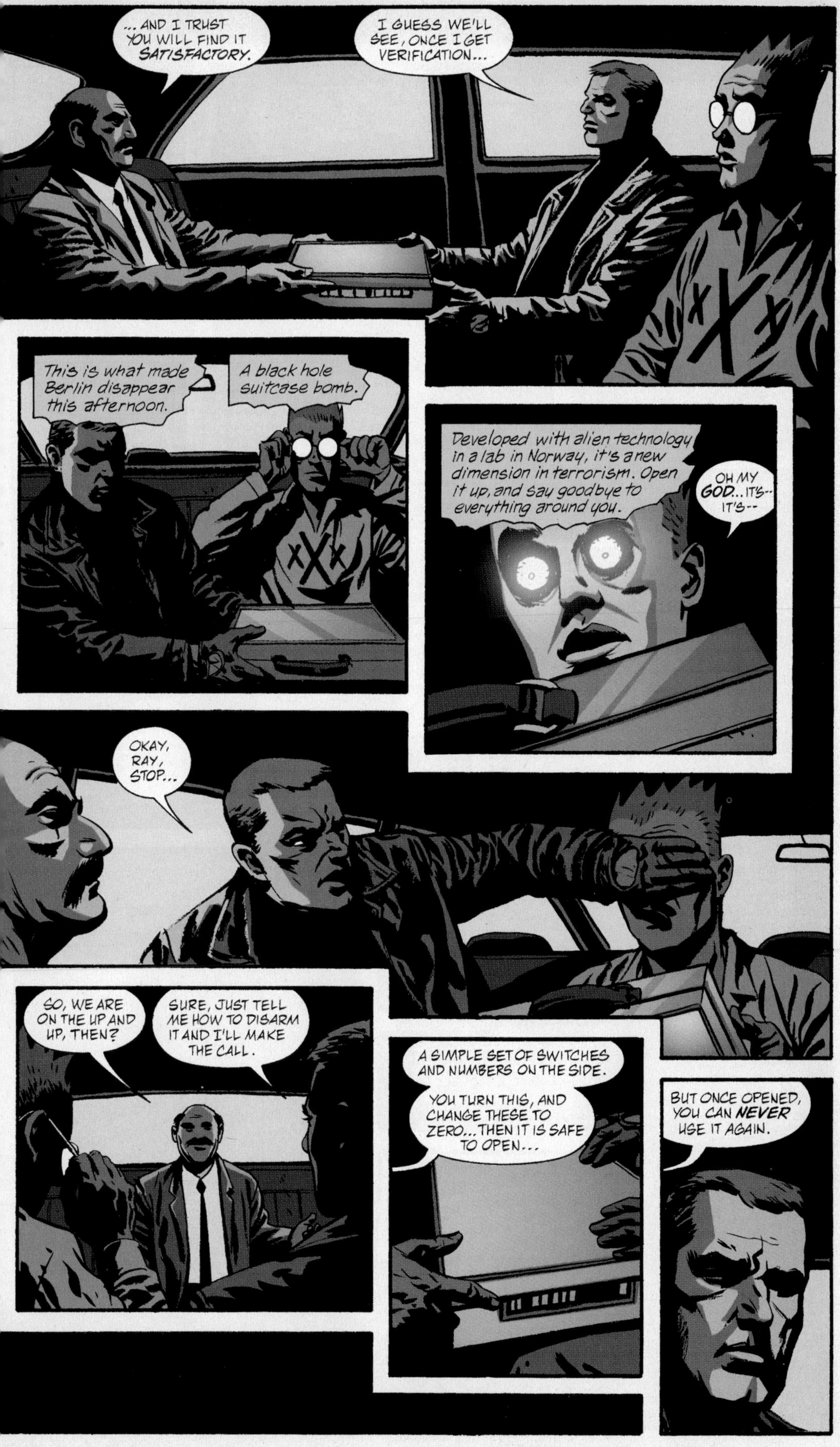
...AND I TRUST YOU WILL FIND IT SATISFACTORY.
I GUESS WE'LL SEE, ONCE I GET VERIFICATION...
This is what made Berlin disappear this afternoon.
A black hole suitcase bomb.
Developed with alien technology in a lab in Norway, it's a new dimension in terrorism. Open it up, and say goodbye to everything around you.
OH MY GOD... IT'S-- IT'S--
OKAY, RAY, STOP...
SO, WE ARE ON THE UP AND UP, THEN?
SURE, JUST TELL ME HOW TO DISARM IT AND I'LL MAKE THE CALL.
A SIMPLE SET OF SWITCHES AND NUMBERS ON THE SIDE.
YOU TURN THIS, AND CHANGE THESE TO ZERO... THEN IT IS SAFE TO OPEN...
BUT ONCE OPENED, YOU CAN NEVER USE IT AGAIN.

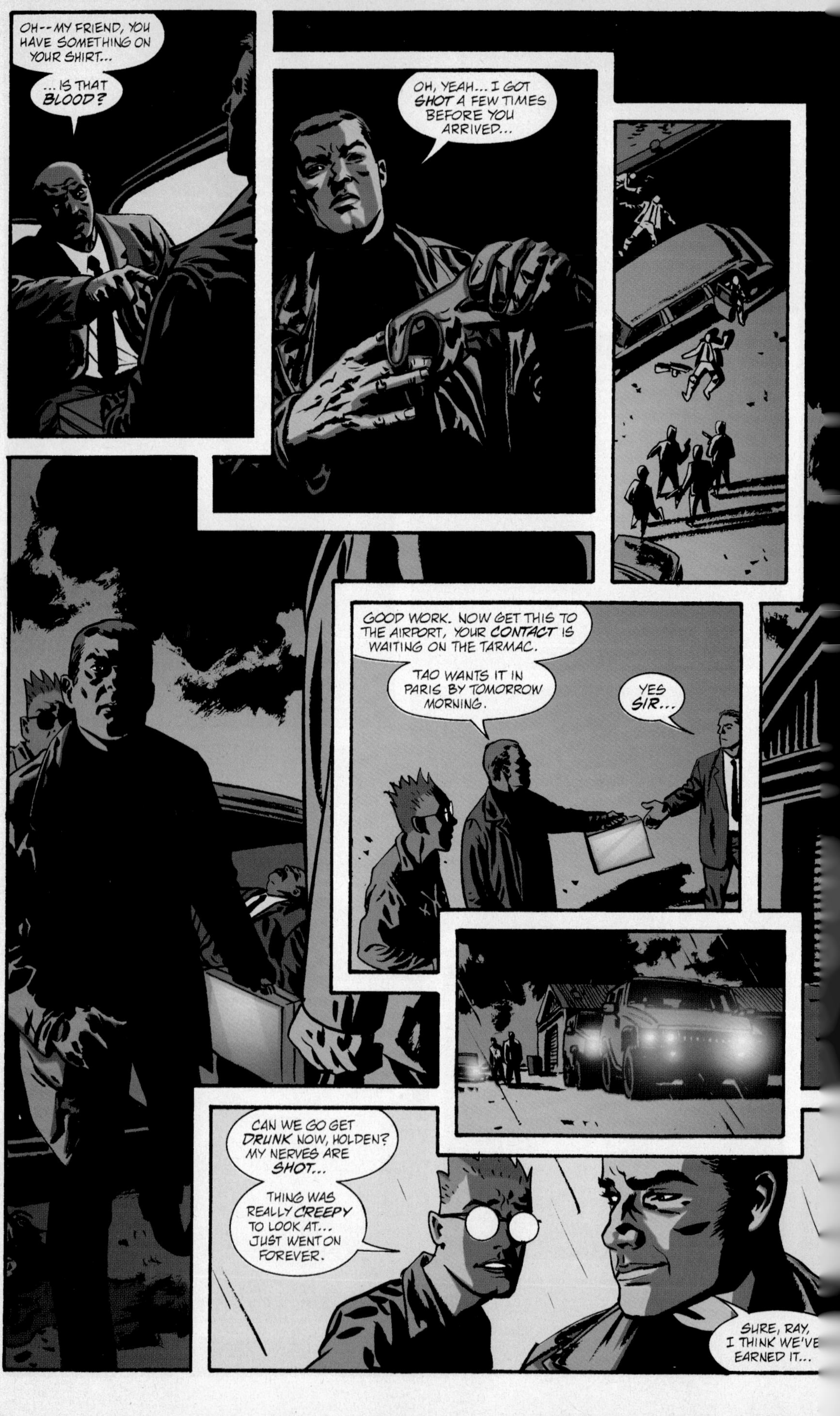
OH--MY FRIEND, YOU HAVE SOMETHING ON YOUR SHIRT...
...IS THAT BLOOD?
OH, YEAH... I GOT SHOT A FEW TIMES BEFORE YOU ARRIVED...
GOOD WORK. NOW GET THIS TO THE AIRPORT, YOUR CONTACT IS WAITING ON THE TARMAC.
TAO WANTS IT IN PARIS BY TOMORROW MORNING.
YES SIR...
CAN WE GO GET DRUNK NOW, HOLDEN? MY NERVES ARE SHOT...
THING WAS REALLY CREEPY TO LOOK AT... JUST WENT ON FOREVER.
SURE, RAY, I THINK WE'VE EARNED IT...

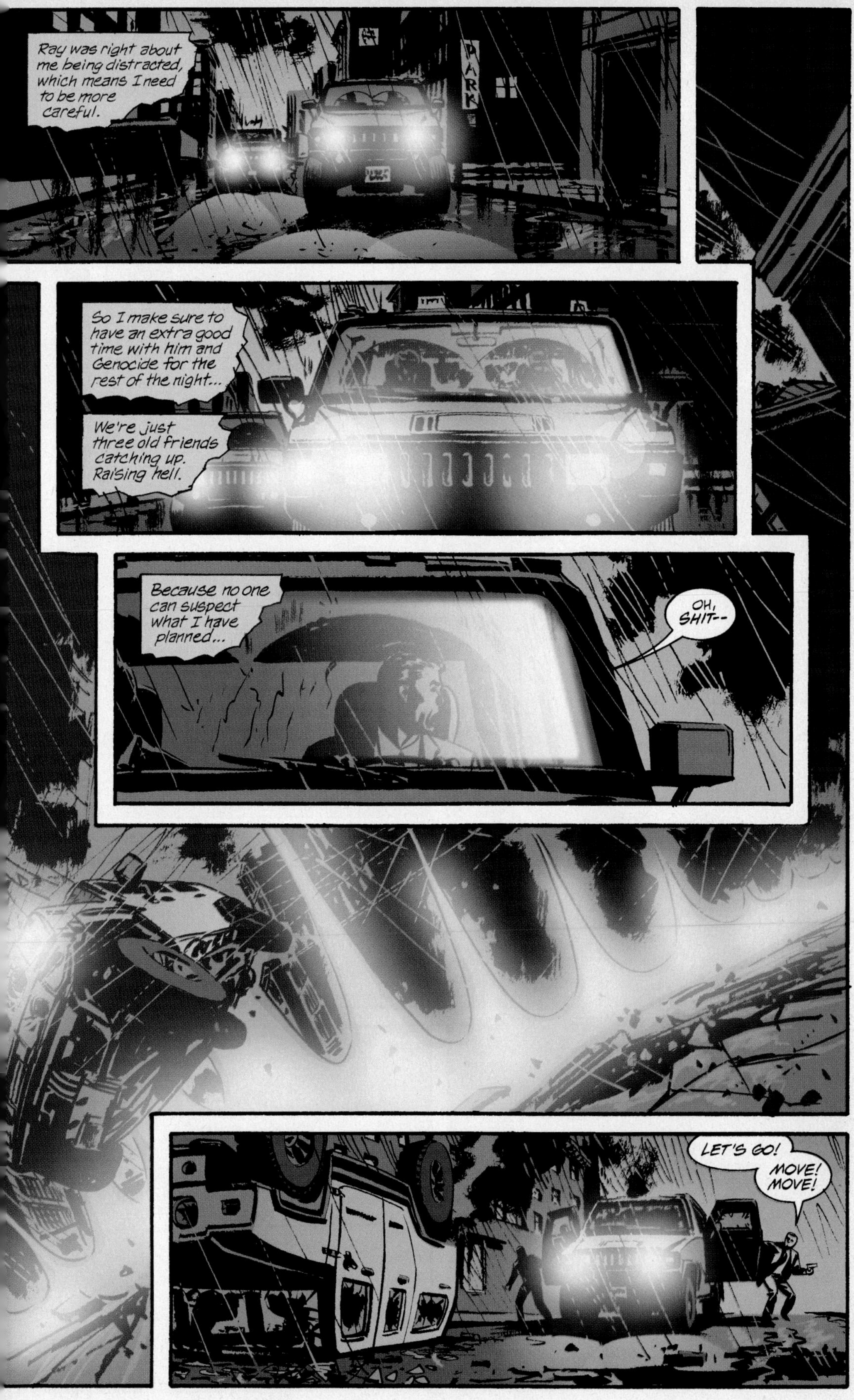

Ray was right about me being distracted, which means I need to be more careful.
So I make sure to have an extra good time with him and Genocide for the rest of the night...
We're just three old friends catching up. Raising hell.
Because no one can suspect what I have planned...
OH, SHIT--
LET'S GO!
MOVE! MOVE!

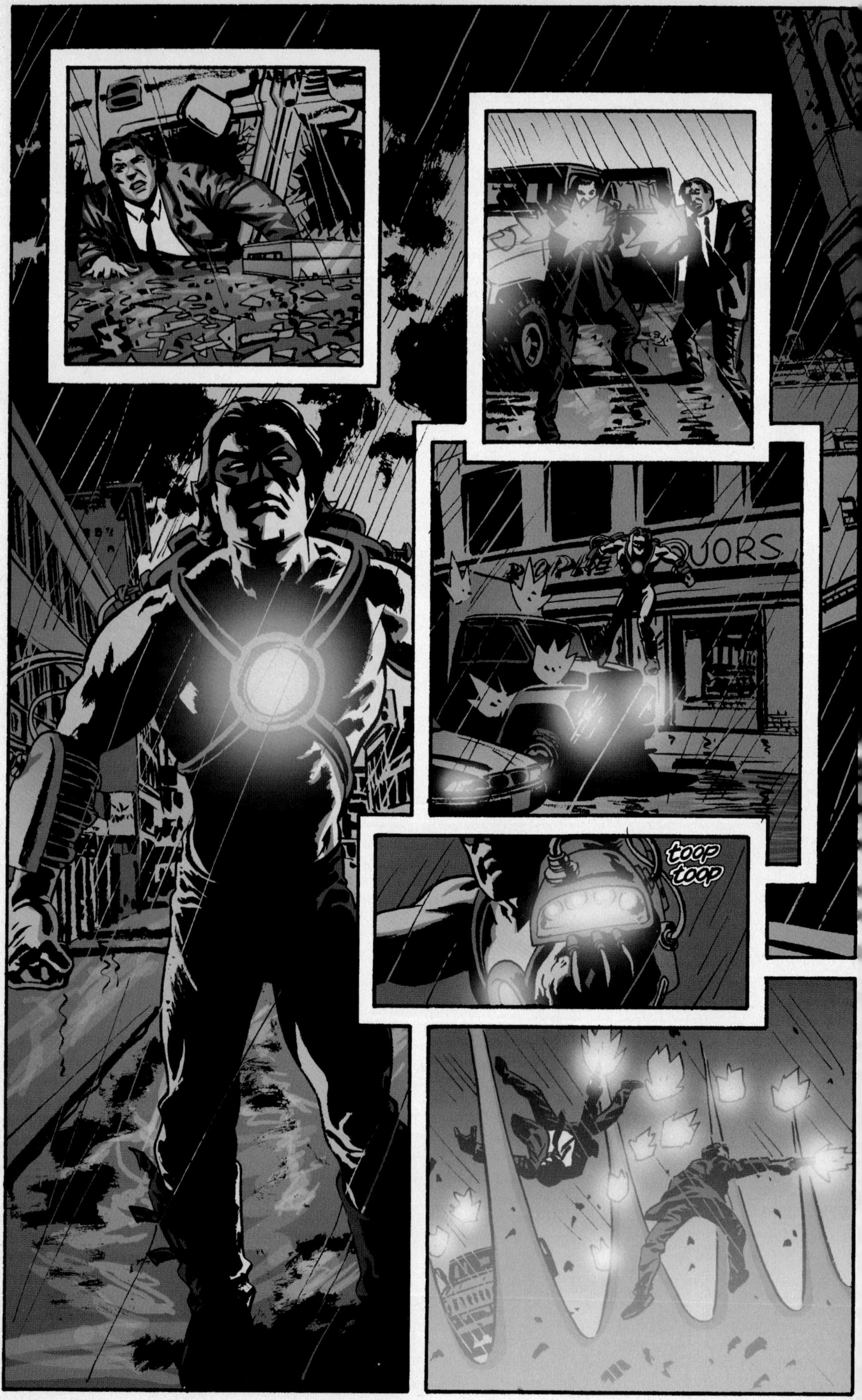
toop
toop

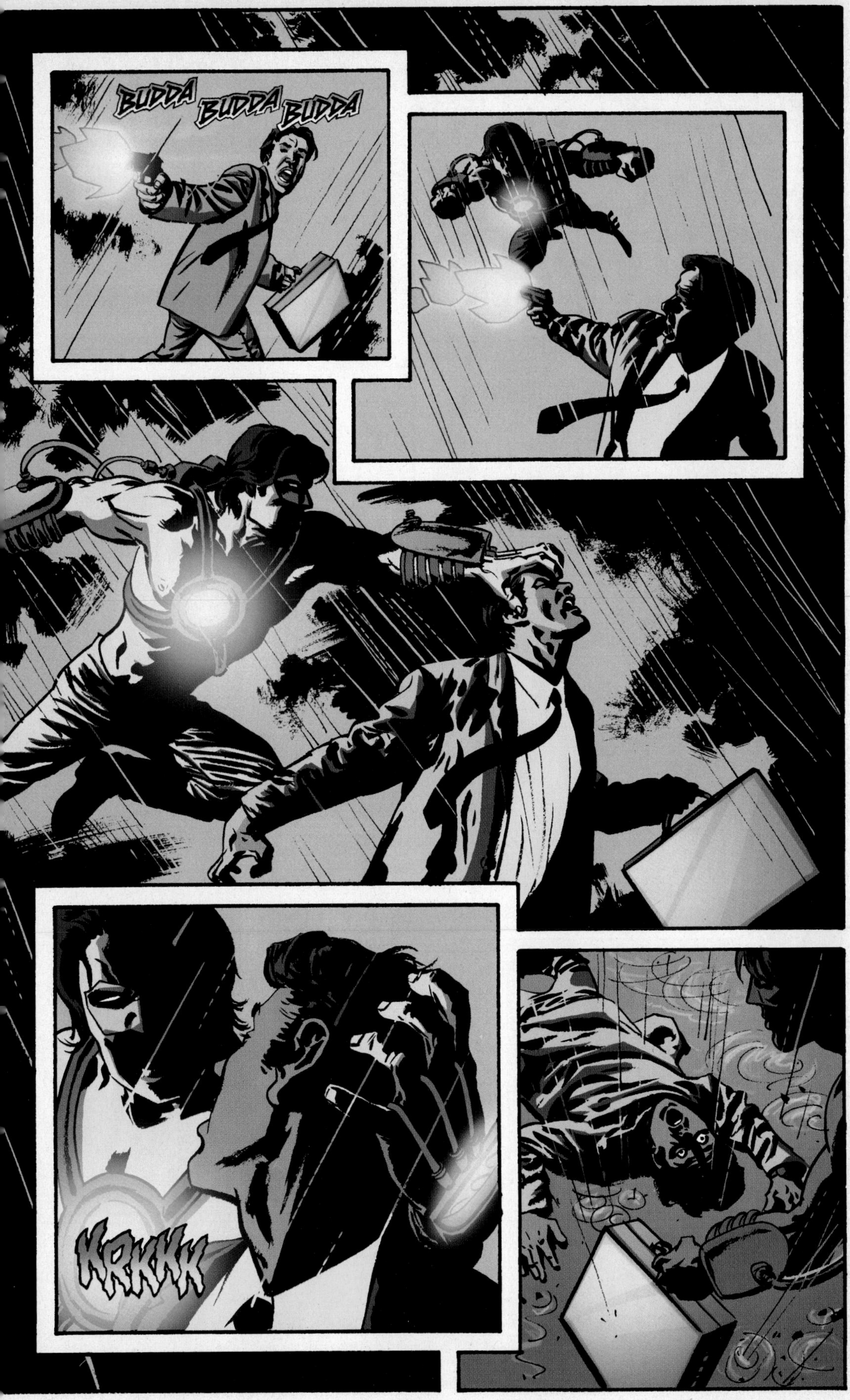
BUDDA BUDDA BUDDA
KRKKK

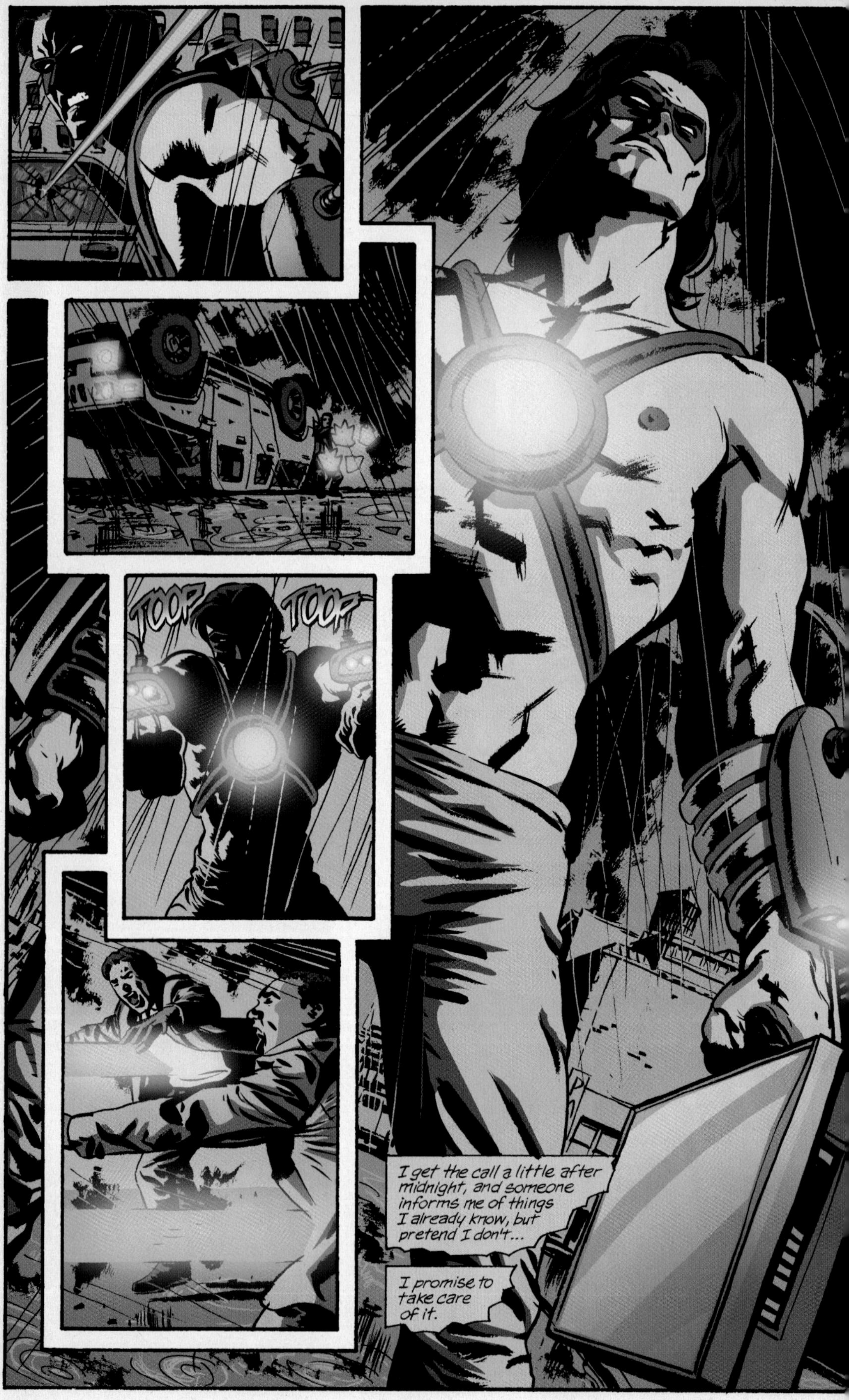
TOOP
TOOP
I get the call a little after midnight, and someone informs me of things I already know, but pretend I don't...
I promise to take care of it.

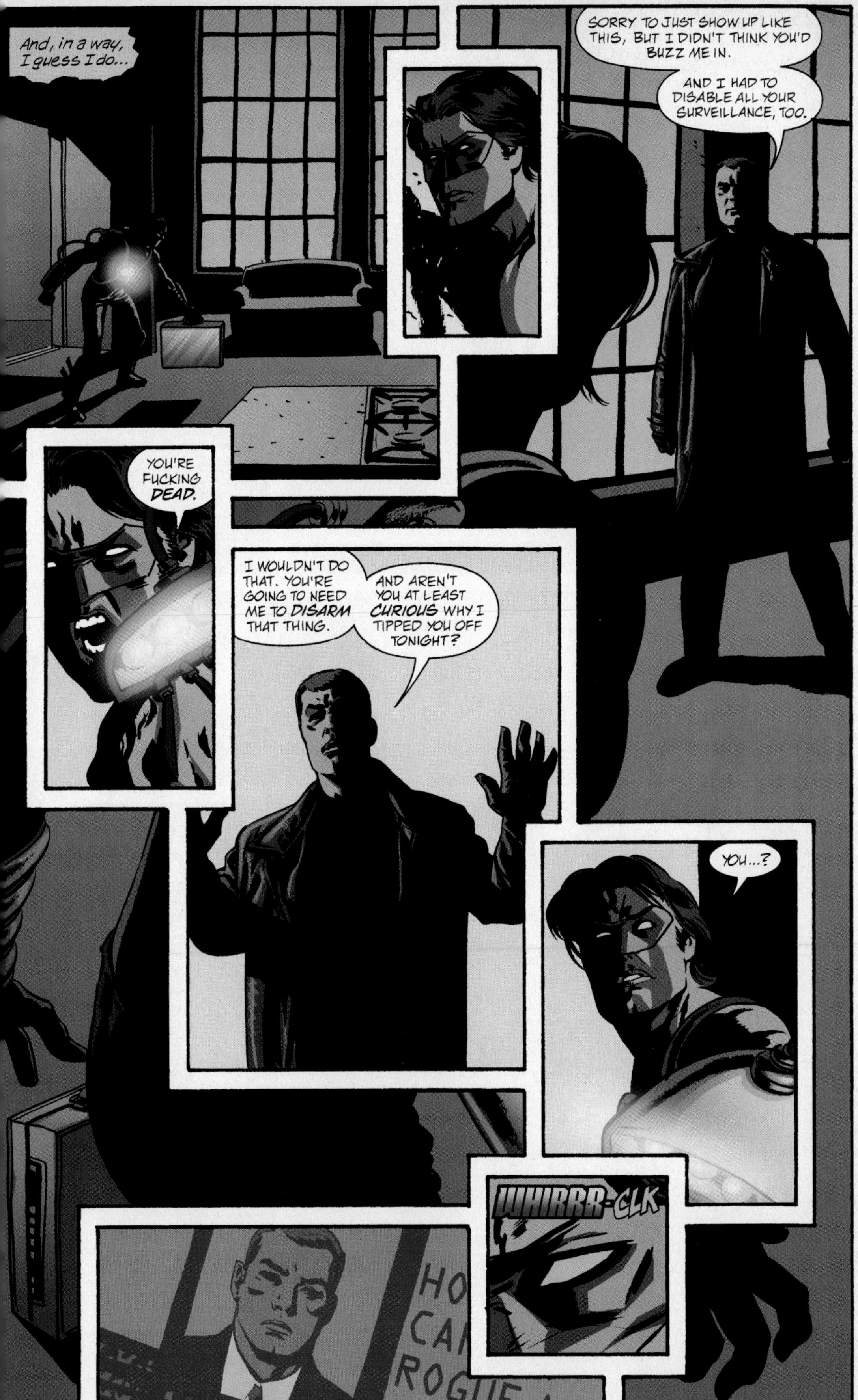
And, in a way, I guess I do...
SORRY TO JUST SHOW UP LIKE THIS, BUT I DIDN'T THINK YOU'D BUZZ ME IN.
AND I HAD TO DISABLE ALL YOUR SURVEILLANCE, TOO.
YOU'RE FUCKING DEAD.
I WOULDN'T DO THAT. YOU'RE GOING TO NEED ME TO DISARM THAT THING.
AND AREN'T YOU AT LEAST CURIOUS WHY I TIPPED YOU OFF TONIGHT?
YOU...?
WHIRRR-CLK
ROGUE

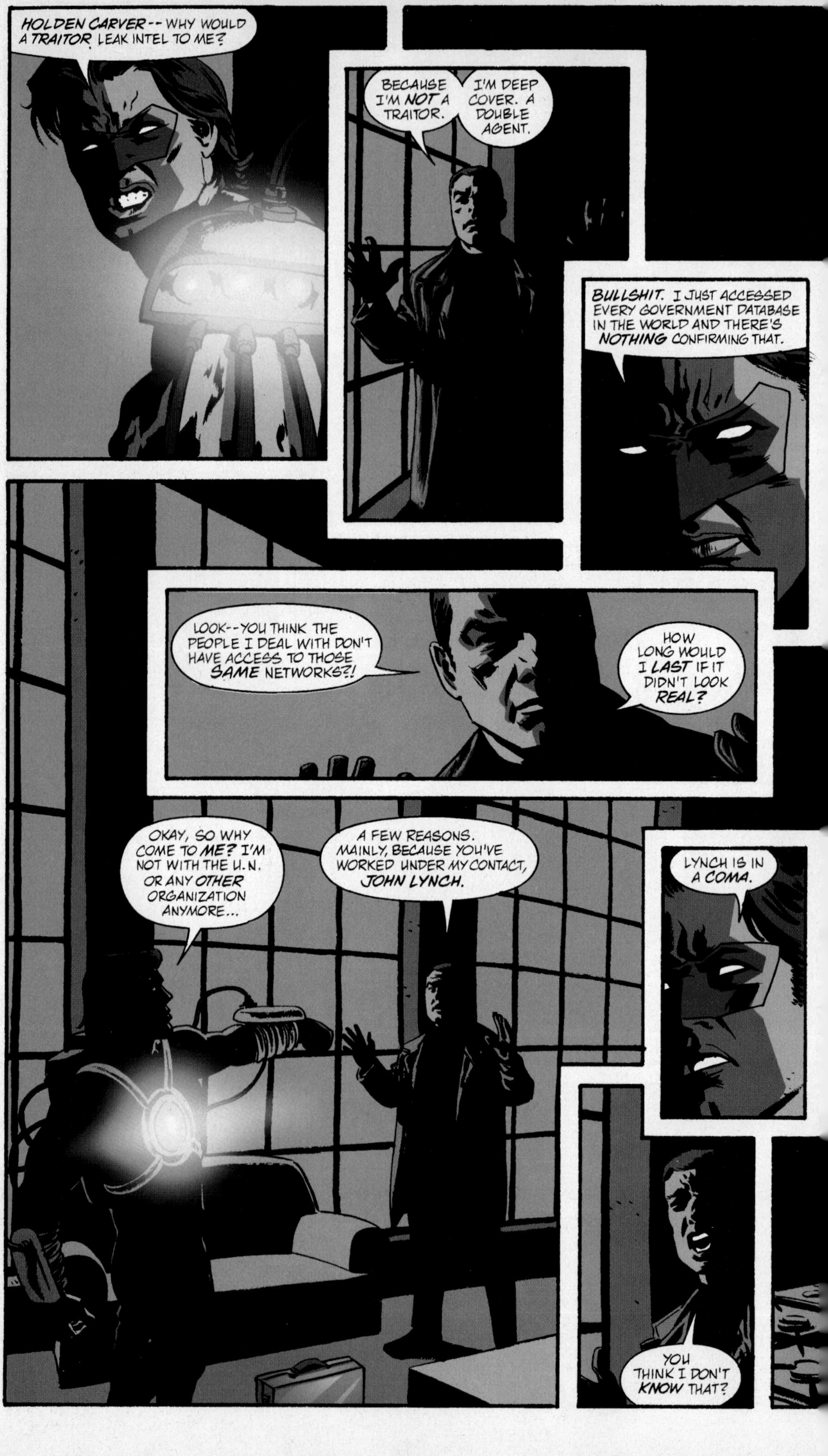
HOLDEN CARVER-- WHY WOULD A TRAITOR LEAK INTEL TO ME?
BECAUSE I'M NOT A TRAITOR.
I'M DEEP COVER. A DOUBLE AGENT.
BULLSHIT. I JUST ACCESSED EVERY GOVERNMENT DATABASE IN THE WORLD AND THERE'S NOTHING CONFIRMING THAT.
LOOK--YOU THINK THE PEOPLE I DEAL WITH DON'T HAVE ACCESS TO THOSE SAME NETWORKS?!
HOW LONG WOULD I LAST IF IT DIDN'T LOOK REAL?
OKAY, SO WHY COME TO ME? I'M NOT WITH THE U.N. OR ANY OTHER ORGANIZATION ANYMORE...
A FEW REASONS. MAINLY, BECAUSE YOU'VE WORKED UNDER MY CONTACT, JOHN LYNCH.
LYNCH IS IN A COMA.
YOU THINK I DON'T KNOW THAT?

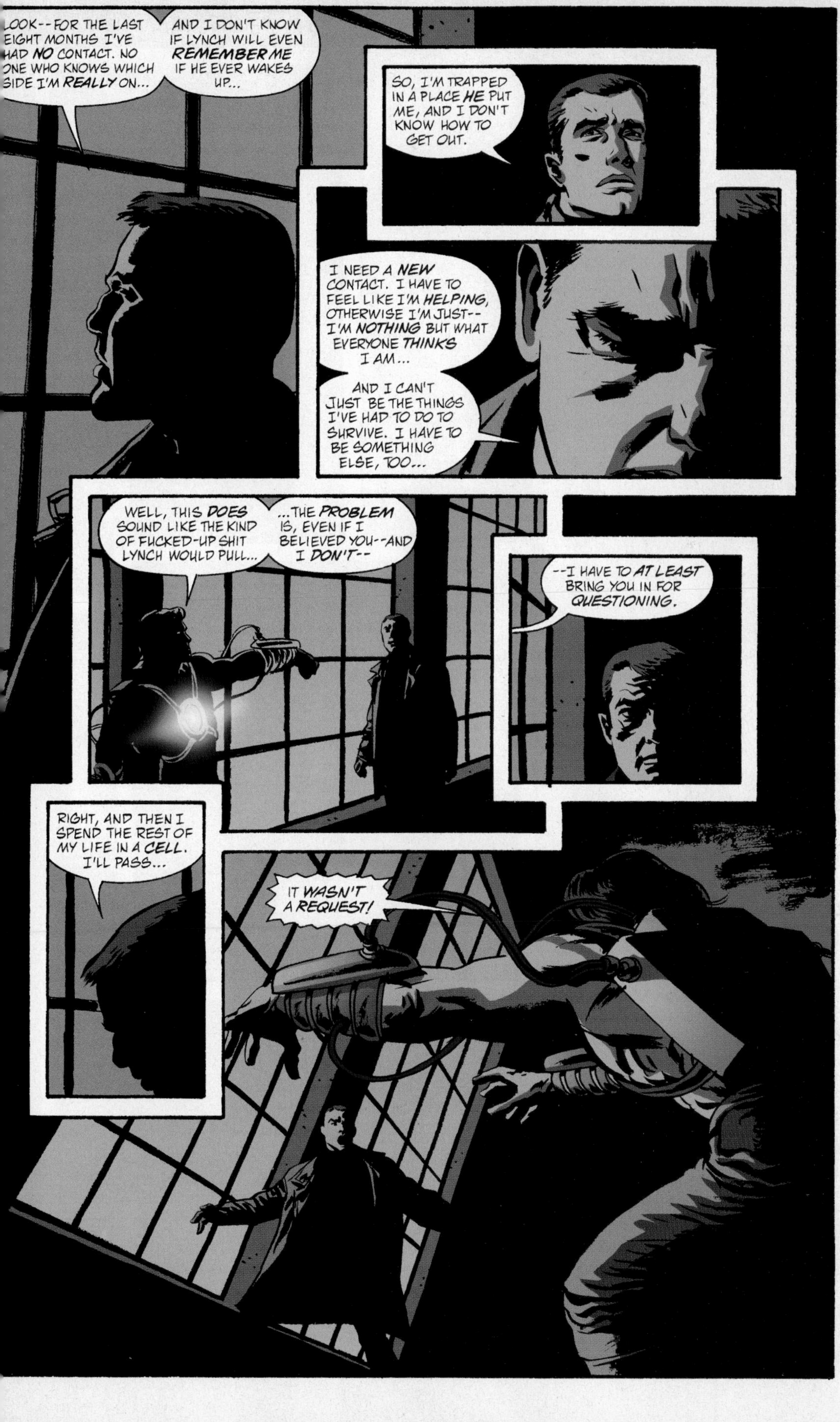
LOOK--FOR THE LAST EIGHT MONTHS I'VE HAD NO CONTACT. NO ONE WHO KNOWS WHICH SIDE I'M REALLY ON...
AND I DON'T KNOW IF LYNCH WILL EVEN REMEMBER ME IF HE EVER WAKES UP...
SO, I'M TRAPPED IN A PLACE HE PUT ME, AND I DON'T KNOW HOW TO GET OUT.
I NEED A NEW CONTACT. I HAVE TO FEEL LIKE I'M HELPING, OTHERWISE I'M JUST-- I'M NOTHING BUT WHAT EVERYONE THINKS I AM...
AND I CAN'T JUST BE THE THINGS I'VE HAD TO DO TO SURVIVE. I HAVE TO BE SOMETHING ELSE, TOO...
WELL, THIS DOES SOUND LIKE THE KIND OF FUCKED-UP SHIT LYNCH WOULD PULL...
...THE PROBLEM IS, EVEN IF I BELIEVED YOU--AND I DON'T--
--I HAVE TO AT LEAST BRING YOU IN FOR QUESTIONING.
RIGHT, AND THEN I SPEND THE REST OF MY LIFE IN A CELL. I'LL PASS...
IT WASN'T A REQUEST!

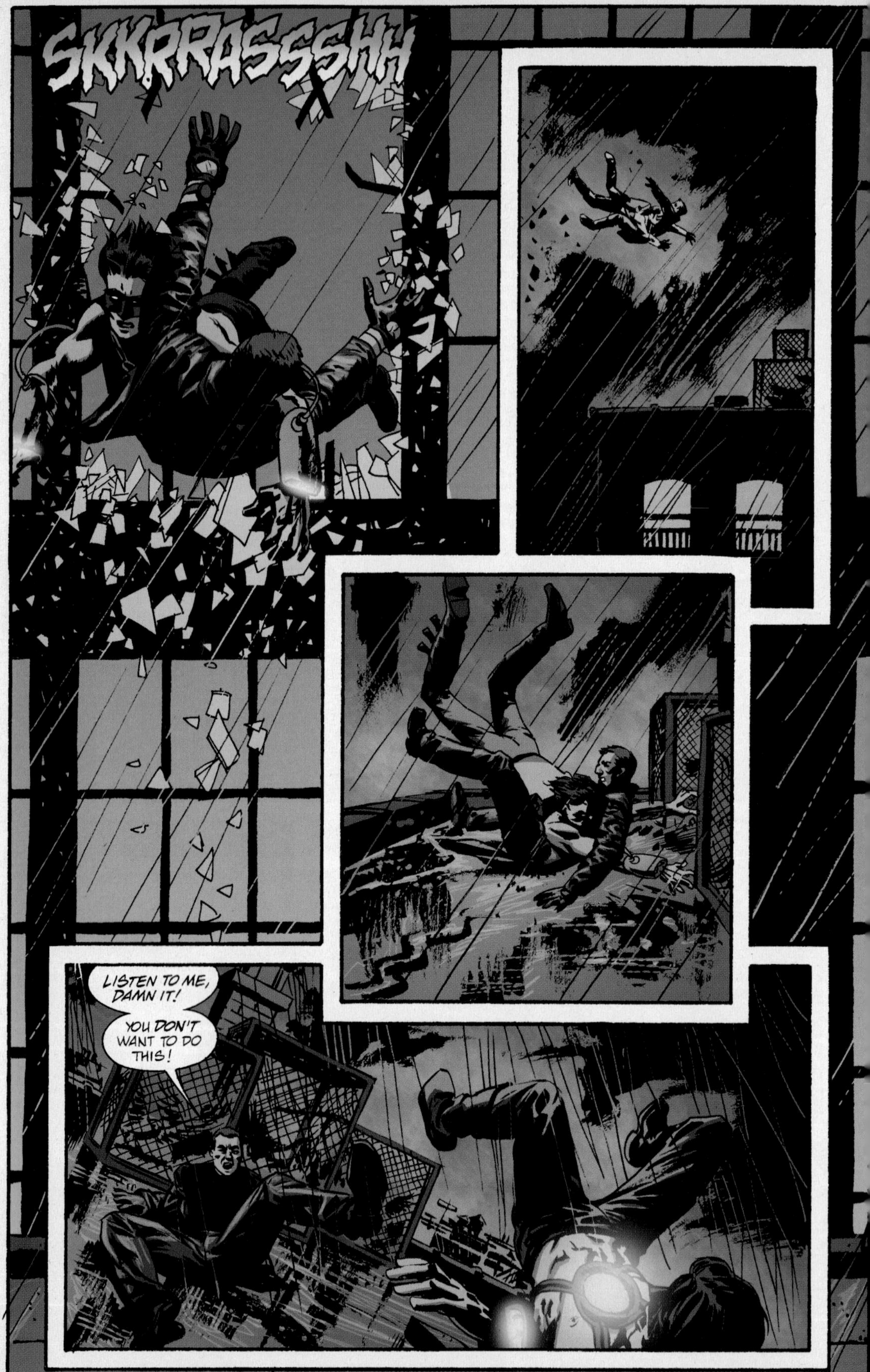
SKKRASSSHH
LISTEN TO ME, DAMN IT!
YOU DON'T WANT TO DO THIS!

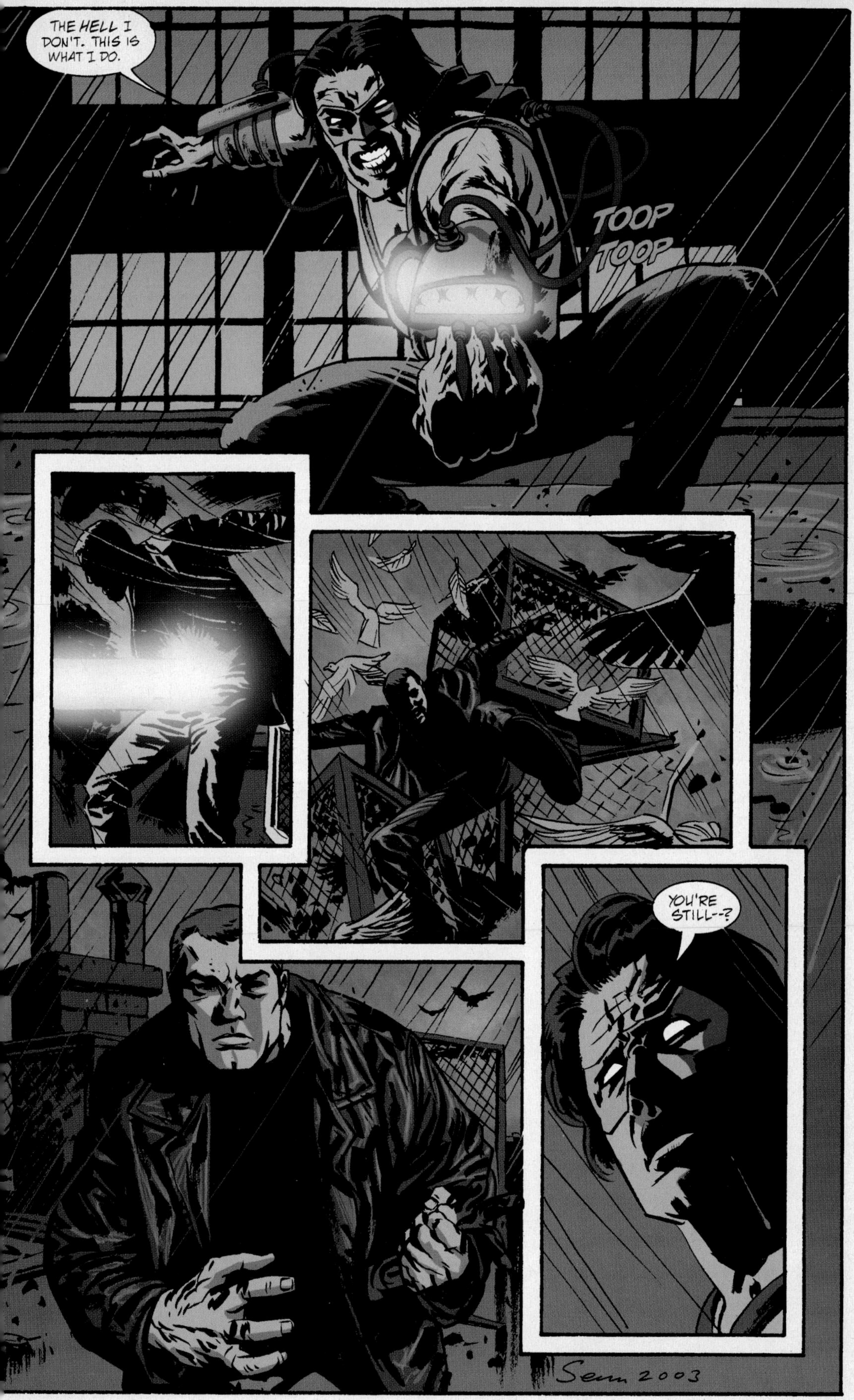
THE HELL I DON'T. THIS IS WHAT I DO.
TOOP TOOP
YOU'RE STILL--?
Sean 2003

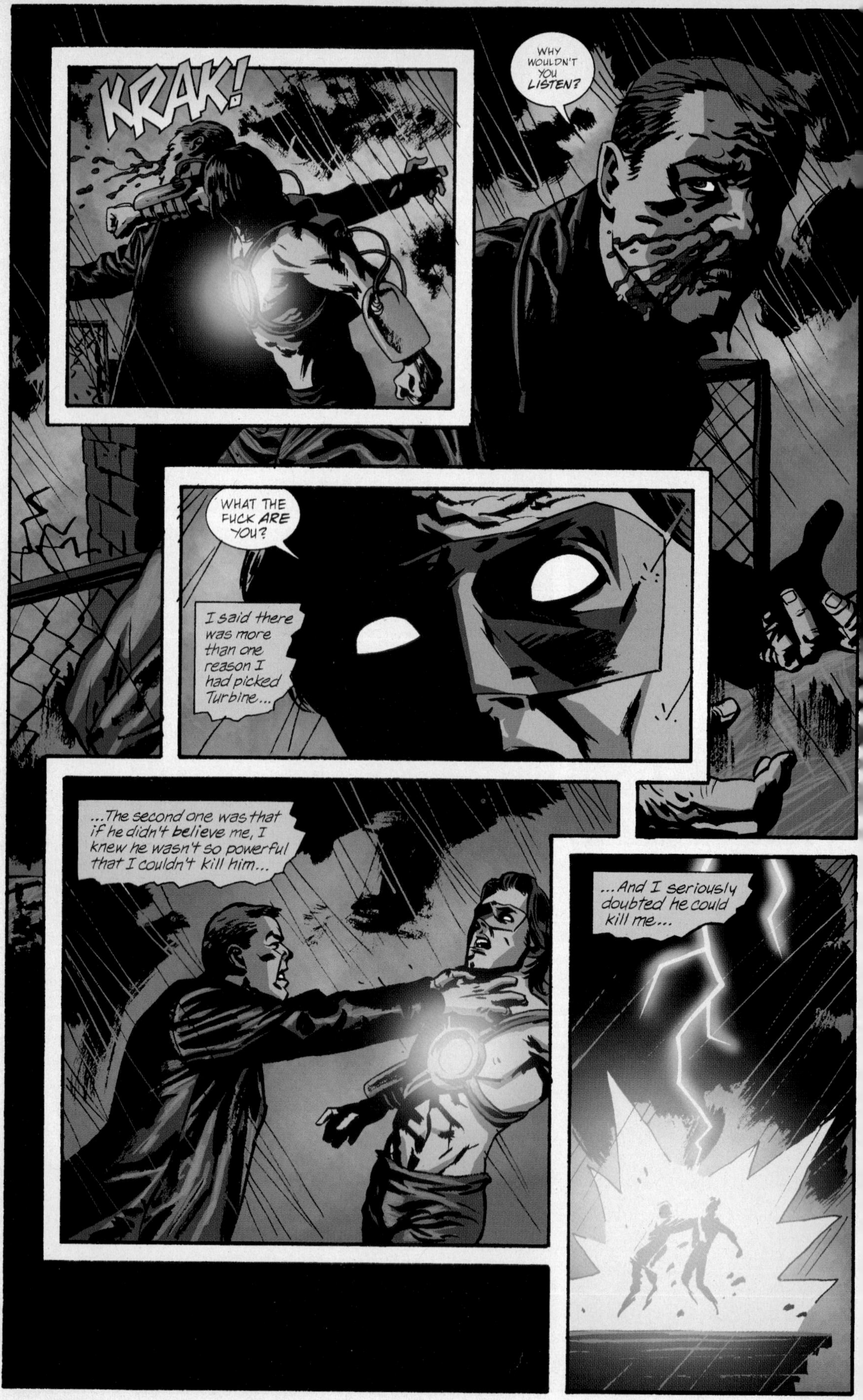
KRAK!
WHY WOULDN'T YOU LISTEN?
WHAT THE FUCK ARE YOU?
I said there was more than one reason I had picked Turbine...
...The second one was that if he didn't believe me, I knew he wasn't so powerful that I couldn't kill him...
...And I seriously doubted he could kill me...

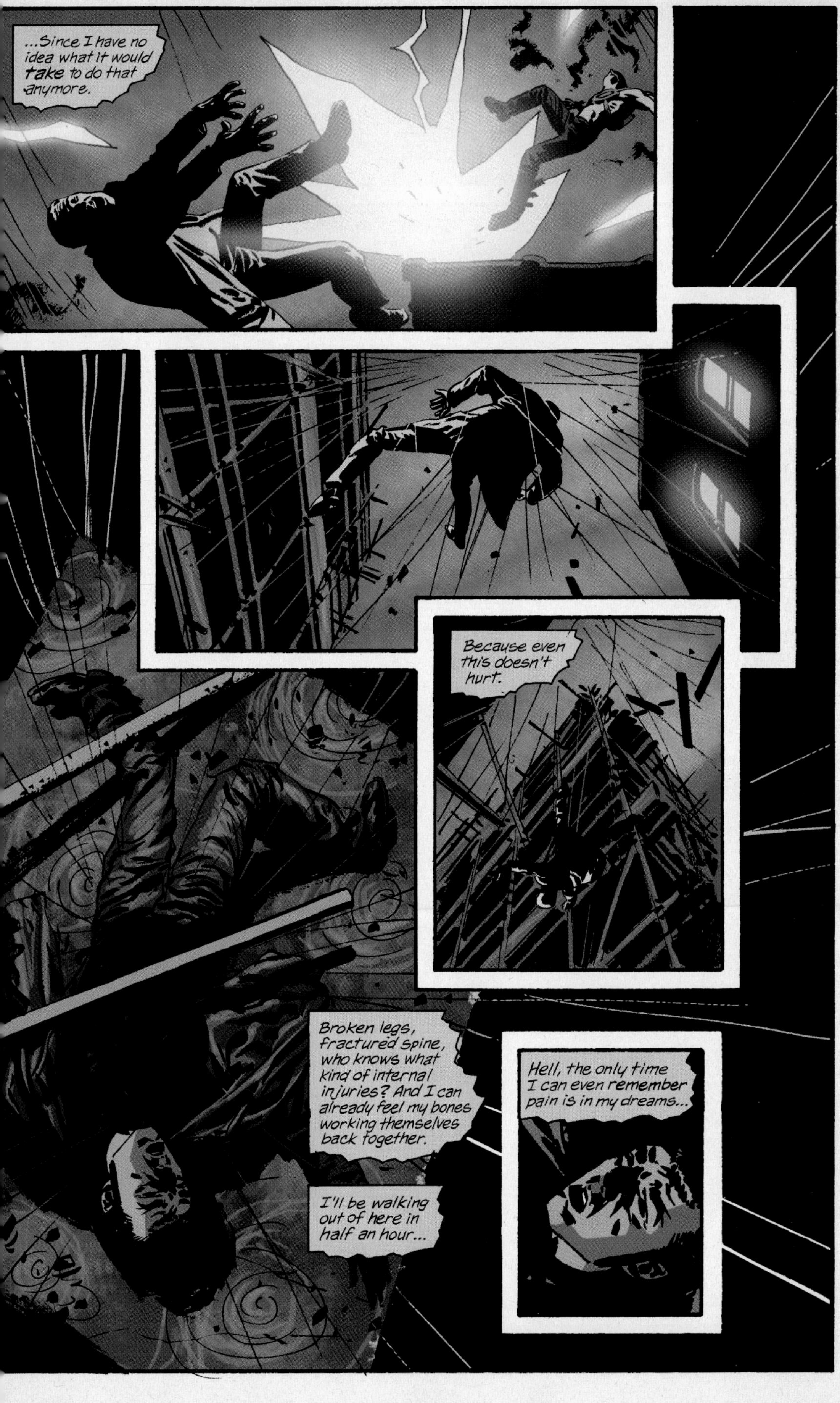

...Since I have no idea what it would take to do that anymore.
Because even this doesn't hurt.
Broken legs, fractured spine, who knows what kind of internal injuries? And I can already feel my bones working themselves back together.
I'll be walking out of here in half an hour...
Hell, the only time I can even remember pain is in my dreams...

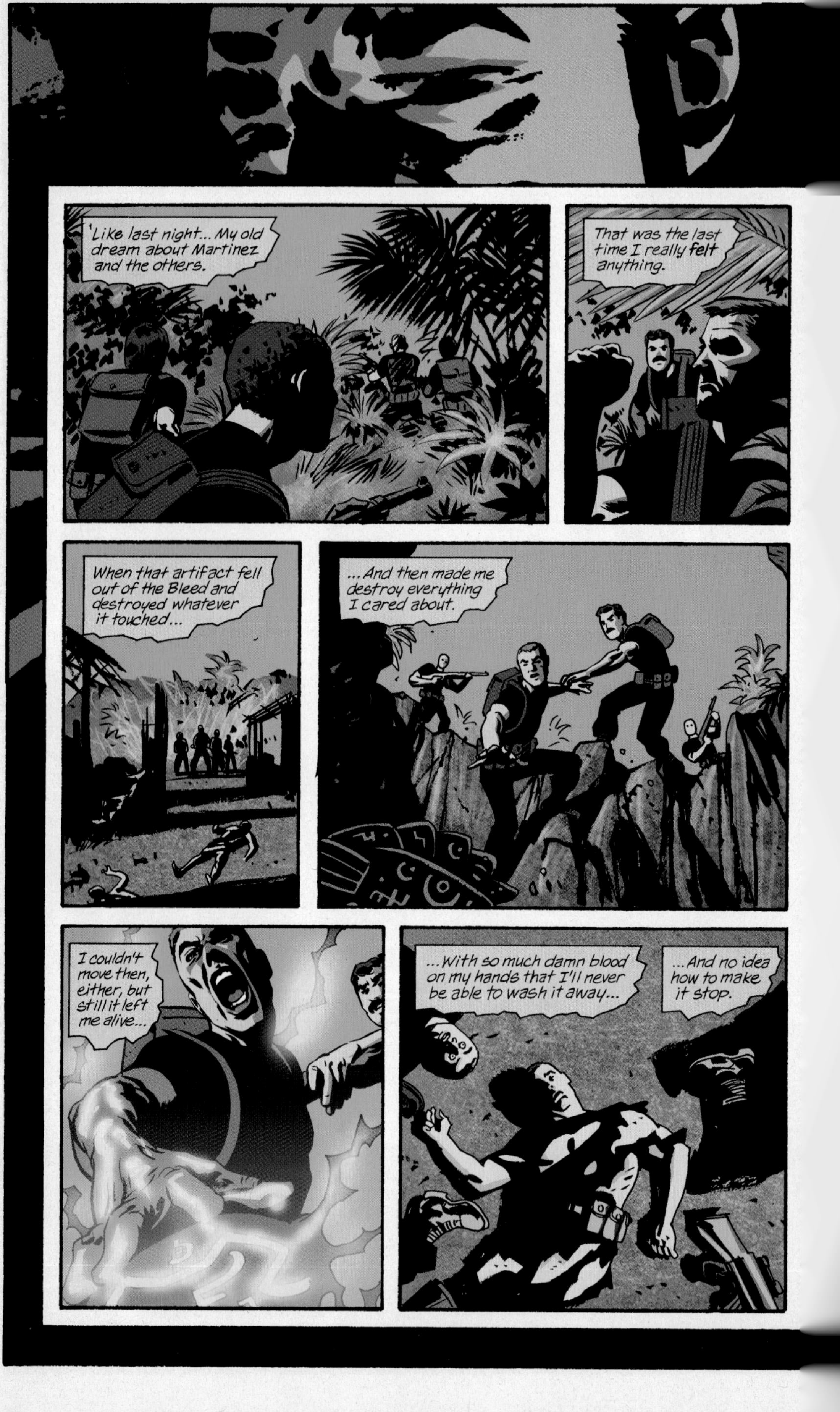
Like last night... My old dream about Martinez and the others.
That was the last time I really felt anything.
When that artifact fell out of the Bleed and destroyed whatever it touched...
...And then made me destroy everything I cared about.
I couldn't move then, either, but still it left me alive...
...With so much damn blood on my hands that I'll never be able to wash it away...
...And no idea how to make it stop.

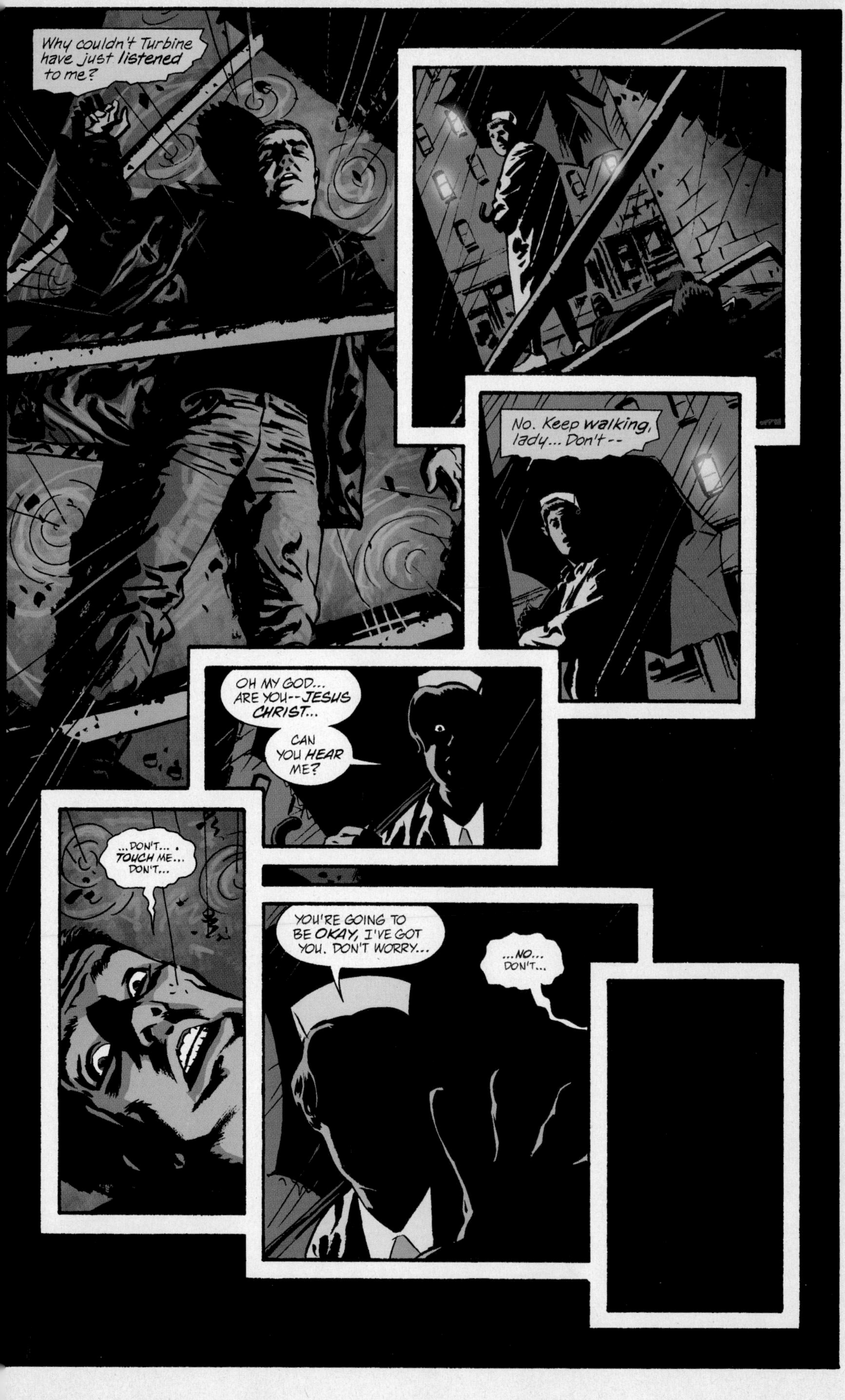
Why couldn't Turbine have just listened to me?
No. Keep walking, lady... Don't--
OH MY GOD... ARE YOU--JESUS CHRIST...
CAN YOU HEAR ME?
...DON'T... TOUCH ME... DON'T...
YOU'RE GOING TO BE OKAY, I'VE GOT YOU. DON'T WORRY...
...NO... DON'T...

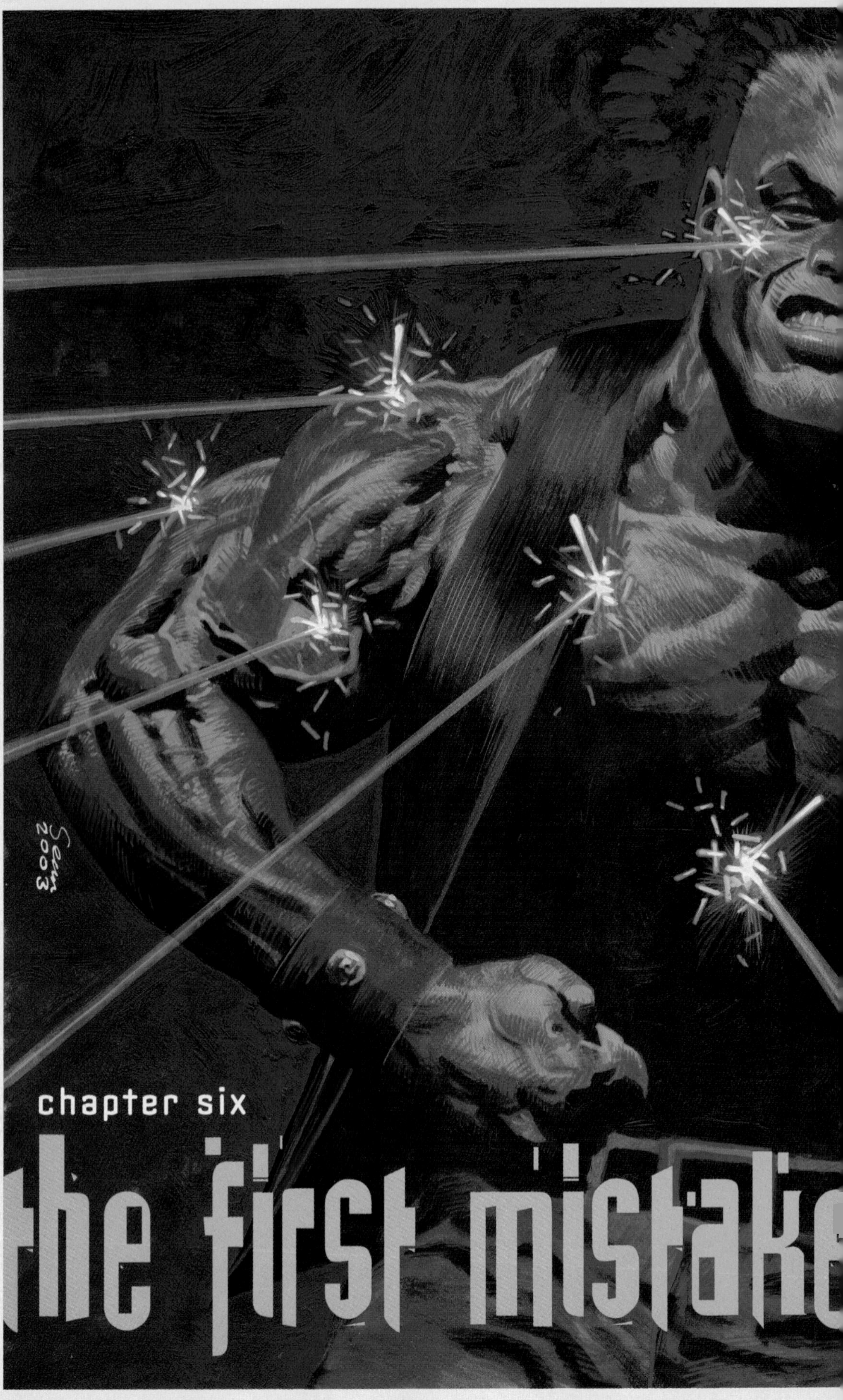
Sean 2003

chapter six

the first mistake

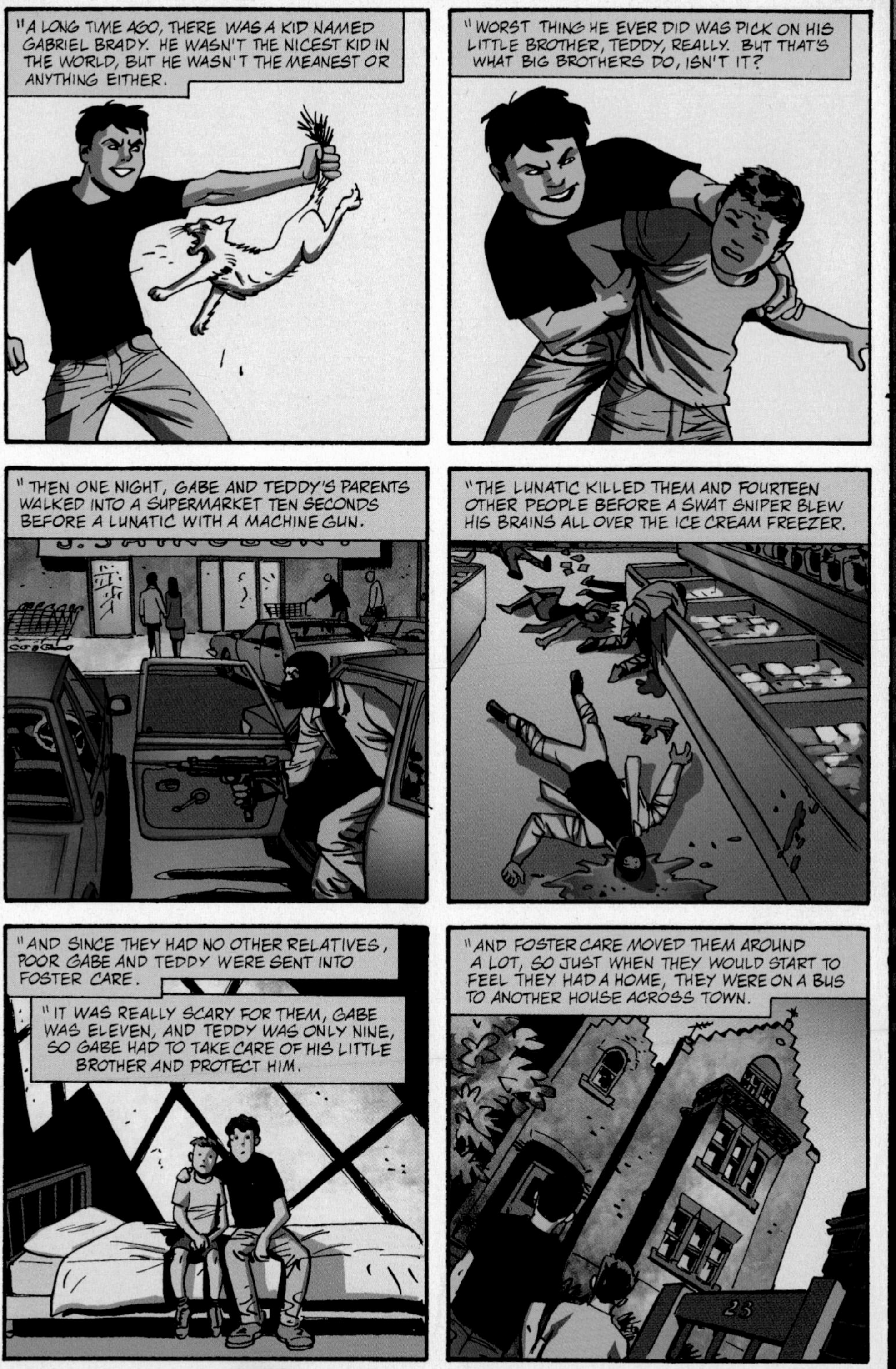
"A LONG TIME AGO, THERE WAS A KID NAMED GABRIEL BRADY. HE WASN'T THE NICEST KID IN THE WORLD, BUT HE WASN'T THE MEANEST OR ANYTHING EITHER.
"WORST THING HE EVER DID WAS PICK ON HIS LITTLE BROTHER, TEDDY, REALLY. BUT THAT'S WHAT BIG BROTHERS DO, ISN'T IT?
"THEN ONE NIGHT, GABE AND TEDDY'S PARENTS WALKED INTO A SUPERMARKET TEN SECONDS BEFORE A LUNATIC WITH A MACHINE GUN.
"THE LUNATIC KILLED THEM AND FOURTEEN OTHER PEOPLE BEFORE A SWAT SNIPER BLEW HIS BRAINS ALL OVER THE ICE CREAM FREEZER.
"AND SINCE THEY HAD NO OTHER RELATIVES, POOR GABE AND TEDDY WERE SENT INTO FOSTER CARE.
"IT WAS REALLY SCARY FOR THEM, GABE WAS ELEVEN, AND TEDDY WAS ONLY NINE, SO GABE HAD TO TAKE CARE OF HIS LITTLE BROTHER AND PROTECT HIM.
"AND FOSTER CARE MOVED THEM AROUND A LOT, SO JUST WHEN THEY WOULD START TO FEEL THEY HAD A HOME, THEY WERE ON A BUS TO ANOTHER HOUSE ACROSS TOWN.
23

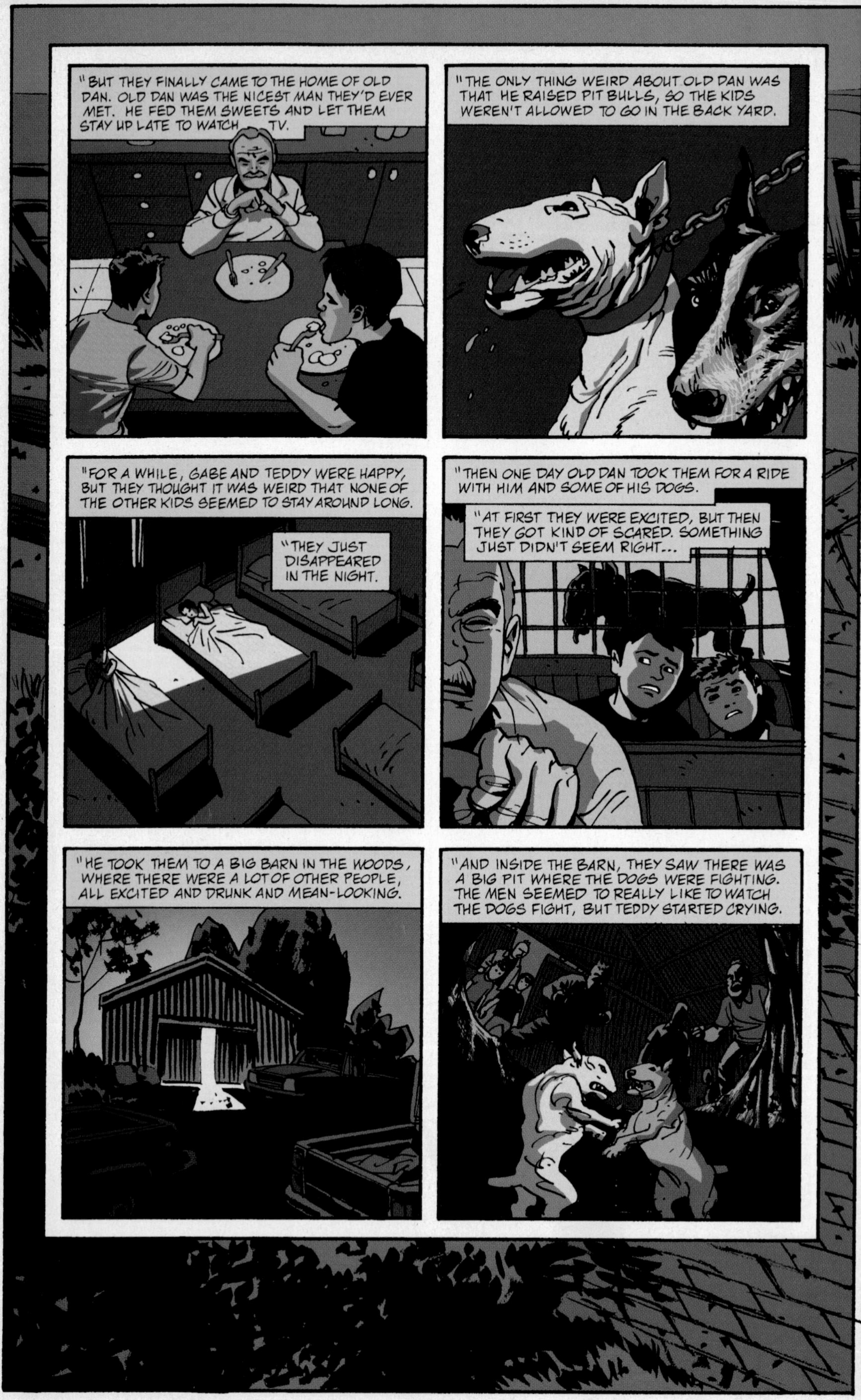
"BUT THEY FINALLY CAME TO THE HOME OF OLD DAN. OLD DAN WAS THE NICEST MAN THEY'D EVER MET. HE FED THEM SWEETS AND LET THEM STAY UP LATE TO WATCH TV.
"THE ONLY THING WEIRD ABOUT OLD DAN WAS THAT HE RAISED PIT BULLS, SO THE KIDS WEREN'T ALLOWED TO GO IN THE BACK YARD.
"FOR A WHILE, GABE AND TEDDY WERE HAPPY, BUT THEY THOUGHT IT WAS WEIRD THAT NONE OF THE OTHER KIDS SEEMED TO STAY AROUND LONG.
"THEY JUST DISAPPEARED IN THE NIGHT.
"THEN ONE DAY OLD DAN TOOK THEM FOR A RIDE WITH HIM AND SOME OF HIS DOGS.
"AT FIRST THEY WERE EXCITED, BUT THEN THEY GOT KIND OF SCARED. SOMETHING JUST DIDN'T SEEM RIGHT...
"HE TOOK THEM TO A BIG BARN IN THE WOODS, WHERE THERE WERE A LOT OF OTHER PEOPLE, ALL EXCITED AND DRUNK AND MEAN-LOOKING.
"AND INSIDE THE BARN, THEY SAW THERE WAS A BIG PIT WHERE THE DOGS WERE FIGHTING. THE MEN SEEMED TO REALLY LIKE TO WATCH THE DOGS FIGHT, BUT TEDDY STARTED CRYING.

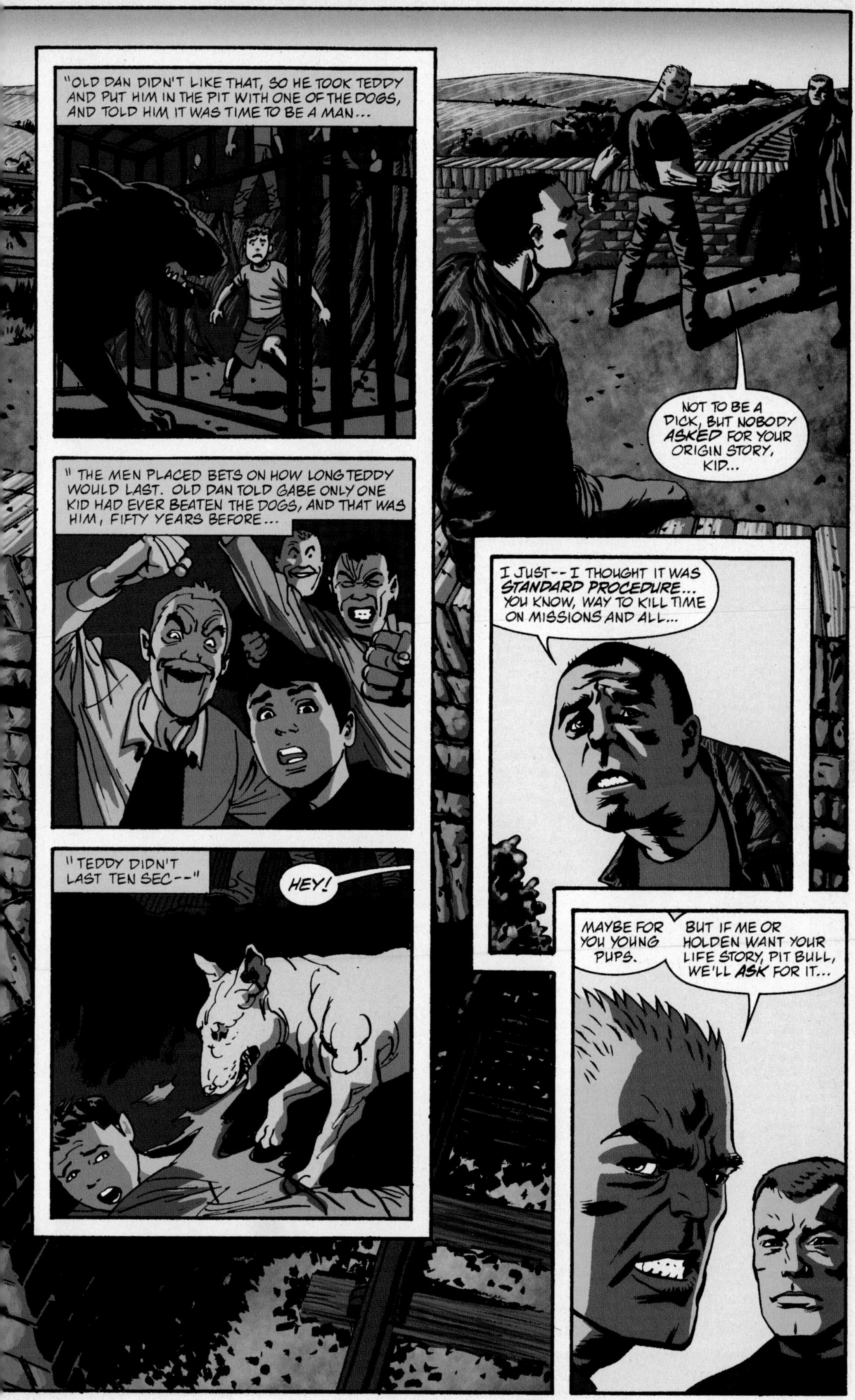
"OLD DAN DIDN'T LIKE THAT, SO HE TOOK TEDDY AND PUT HIM IN THE PIT WITH ONE OF THE DOGS, AND TOLD HIM IT WAS TIME TO BE A MAN...
NOT TO BE A DICK, BUT NOBODY ASKED FOR YOUR ORIGIN STORY, KID...
" THE MEN PLACED BETS ON HOW LONG TEDDY WOULD LAST. OLD DAN TOLD GABE ONLY ONE KID HAD EVER BEATEN THE DOGS, AND THAT WAS HIM, FIFTY YEARS BEFORE...
I JUST-- I THOUGHT IT WAS STANDARD PROCEDURE... YOU KNOW, WAY TO KILL TIME ON MISSIONS AND ALL...
" TEDDY DIDN'T LAST TEN SEC--"
HEY!
MAYBE FOR YOU YOUNG PUPS.
BUT IF ME OR HOLDEN WANT YOUR LIFE STORY, PIT BULL, WE'LL ASK FOR IT...

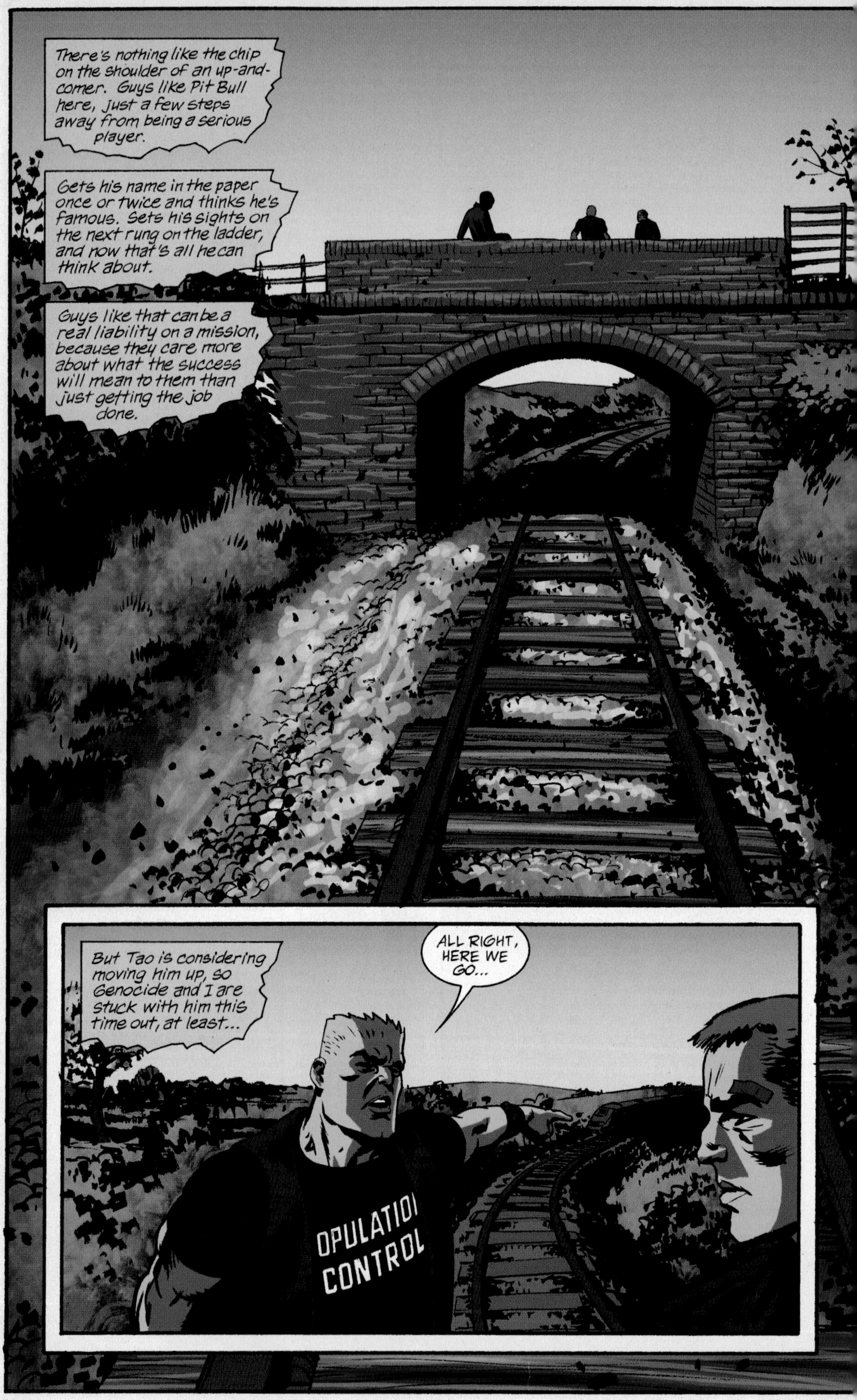
There's nothing like the chip on the shoulder of an up-and-comer. Guys like Pit Bull here, just a few steps away from being a serious player.
Gets his name in the paper once or twice and thinks he's famous. Sets his sights on the next rung on the ladder, and now that's all he can think about.
Guys like that can be a real liability on a mission, because they care more about what the success will mean to them than just getting the job done.
But Tao is considering moving him up, so Genocide and I are stuck with him this time out, at least...
ALL RIGHT, HERE WE GO...
OPULATIO CONTROL

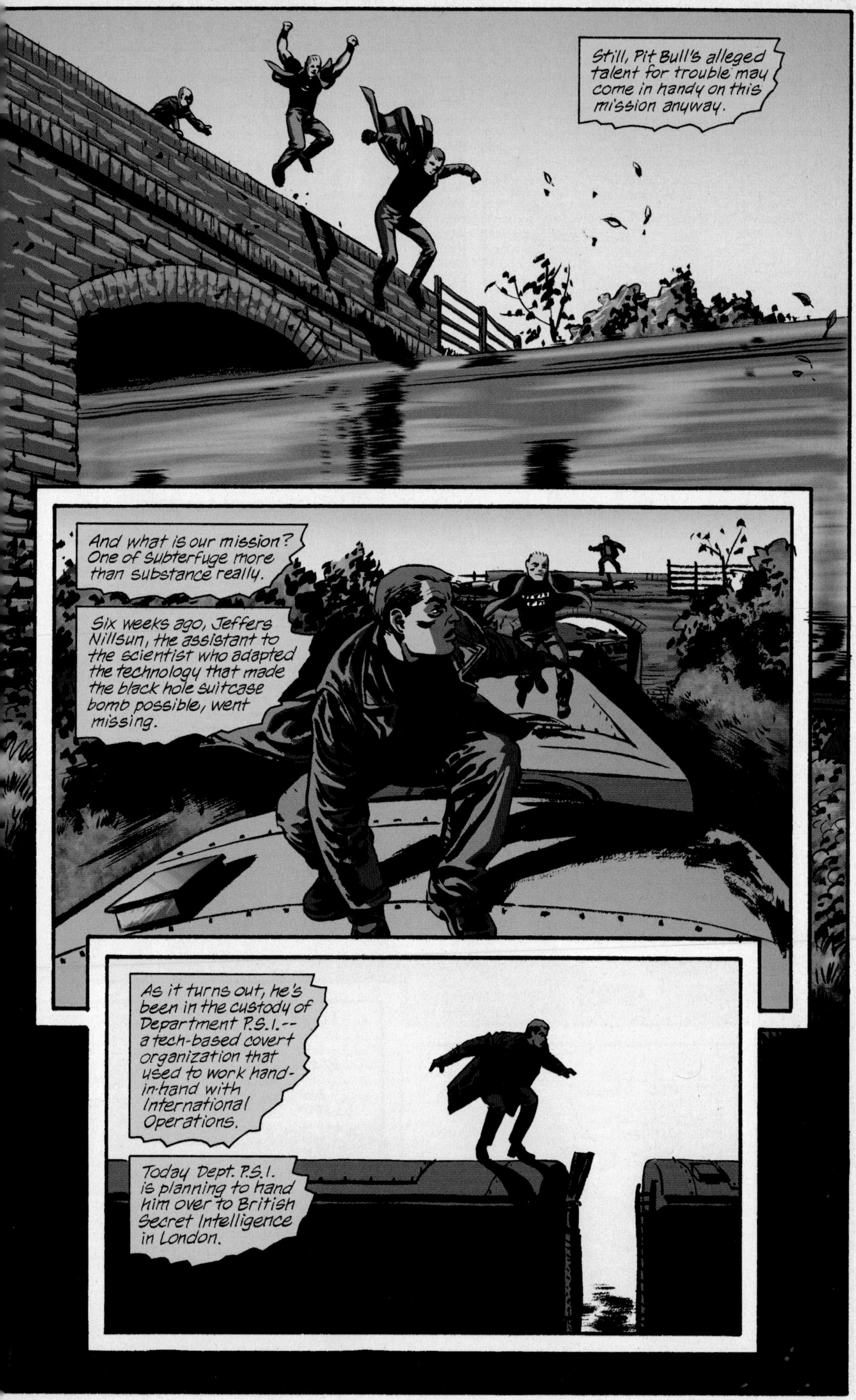
Still, Pit Bull's alleged talent for trouble may come in handy on this mission anyway.
And what is our mission? One of subterfuge more than substance really.
Six weeks ago, Jeffers Nillsun, the assistant to the scientist who adapted the technology that made the black hole suitcase bomb possible, went missing.
As it turns out, he's been in the custody of Department P.S.I.-- a tech-based covert organization that used to work hand-in-hand with International Operations.
Today Dept. P.S.I. is planning to hand him over to British Secret Intelligence in London.

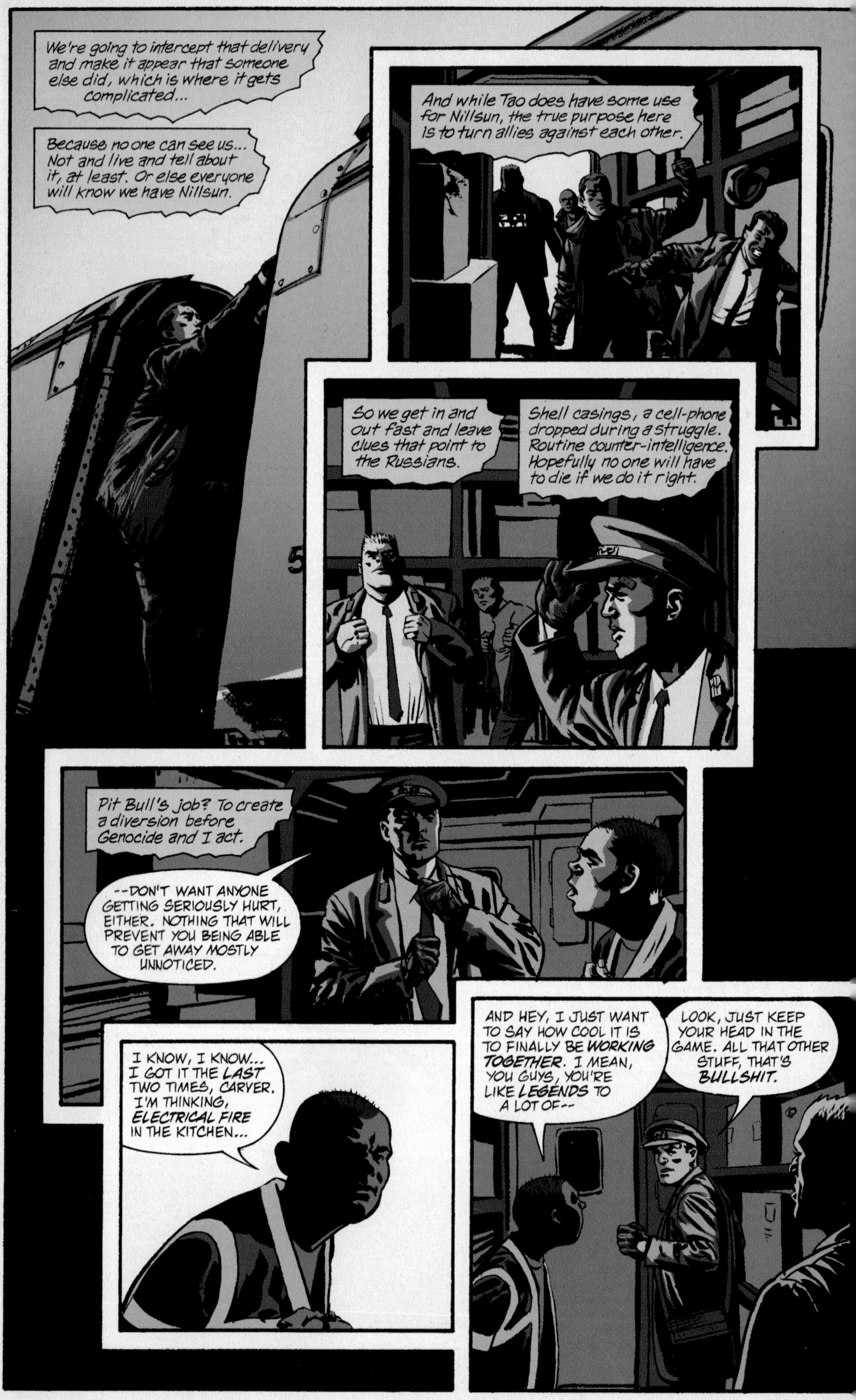
We're going to intercept that delivery and make it appear that someone else did, which is where it gets complicated...
Because no one can see us... Not and live and tell about it, at least. Or else everyone will know we have Nillsun.
And while Tao does have some use for Nillsun, the true purpose here is to turn allies against each other.
So we get in and out fast and leave clues that point to the Russians.
Shell casings, a cell-phone dropped during a struggle. Routine counter-intelligence. Hopefully no one will have to die if we do it right.
Pit Bull's job? To create a diversion before Genocide and I act.
--DON'T WANT ANYONE GETTING SERIOUSLY HURT, EITHER. NOTHING THAT WILL PREVENT YOU BEING ABLE TO GET AWAY MOSTLY UNNOTICED.
I KNOW, I KNOW... I GOT IT THE LAST TWO TIMES, CARVER. I'M THINKING, ELECTRICAL FIRE IN THE KITCHEN...
AND HEY, I JUST WANT TO SAY HOW COOL IT IS TO FINALLY BE WORKING TOGETHER. I MEAN, YOU GUYS, YOU'RE LIKE LEGENDS TO A LOT OF--
LOOK, JUST KEEP YOUR HEAD IN THE GAME. ALL THAT OTHER STUFF, THAT'S BULLSHIT.

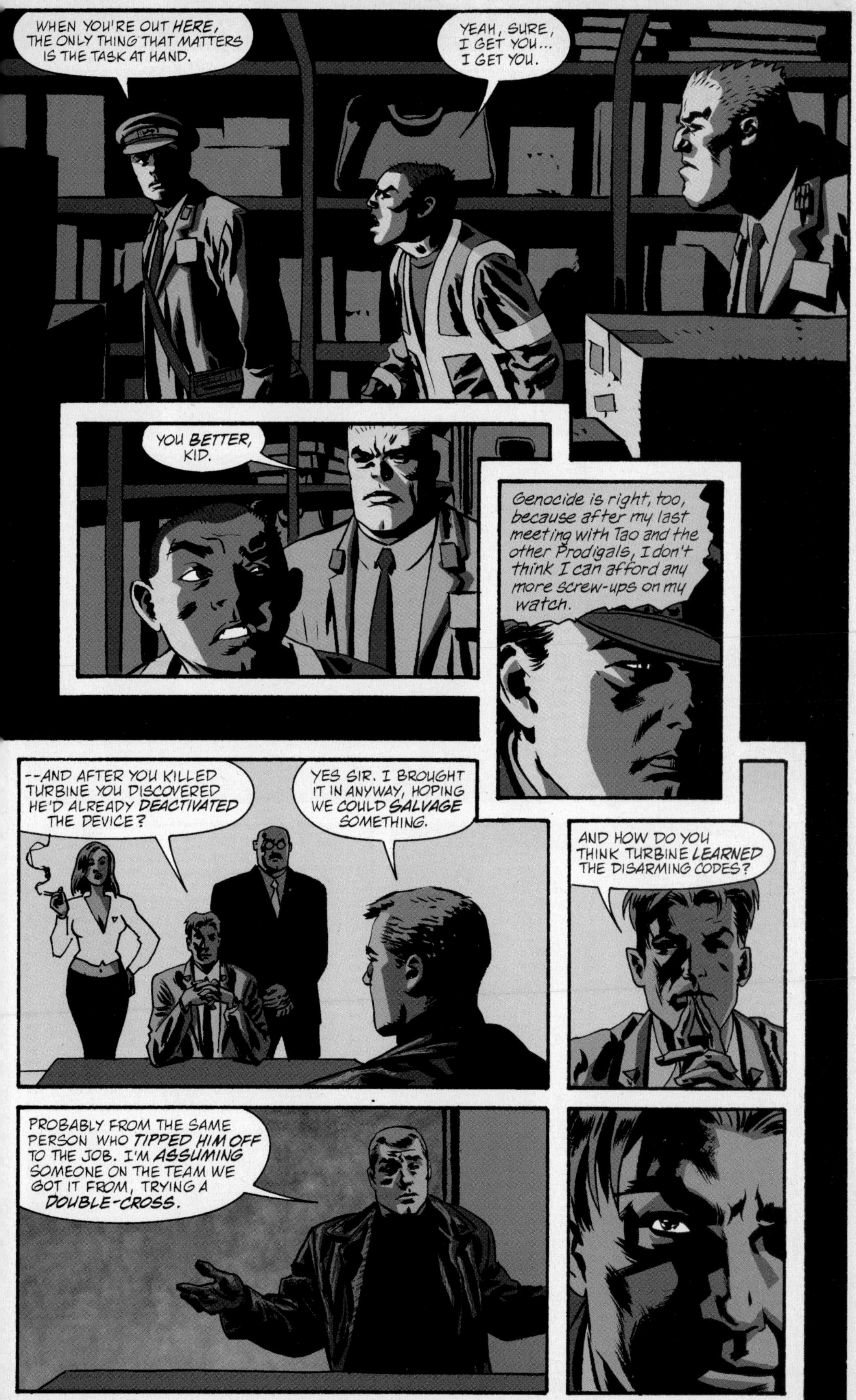
WHEN YOU'RE OUT HERE, THE ONLY THING THAT MATTERS IS THE TASK AT HAND.
YEAH, SURE, I GET YOU... I GET YOU.
YOU BETTER, KID.
Genocide is right, too, because after my last meeting with Tao and the other Prodigals, I don't think I can afford any more screw-ups on my watch.
--AND AFTER YOU KILLED TURBINE YOU DISCOVERED HE'D ALREADY DEACTIVATED THE DEVICE?
YES SIR. I BROUGHT IT IN ANYWAY, HOPING WE COULD SALVAGE SOMETHING.
AND HOW DO YOU THINK TURBINE LEARNED THE DISARMING CODES?
PROBABLY FROM THE SAME PERSON WHO TIPPED HIM OFF TO THE JOB. I'M ASSUMING SOMEONE ON THE TEAM WE GOT IT FROM, TRYING A DOUBLE-CROSS.

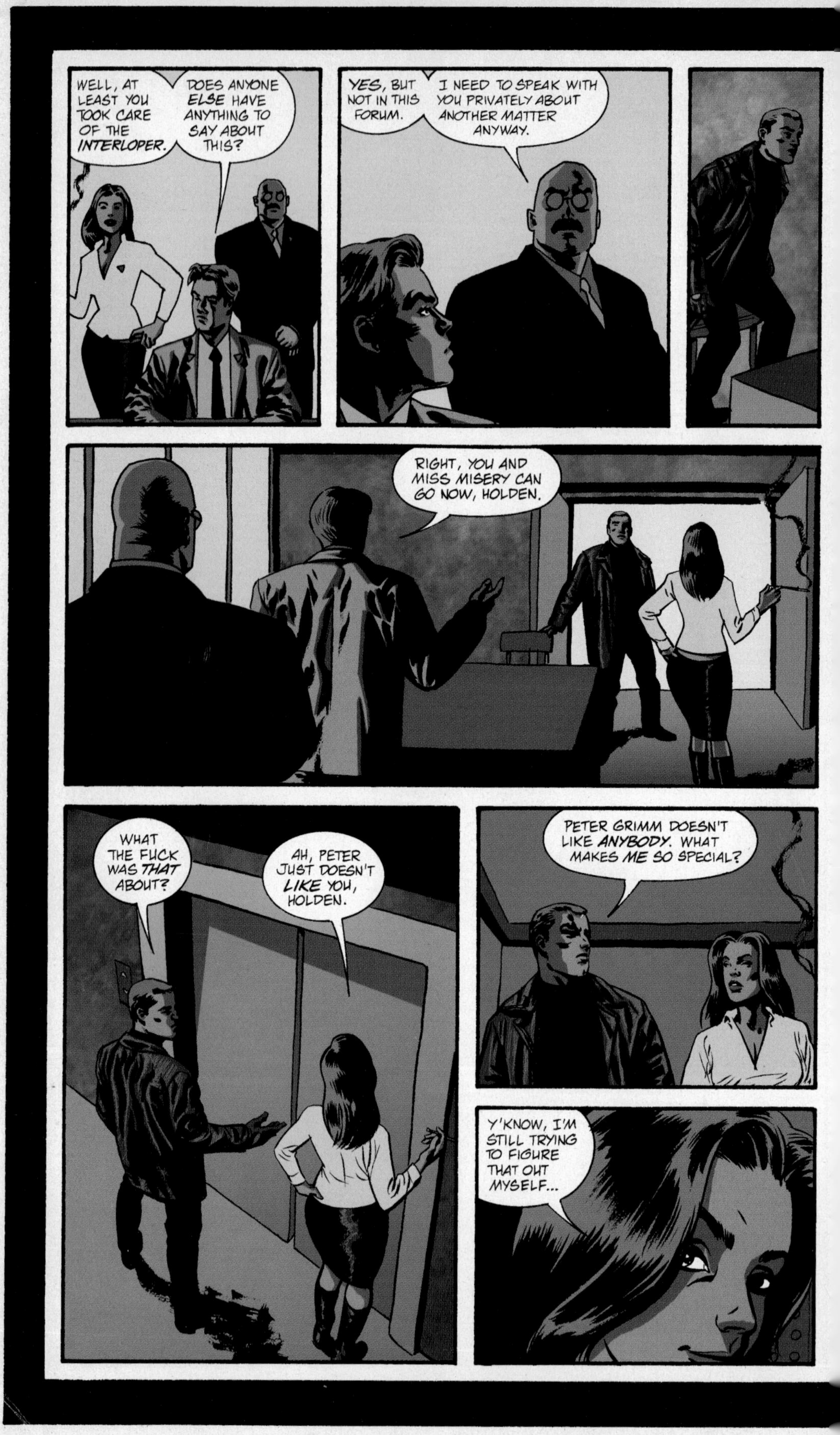
WELL, AT LEAST YOU TOOK CARE OF THE INTERLOPER.
DOES ANYONE ELSE HAVE ANYTHING TO SAY ABOUT THIS?
YES, BUT NOT IN THIS FORUM.
I NEED TO SPEAK WITH YOU PRIVATELY ABOUT ANOTHER MATTER ANYWAY.
RIGHT, YOU AND MISS MISERY CAN GO NOW, HOLDEN.
WHAT THE FUCK WAS THAT ABOUT?
AH, PETER JUST DOESN'T LIKE YOU, HOLDEN.
PETER GRIMM DOESN'T LIKE ANYBODY. WHAT MAKES ME SO SPECIAL?
Y'KNOW, I'M STILL TRYING TO FIGURE THAT OUT MYSELF...

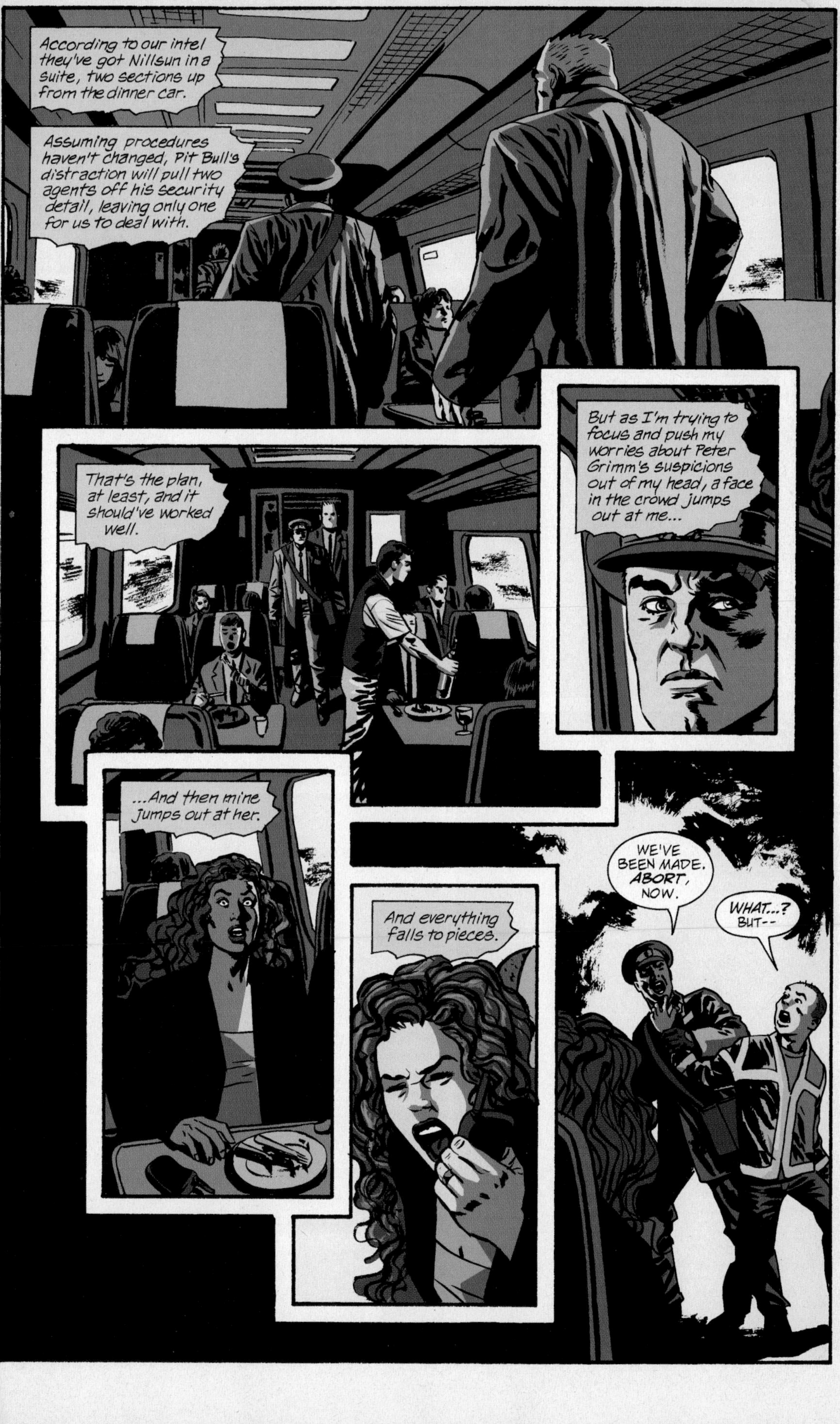
According to our intel they've got Nillsun in a suite, two sections up from the dinner car.
Assuming procedures haven't changed, Pit Bull's distraction will pull two agents off his security detail, leaving only one for us to deal with.
That's the plan, at least, and it should've worked well.
But as I'm trying to focus and push my worries about Peter Grimm's suspicions out of my head, a face in the crowd jumps out at me...
...And then mine jumps out at her.
And everything falls to pieces.
WE'VE BEEN MADE. ABORT, NOW.
WHAT...? BUT--

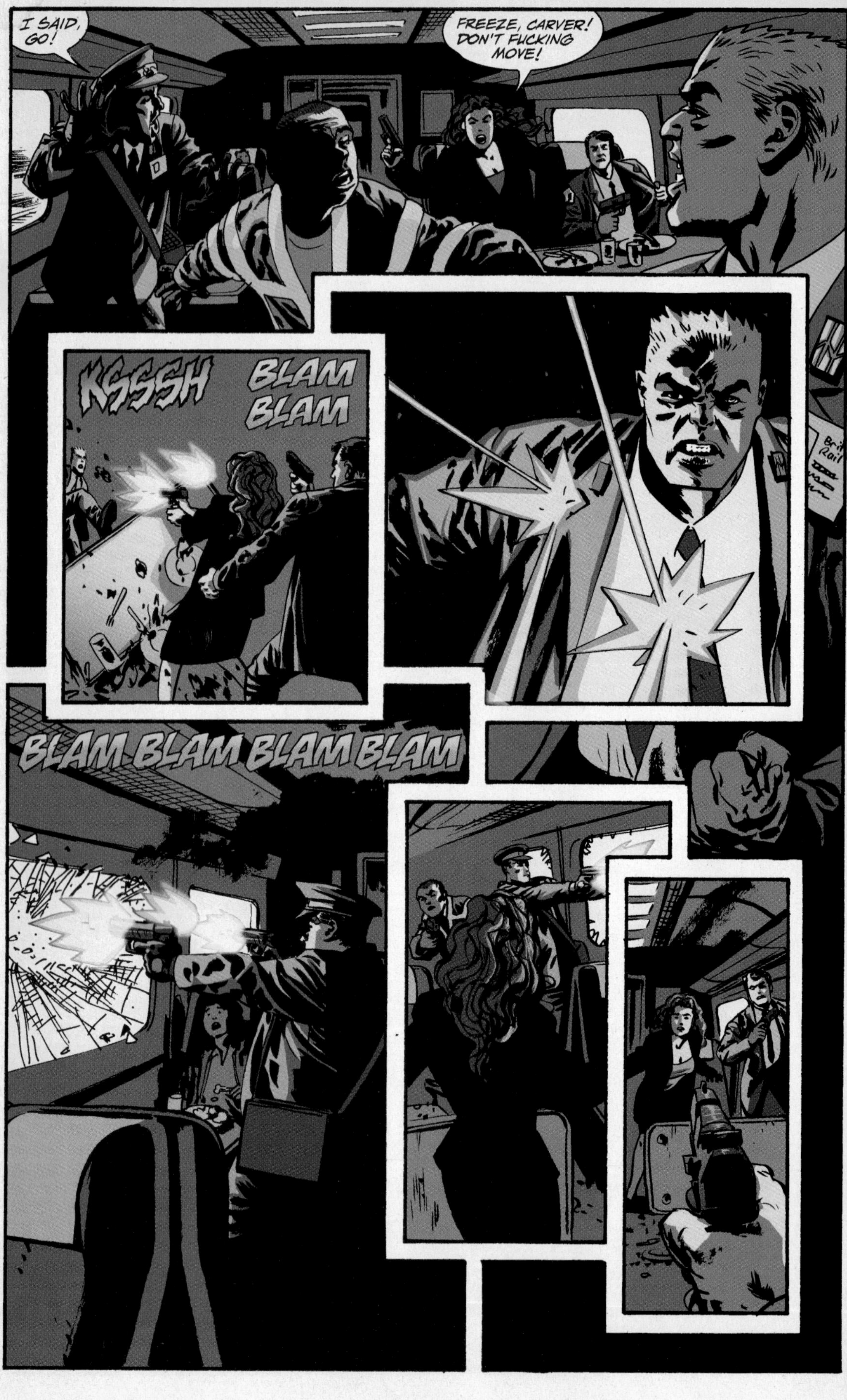
I SAID, GO!
FREEZE, CARVER! DON'T FUCKING MOVE!
KSSSH
BLAM BLAM
BLAM BLAM BLAM BLAM

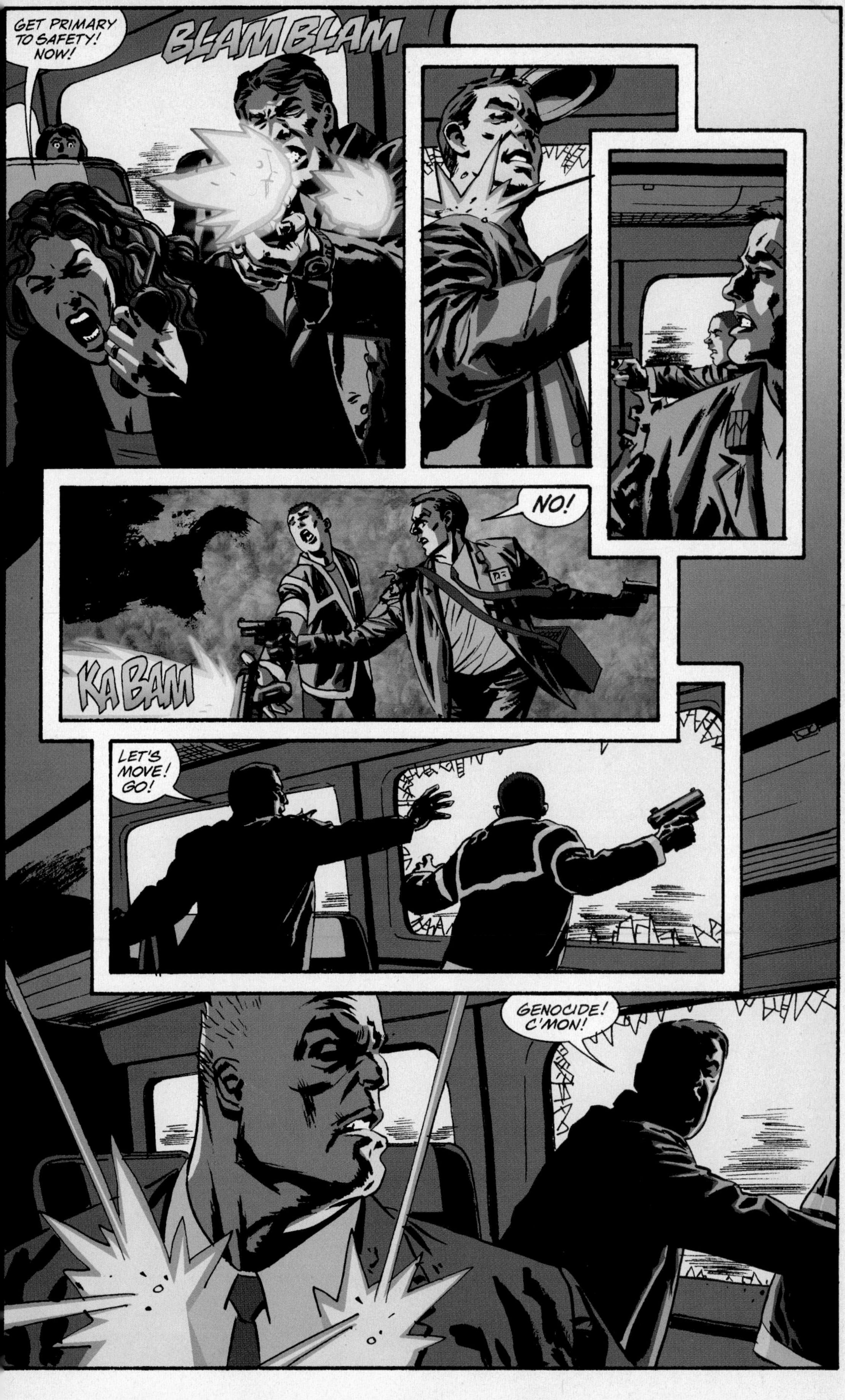
GET PRIMARY TO SAFETY! NOW!
BLAM BLAM
NO!
KA BAM
LET'S MOVE! GO!
GENOCIDE! C'MON!

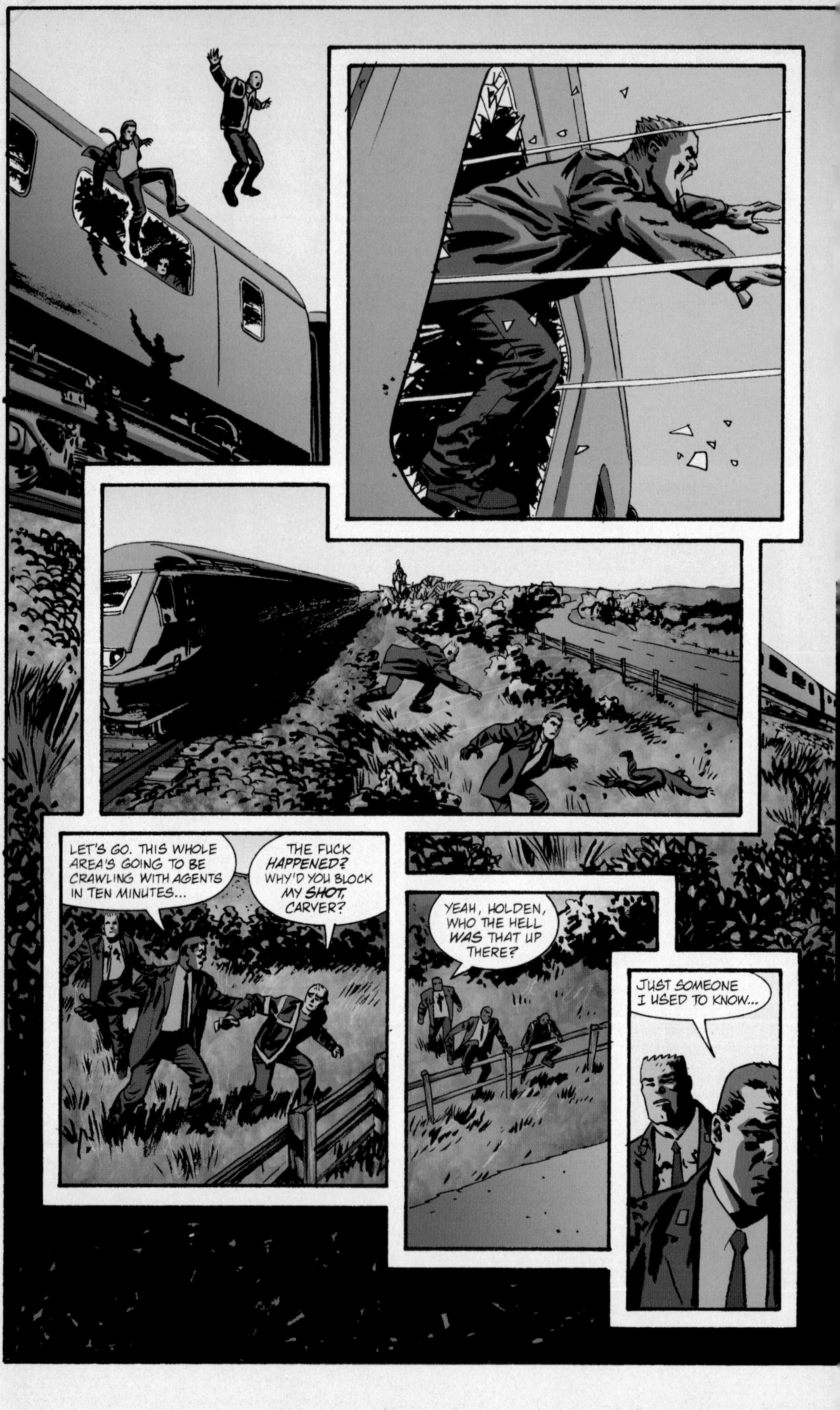
LET'S GO. THIS WHOLE AREA'S GOING TO BE CRAWLING WITH AGENTS IN TEN MINUTES...
THE FUCK HAPPENED? WHY'D YOU BLOCK MY SHOT, CARVER?
YEAH, HOLDEN, WHO THE HELL WAS THAT UP THERE?
JUST SOMEONE I USED TO KNOW...

In fact, her name was Veronica St. James...

...And in another life, we were engaged.

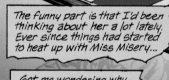

The funny part is that I'd been thinking about her a lot lately. Ever since things had started to heat up with Miss Misery...

Got me wondering why I'd always gone for these "throw caution to the wind" type of women.

And I thought about the first time Veronica and I worked together, Paris in '96. She was my tech liaison from Dept. P.S.I.

It was a boring mission, really. Mostly sitting around a room listening to wire taps and taking pictures of people going in and out of an embassy.

Waiting for the right man to show up so I could take him off the board.

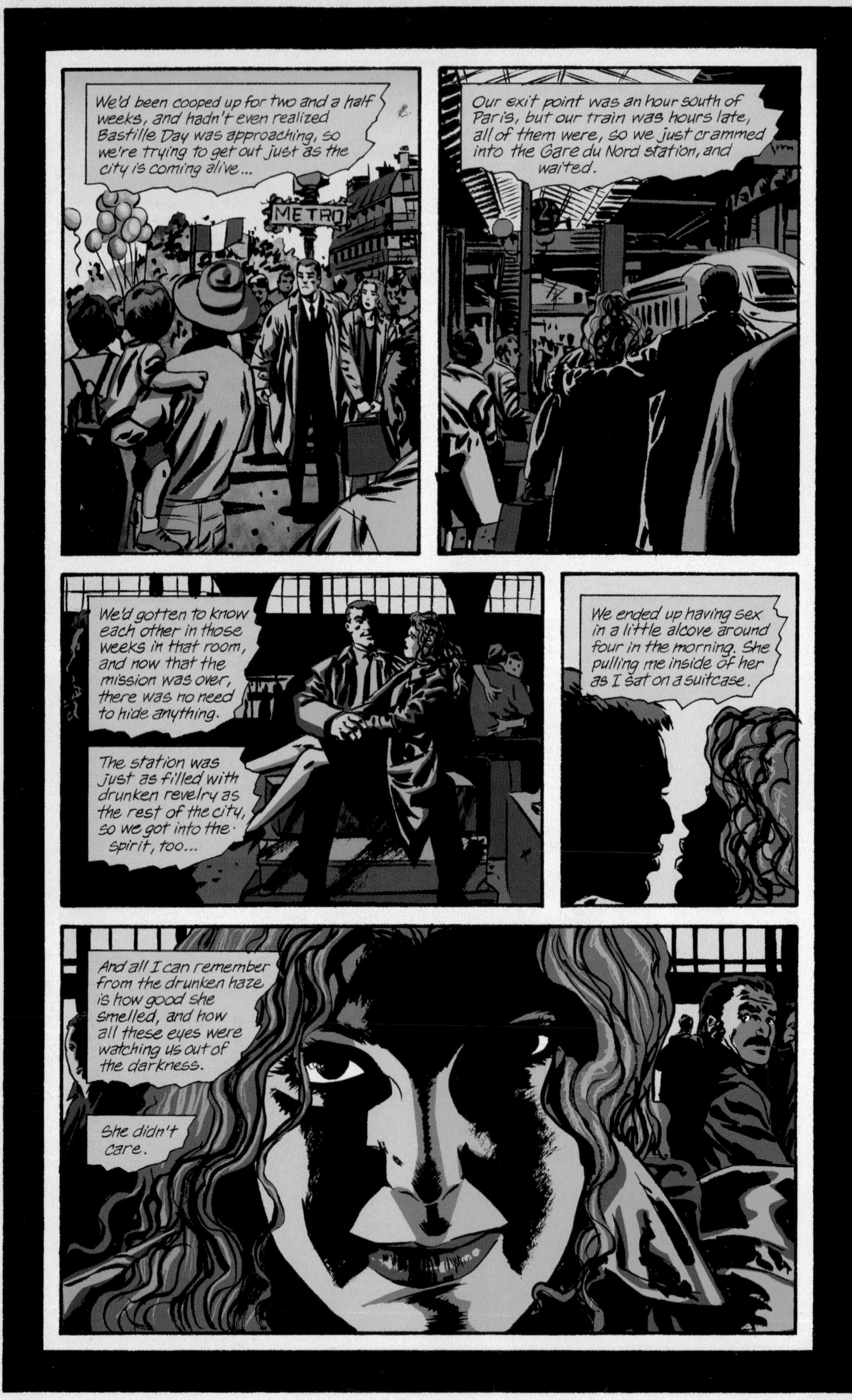
We'd been cooped up for two and a half weeks, and hadn't even realized Bastille Day was approaching, so we're trying to get out just as the city is coming alive...
METRO
Our exit point was an hour south of Paris, but our train was hours late, all of them were, so we just crammed into the Gare du Nord station, and waited.
We'd gotten to know each other in those weeks in that room, and now that the mission was over, there was no need to hide anything.
The station was just as filled with drunken revelry as the rest of the city, so we got into the spirit, too...
We ended up having sex in a little alcove around four in the morning. She pulling me inside of her as I sat on a suitcase.
And all I can remember from the drunken haze is how good she smelled, and how all these eyes were watching us out of the darkness.
She didn't care.

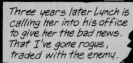

Three years later Lynch is calling her into his office to give her the bad news. That I've gone rogue, traded with the enemy.

I can only imagine her face that day.

Lynch made a point of telling me she was heading up the manhunt operation that was after me. Making sure I wouldn't call her in a drunken moment and tell her the truth.

He didn't have to worry, though... I would never have the guts to call her. Not after the kind of pain I'd put her through.

Of course, I can't tell these guys the real story, so I have to change the details...

--HOPED SHE'D COME *WITH* ME, BUT INSTEAD SHE SPENDS A *YEAR* HUNTING ME DOWN BEFORE THEY LOSE THEIR FUNDING.

WELL, YOU'D'VE LET ME TAKE THAT *SHOT* TODAY, THAT WOULD'VE BEEN THE END OF IT.

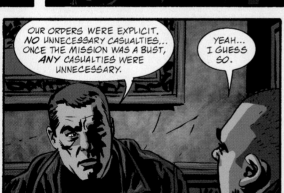

OUR ORDERS WERE EXPLICIT. *NO* UNNECESSARY CASUALTIES... ONCE THE MISSION WAS A BUST, *ANY* CASUALTIES WERE UNNECESSARY.

YEAH... I GUESS SO.

HMMF, GUY WITH HER MUST BE HER *HUSBAND.* HEARD SHE MARRIED ANOTHER AGENT A FEW YEARS BACK...

NOTICE HOW ALL *HIS* SHOTS WERE AIMED AT *ME?*

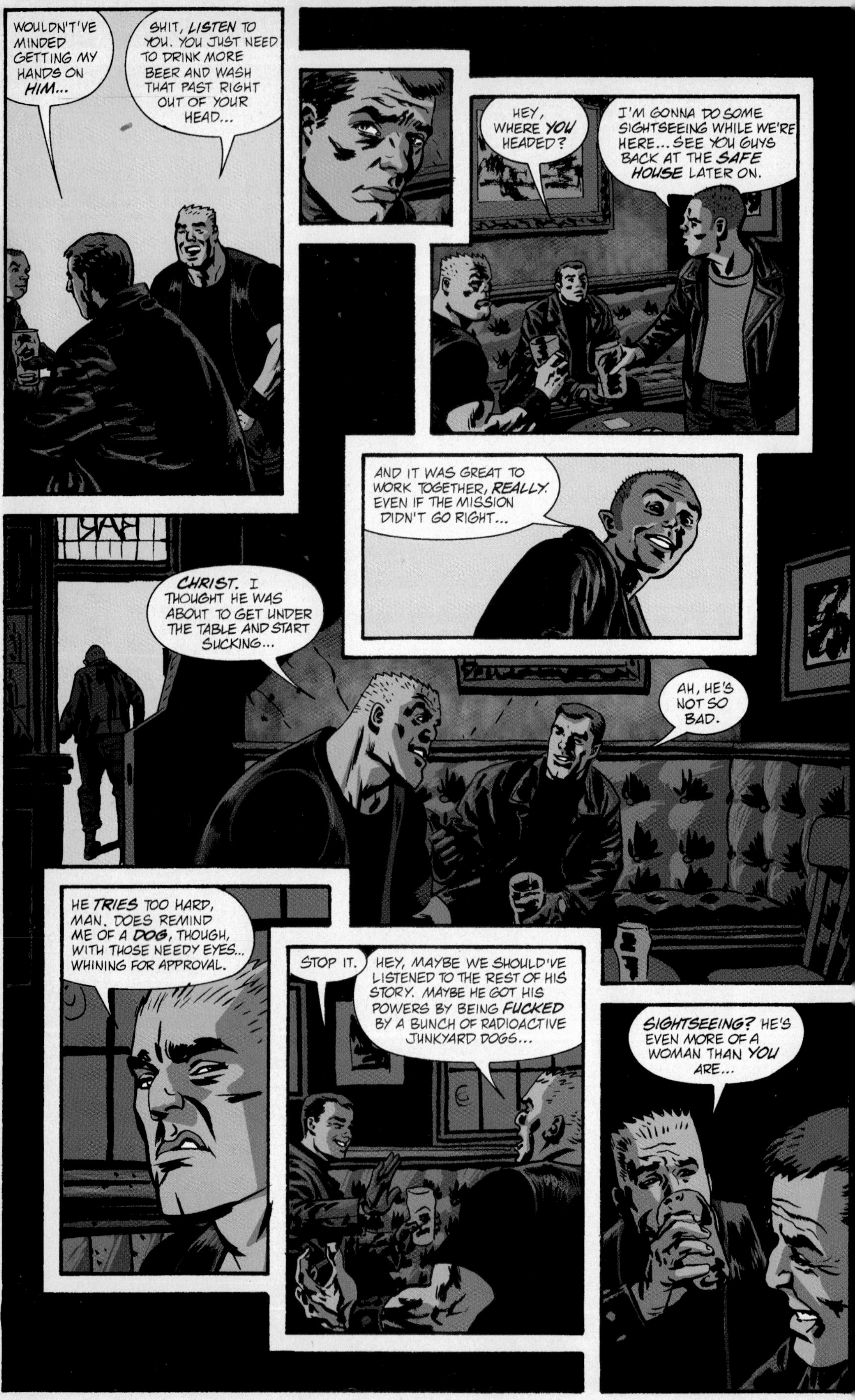

WOULDN'T'VE MINDED GETTING MY HANDS ON HIM...
SHIT, LISTEN TO YOU. YOU JUST NEED TO DRINK MORE BEER AND WASH THAT PAST RIGHT OUT OF YOUR HEAD...
HEY, WHERE YOU HEADED?
I'M GONNA DO SOME SIGHTSEEING WHILE WE'RE HERE... SEE YOU GUYS BACK AT THE SAFE HOUSE LATER ON.
AND IT WAS GREAT TO WORK TOGETHER, REALLY. EVEN IF THE MISSION DIDN'T GO RIGHT...
CHRIST. I THOUGHT HE WAS ABOUT TO GET UNDER THE TABLE AND START SUCKING...
AH, HE'S NOT SO BAD.
HE TRIES TOO HARD, MAN. DOES REMIND ME OF A DOG, THOUGH, WITH THOSE NEEDY EYES... WHINING FOR APPROVAL.
STOP IT.
HEY, MAYBE WE SHOULD'VE LISTENED TO THE REST OF HIS STORY. MAYBE HE GOT HIS POWERS BY BEING FUCKED BY A BUNCH OF RADIOACTIVE JUNKYARD DOGS...
SIGHTSEEING? HE'S EVEN MORE OF A WOMAN THAN YOU ARE...

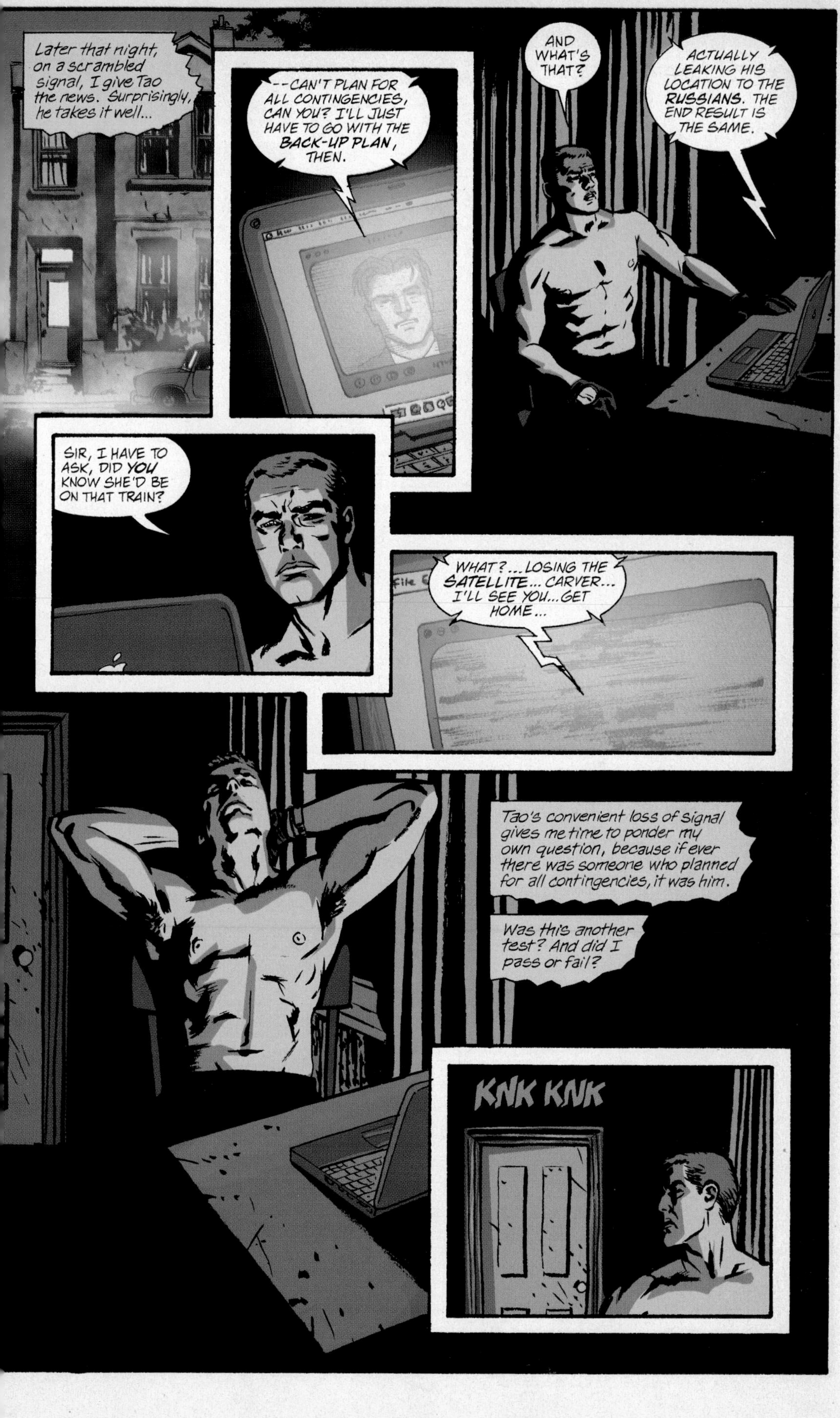
Later that night, on a scrambled signal, I give Tao the news. Surprisingly, he takes it well...
--CAN'T PLAN FOR ALL CONTINGENCIES, CAN YOU? I'LL JUST HAVE TO GO WITH THE BACK-UP PLAN, THEN.
AND WHAT'S THAT?
ACTUALLY LEAKING HIS LOCATION TO THE RUSSIANS. THE END RESULT IS THE SAME.
SIR, I HAVE TO ASK, DID YOU KNOW SHE'D BE ON THAT TRAIN?
WHAT?... LOSING THE SATELLITE... CARVER... I'LL SEE YOU...GET HOME...
Tao's convenient loss of signal gives me time to ponder my own question, because if ever there was someone who planned for all contingencies, it was him.
Was this another test? And did I pass or fail?
KNK KNK

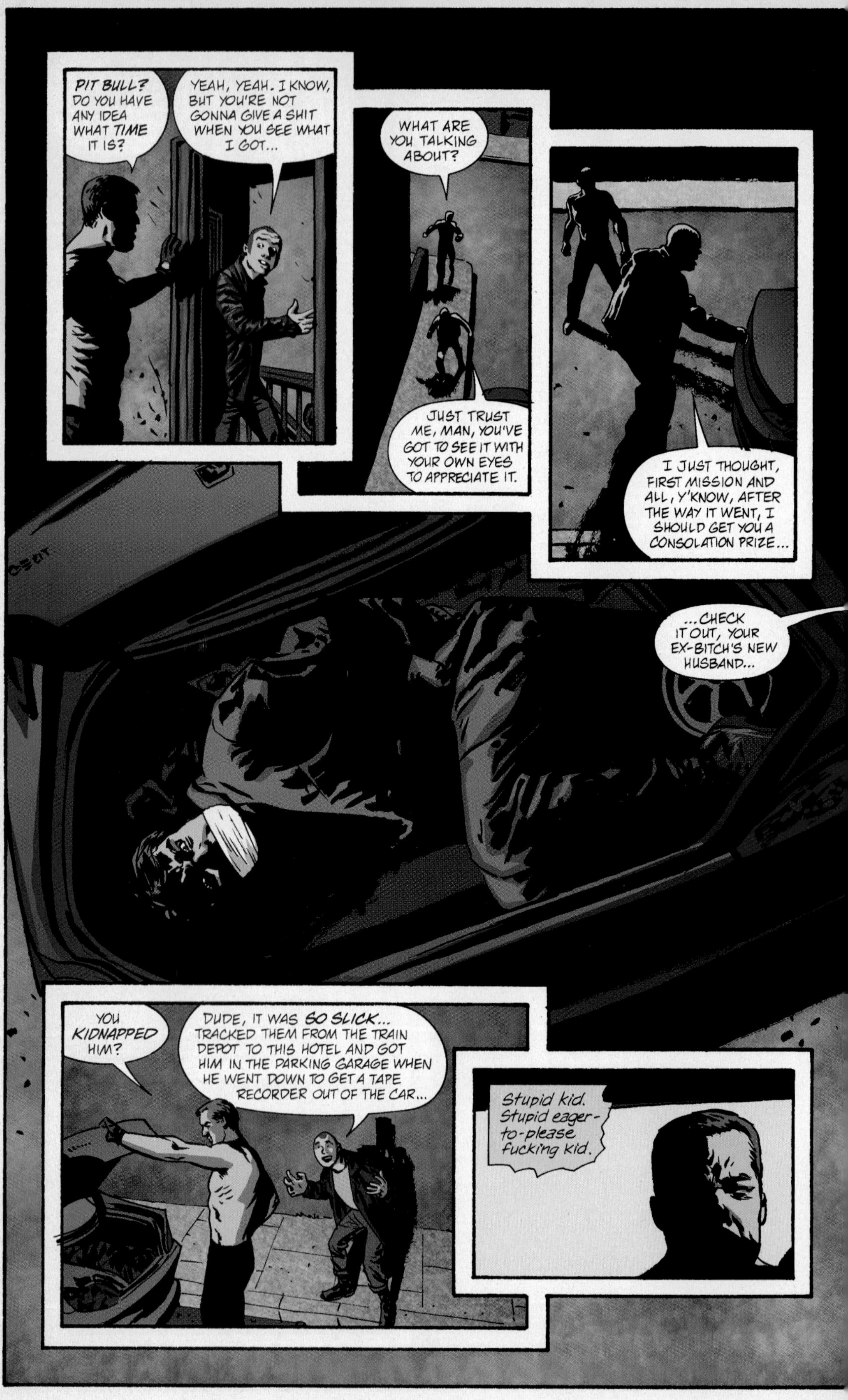
PIT BULL? DO YOU HAVE ANY IDEA WHAT TIME IT IS?
YEAH, YEAH. I KNOW, BUT YOU'RE NOT GONNA GIVE A SHIT WHEN YOU SEE WHAT I GOT...
WHAT ARE YOU TALKING ABOUT?
JUST TRUST ME, MAN, YOU'VE GOT TO SEE IT WITH YOUR OWN EYES TO APPRECIATE IT.
I JUST THOUGHT, FIRST MISSION AND ALL, Y'KNOW, AFTER THE WAY IT WENT, I SHOULD GET YOU A CONSOLATION PRIZE...
...CHECK IT OUT, YOUR EX-BITCH'S NEW HUSBAND...
YOU KIDNAPPED HIM?
DUDE, IT WAS SO SLICK... TRACKED THEM FROM THE TRAIN DEPOT TO THIS HOTEL AND GOT HIM IN THE PARKING GARAGE WHEN HE WENT DOWN TO GET A TAPE RECORDER OUT OF THE CAR...
Stupid kid. Stupid eager-to-please fucking kid.

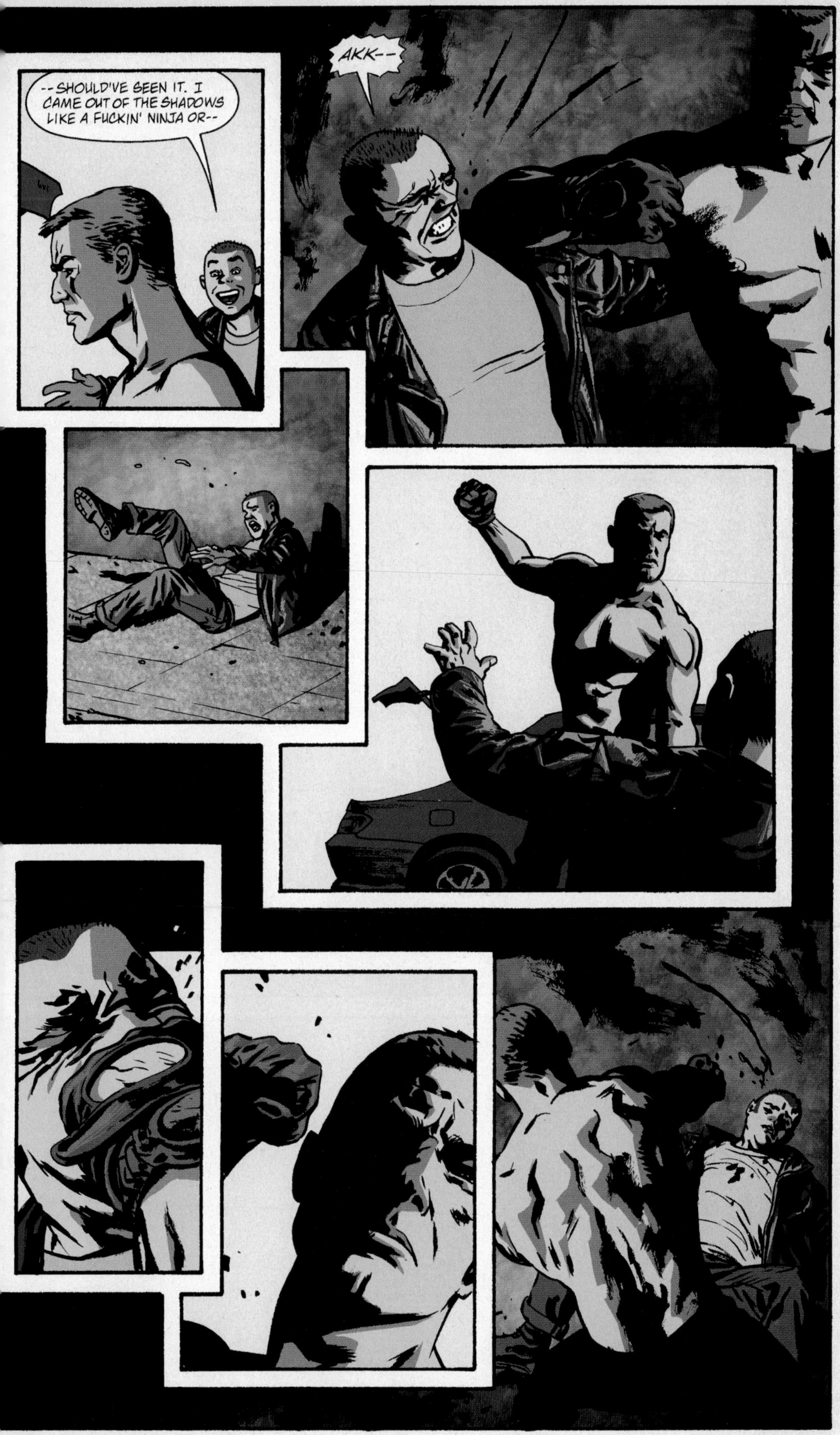
-- SHOULD'VE SEEN IT. I CAME OUT OF THE SHADOWS LIKE A FUCKIN' NINJA OR--
AKK--

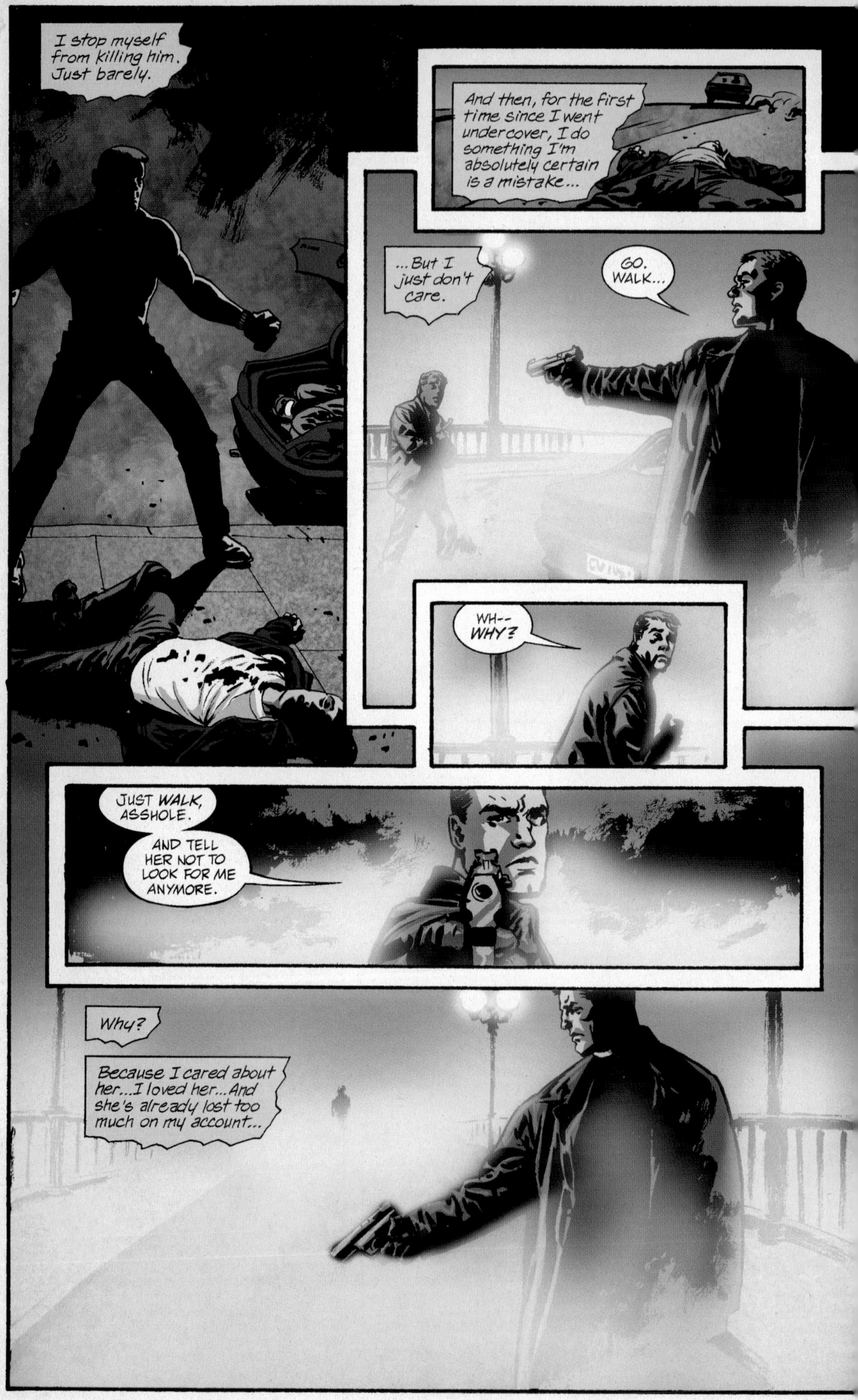
I stop myself from killing him. Just barely.
And then, for the first time since I went undercover, I do something I'm absolutely certain is a mistake...
...But I just don't care.
GO. WALK...
WH-- WHY?
JUST WALK, ASSHOLE.
AND TELL HER NOT TO LOOK FOR ME ANYMORE.
Why?
Because I cared about her...I loved her...And she's already lost too much on my account...

Award-winning writer Ed Brubaker has spent the last ten years in the Witness Protection Program, where, since the initial publication of his tell-all biography "A Complete Lowlife" about his time on the wrong side of the law, he's become an international celebrity. His work has been translated into 14 languages and nominated for numerous awards, including the Eisner and the Harvey. He doesn't give interviews or allow his picture to be taken, for obvious reasons.

Sean Phillips just draws what he is told and tries to keep his nose clean.

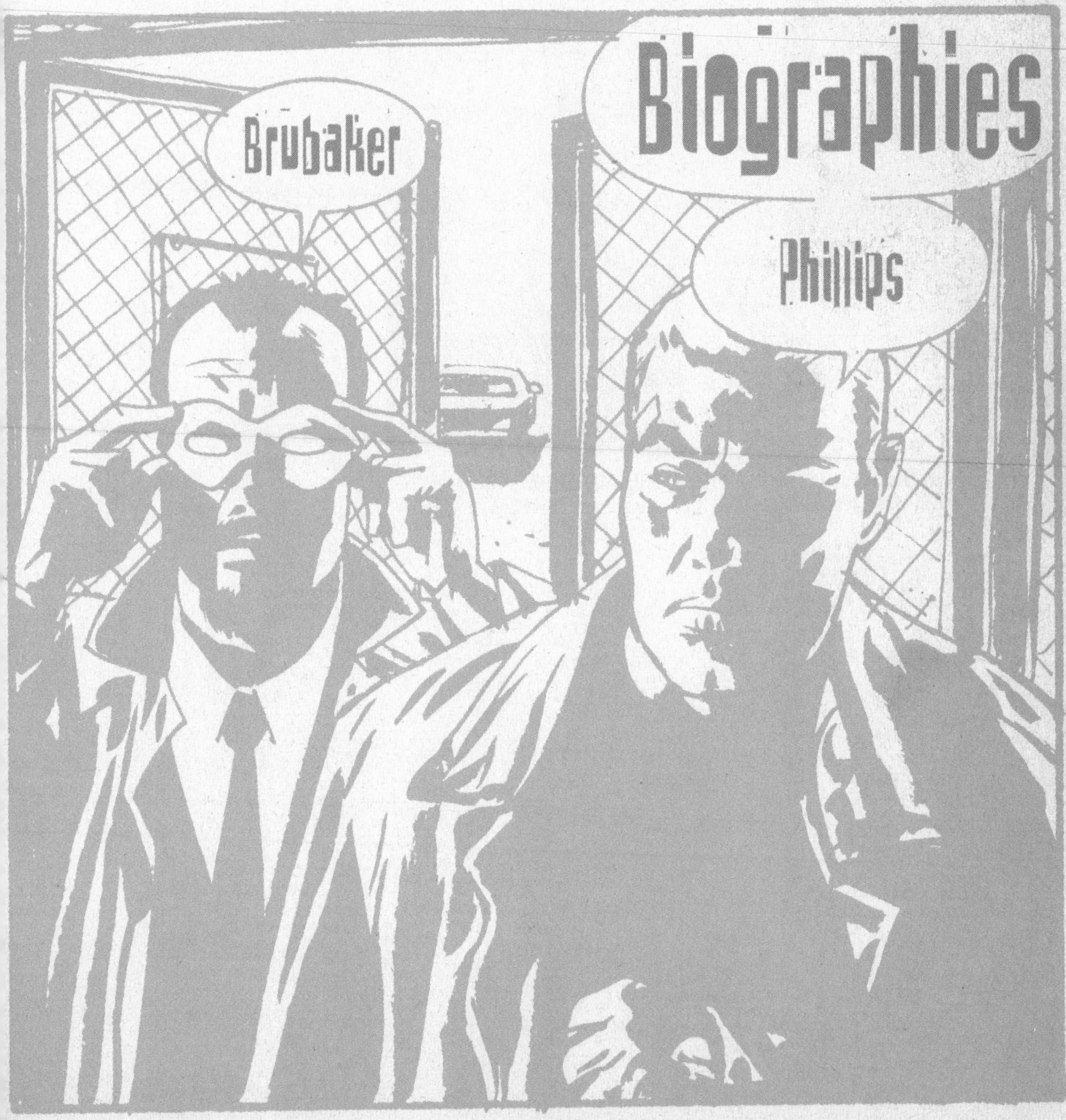
Brubaker
Biographies
Phillips

sleeper
all false moves
Ed Brubaker
Sean Phillips

SLEEPER: All False Moves
Brubaker * Phillips

COLE CASH IS THE GRIFTER
STARRING IN
POINT BLANK
ED BRUBAKER COLIN WILSON

POINT BLANK
Brubaker * Wilson

WILDCATS
BATTERY PARK

WILDCATS Vol 2 BOOKS 1-4
Casey * Phillips

WARREN ELLIS
GLOBAL
FREQUENCY
PLANET ABLAZE

GLOBAL FREQUENCY Vol 1
Ellis * Various

THE AUTHORITY
RELENTLESS

THE AUTHORITY BOOKS 1-5
Various Writers & Artists

21 DOWN
THE CONDUIT
PALMIOTTI GRAY SAIZ

21 DOWN: THE CONDUIT
Palmiotti * Gray * Saiz

backlist

To find more collected editions and monthly comic books from WildStorm and DC Comics, call 1-888-comic book for the nearest comic shop or go to your local bookstore.

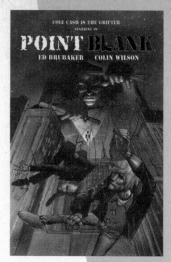